DION FORTUNE
&
THE INNER LIGHT

Other books by Gareth Knight

A Practical Guide to Qabalistic Symbolism
Esoteric Training in Everyday Life
Evoking the Goddess (*aka* The Rose Cross and the Goddess)
Experience of the Inner Worlds
Magic and the Western Mind (*aka* A History of White Magic)
Magical Images and the Magical Imagination
Merlin and the Grail Tradition
Occult Exercises and Practices
Tarot and Magic (*aka* The Treasure House of Images)
The Secret Tradition in Arthurian Legend
The Magical World of the Inklings
The Magical World of the Tarot
The Occult: an Introduction
The Practice of Ritual Magic

Books by Dion Fortune with Gareth Knight

The Magical Battle of Britain
An Introduction to Ritual Magic
The Circuit of Force
Principles of Hermetic Philosophy
Spiritualism and Occultism

Future titles

Practical Occultism

DION FORTUNE
&
THE INNER LIGHT

by

Gareth Knight

THOTH PUBLICATIONS
Loughborough, Leicestershire.

Cover design by Rebecca Mazonowicz

First published in 2000 by
Thoth Publications
64 Leopold Street
Loughborough, LE11 5DN

www.thoth.co.uk
www.thothpublications.com
e-mail: inquiries@thothpublications.co.uk

ISBN 1 870450 45 0

Printed and bound in Great Britain

CONTENTS

PART ONE

THE FORMATIVE YEARS: 1890 – 1922

PART TWO

THE FOUNDATION YEARS: 1922 – 1926

PART THREE:

FORGING THE FRATERNITY: 1926 – 1928

PART FOUR:

THE FRATERNITY AT WORK: 1928 – 1939

PART FIVE:

THE YEARS OF TRANSFORMATION: 1939 – 1946

EPILOGUE:

POST MORTEM INHERITANCE: 1946 - 1999

APPENDIX:

ACKNOWLEDGEMENTS

To the Warden, the Society of the Inner Light, for making available Society archives and giving permission and complete freedom to quote therefrom.

The letters of Dion Fortune to Israel Regardie were made available through the courtesy of Mrs. Maria Babwhasingh.

To Simon Buxton, for generously giving his time and the results of his own painstaking research.

To R.A.Gilbert for some valuable leads, corrections and advice.

To Alan Richardson, for his encouragement and material advice from the results of his own research in connection with previous biographies.

To Sander Littel for drawing up a rectified astrological birth chart of Dion Fortune.

To the Librarian of the Royal College of Psychiatry for her courtesy.

And not least, to those whose published work has helped to fill in some of the picture from their own perspectives, particularly:

Patrick Benham: "The Avalonians" (Gothic Image, Glastonbury 1993)

Janine Chapman: "Quest for Dion Fortune" (Weiser, York Beach 1993)

Charles Fielding and Carr Collins: "The Story of Dion Fortune" (Weiser, York Beach 1985 & Thoth, Loughborough 1998)

Alan Richardson: "Priestess – The Life and Magic of Dion Fortune" (Aquarian, Wellingborough, 1987)

Alan Richardson: "Dancers to the Gods" (Aquarian, Wellingborough, 1985)

Theopholis E. M. Boll: "May Sinclair and the Medico-Psychological Clinic of London" from "Proceedings of the American Philosophical Society", Vol. 106, No. 4, August 1962.

— Part One —

THE FORMATIVE YEARS 1890-1922

1

Childhood of an Adept

Sarah Firth felt there was something strange about her daughter Violet's birth in the early hours of 6th December 1890. She confided these thoughts, in later years, to her friend Kitty Tudor Pole, and also to her daughter herself, who passed on the story, half jokingly, in an article in "The Occult Review", and also wrote up the idea as the circumstances of birth of the heroine of two of her novels, "The Sea Priestess" and "Moon Magic":

> I was supposed to have died as a baby. I was declared dead and lay dead for many hours in my mother's lap, for she could not be persuaded to put me down, and at dawn I revived but the eyes that looked at my mother, she told me many years afterward when I asked her the cause of my strangeness, were not the eyes of a child, and she knew with the unerring instinct of a mother that I was not the same one.

Lilith Le Fay Morgan, also known as Vivien, was a character with whom she identified to some degree. A woman of strange powers who had magical links with a lost continent to the far West across the Atlantic, who cut through the conventions of the sleepy west country town where Violet spent her early teens, and built a temple at the end of the spur of land that stretches into the sea and is known today as Brean Down.

Sarah Firth probably told this incident of her birth to Violet in about 1922, at much the same time as she told it to Kitty Tudor Pole, who was herself interested in psychic things. It may have been that it went some way to account for the concern she felt at Violet becoming increasingly involved in occultism with a penchant for trance mediumship.

It is hardly likely that she thought her daughter to be a "changeling" in the sense of being a fairy's child. She was an intelligent and cultivated woman, married to a solicitor, part of an extended family proud of their down to earth, sensible and respectable Yorkshire origins. They ran, at the time of Violet's birth, the Craigside Hydrotherapeutic Establishment at Llandudno in North Wales, an up-market watering place with heated pools and resident medical practitioner.

Violet was certainly highly imaginative as a child. In later life she recounted some of the images that arose in her mind at the age of four, and wondered if they were memories of a previous life in some ancient civilisation.

In not a few people there linger memories of past lives. Shadowy and fragmentary, like the memories of a home left in early childhood, the picture images survive. Far less rare than we realise are these memories of the past. Many children have them, and the romancings of childhood are not infrequently recollections.

Life soon buries these dim memory pictures under layer upon layer of fresh impressions and absorbing interests. There are some children, however, who find a strange fascination in these pictures of the past that rise unbidden into consciousness, and who dwell upon them, until they develop into whole landscapes and life histories. The child himself may regard them as nothing but story-tellings that amuse his idleness; the adolescent may forget them altogether, but sometimes there comes a day when an interest in transcendental subjects may lead him to dip into the literature of occultism, and in the investigations of some psychic into the records of the lost continents, or the researches of some scientist into their surviving relics, he may suddenly find he has come face to face with his own long-forgotten imaginings.

What are they worth, those musings of childhood when the brightly coloured pictures raise one after the other in the magic lantern of the mind? If we could collect them altogether, might we not

*be able to reconstruct some picture of the lost civilisation
that history has forgotten?*

Among the pictures that formed unbidden in her mind between
waking and sleeping was the recurring image of a sandy foreshore
with a level plain behind it and mountains rising abruptly in the
distance. A sluggish river made its way across the plain; a few
queer looking trees like feather dusters straggled at intervals along
its banks. It was not safe to go near the trees because of dangerous
beasts lurking in the river that might eat you. For the same reason it
was not safe to go too near the waters of the shallow sea that
rippled over the sands. Things like giant jellyfish were believed to
swim there, and fat black shiny porpoise-like backs could
sometimes be seen further out.

There was glowing warmth, a lush grassy vegetation. The sky
was a very dark indigo blue; and strangest of all, the sun was
copper coloured – which made a great impression upon her.

People lived near the seashore; very poor people who were fishers.
They lived in little low round huts made of basketwork; and went
out fishing in small round baskets too. Very often they did not come
back because they themselves had been eaten. It was dangerous to
go near their huts, because the fishermen themselves ate strange
children when they could get them. For the most part the seashore
was bathed in broiling stewing sunshine, but sometimes swept by
terrific storms, that came on suddenly.

Home was some miles inland, in a cave at the base of the
mountain. Here the broken country was so densely wooded that
there was a perpetual green twilight under the trees. Within the
shelter of the caves, firelight flickered on companions clad in shaggy
skins, whilst the high-cleft roofs led up into darkness.

However, as far as her present life was concerned, at the age of
twelve she moved with her family down to Somerset. This is the
country of her novel "The Sea Priestess" with a seaboard facing
directly upon the Atlantic, and the knolls and tors that once had
been islands rising up above the ancient marshes. Brean Down and
Bleadon Hill (or perhaps Brent Knoll) feature in the novel as Bell
Head and Bell Knowle, while just up river across the moors is
Glastonbury, which played a major part in her life, and where she
established a centre for her work at the foot of the famous Tor.

Here she began to show her literary talents. An indulgent family financed the publication of two slim volumes of her childhood verse and prose, "Violets" and "More Violets". It was not the work of an infant prodigy but was noticed by "The Girl's Realm", a national magazine, in its May issue of 1906. It printed her portrait and a sample poem, accompanied by a somewhat cautious and patronising panegyric from the editor.

Violet is a lover of Nature, and it is when her childish muse sings of Nature that we listen with most pleasure. Life, with its puzzles and problems, is not to be fathomed by the plummet line of a child's intelligence, no matter how gifted that child may be. But a child is near to Nature's heart and to it... she whispers her secrets and sings her sweetest songs. So we turn the pages of "Violets", as the little volume is aptly named, and wonder whether Time, the Tester of all things, has indeed in store for us another Elizabeth Barrett Browning, or another Emily Bronte. And meanwhile wise little Violet Firth works hard at her school at Weston-super-Mare all the term, and reserves verse making for her holidays.

No doubt the advice was sound and commonsensical. Whatever your aspirations to fame and fortune do not neglect your daytime job! Above all, do not get ideas above your station! However, one wonders what prescience caused the editor to make the remarks she did, for little Violet would eventually plunge head first into fathoming life's puzzles and problems - with the somewhat unorthodox tools of psychoanalysis, mediumship and ceremonial magic!

If she could be compared to any mid-Victorian ladies it would more appropriately have been, not the literary figures of Elizabeth Barrett Browning or Emily Bronte, but the campaigning visionary, Anna Bonus Kingsford. Both she and Kingsford were champions of a Western Esoteric Tradition. Anna Kingsford aided MacGregor Mathers just as Dion Fortune helped Israel Regardie. Both had their problems with certain elements of the Theosophical Society, and both were materially assisted by a devoted older man as general factotum, Anna Kingsford by Edward Maitland, and Dion Fortune by Charles Loveday.

A couple of verses from "The Song of the Sea" give a certain hint of the future author of "The Sea Priestess", particularly in the ebb and flow of the rhythm of the verse, but there is some way to go before such sentiments are elevated into a Rite of Isis.

What are the billows murmuring?
Singing so soft and low,
As, retreating, they bare the sea-sands fair
With a ceaseless ebb and flow:

Do they sing of the South Sea Islands
Where the feathery palm-trees grow?
Or the Northern Sound, where they're chained and bound
With the bonds of the King of the Snow?...

Violet Firth's Welsh place of birth did not cause her to identify particularly with Celtic culture. Family pride was strong, conscious of their descent from Yorkshire steel makers. Family tradition had it that there had been Firths in Sheffield since 1532, and that their name derived from the Norse "fjord" and Scandinavian origins, although it is a quite common name throughout Yorkshire and Lancashire and comes from the Old English word for a woodland. However, throughout her life Violet Firth always saw herself as a flaxen haired blue-eyed daughter of the Vikings - although she did later marry a dark and very Celtic Welshman – Thomas Penry Evans.

By the time she was fourteen her parents had become converted to Christian Science, the new American religion of Mary Baker Eddy. Its creed that healing was a function of the spirit impressed Violet but did not claim her as a convert. Her later view was that Mrs. Eddy had empirically stumbled upon certain powers of the mind that she had elevated into a religion. And this not without good reason, for without a reverent approach such powers could be degraded into methods of mental manipulation for personal ends. The strand of Christian religious commitment that remained in the background, and sometimes the foreground, of all her later occult work, may well have had its roots in this realisation.

Her grandparents died when she was sixteen and her mother and father moved to London, first to the well heeled western suburb of Bedford Park, then closer in to town to various Kensington addresses in Horbury Crescent and Queens Gate Gardens, or Hanover Square in the heart of the West End.

Sarah Jane (or "Jennie") Firth was officially listed as a Christian Science practitioner in 1920-22, and was therefore a healer available to the general public. At this time they were living in Westminster Bridge Road. However, in 1922 she and her husband resigned from church membership, without giving a reason, and moved to Letchworth in Hertfordshire.

They had obviously become attracted to the Garden City movement. Letchworth was the first Garden City, built on the vision of Ebenezer Howard, who in a book of 1898, "Tomorrow – a Peaceful Path to Real Reform" launched the idea of a new type of planned city which combined the joys of the countryside with the comforts of the town; a town without slums where people could live and work in a pleasant environment and take pride in their surroundings.

In 1903 he formed an Association and purchased land at Letchworth to start such an enterprise, and by 1905 was living there, in Homesgarth, a communal housing project for professional people with common central heating system and dining area.

It was here that the Firths moved in 1922, although it was now less of a communal project, and had been renamed Sollershott Hall. Here they came into contact with Kitty Tudor Pole and Alice Buckton, both of whom happened to have strong associations with Glastonbury.

Kitty's parents had became interested in Letchworth in 1908 and had built a house there called Tudor Cottage, not far from where the Firths now lived.

Kitty Tudor Pole's link with Glastonbury went back seventeen years. She had been one of three "guardians of the Grail" in a celebrated incident wherein a Dr. John Goodchild had bought an antique cup in Italy in 1885 and, apparently psychically inspired, had hidden it on the marshes near Glastonbury at a spot known as Bride's Well in 1898. He used to visit the spot each year thereafter in a kind of personal pilgrimage. In 1905, also apparently in response to psychic impressions, it had been discovered by two sisters, Janet and Christine Allen, and their friends Wellesley and Katherine ("Kitty") Tudor Pole.

The Cup was invested with Grail-like associations, and some even regarded it as the original Holy Grail, but though it was antique it was more in the nature of a magnetically charged symbolic object. The Allen girls and Kitty came to be regarded as its three guardian maidens, called the Triad, and it was preserved and revered in an oratory at York Crescent, Clifton, near Bristol, where the Tudor Poles lived.

Kitty and her parents, who had spent the war period in Ireland, returned to Tudor Cottage in 1921 and thus were close neighbours of the Firths. Kitty continued to make personal pilgrimages to Glastonbury, although for the most part the Cup remained in the custody of her brother Wellesley who had a variety of homes over the years.

Alice Buckton was a close friend of Kitty, an educationist, a mystical poet and playwright of no mean ability, a supporter of the arts and crafts movement, and an ardent feminist and Christian socialist, who for thirty years was one of the great characters, even an institution, of Glastonbury. She had been drawn to Glastonbury in 1907 when she heard Wellesley Tudor Pole speak about the Cup and the Grail. Fired with the vision of setting up a women's community at Glastonbury, she managed to buy Chalice Well in 1912, a former Roman Catholic seminary, and by 1914 had converted it into a hostel for paying guests and a general arts and crafts commune. There she remained until her death in 1944. Eventually Wellesley Tudor Pole and others formed a Trust to maintain Chalice Well as a holy site in the form in which it remains today.

The full intriguing story of the Grail Cup, the Tudor Poles and Alice Buckton has been ably described in Patrick Benham's "The Avalonians" (Gothic Image 1993). Whilst they were of a generation before Dion Fortune, and were certainly not into the full blooded occultism with which she became associated, it would seem that their influence may have had a long lasting effect upon her, and may well have drawn her to Glastonbury in the first instance.

It was another longstanding friend of the family who influenced her in the magical direction. This was Maiya Curtis-Webb, the wife of a doctor with psychiatric interests, who was a leading member of the Alpha et Omega, an offshoot of the Hermetic Order of the Golden Dawn, into which Violet Firth was later initiated.

However magical interests did not immediately appeal to her until her psychical awakening at the age of twenty-six. In her teenage years she was probably pretty headstrong; when she was twenty her parents thought it a good idea to enrol her at a residential college. It was one, which claimed to cater for young ladies who might have minor emotional problems, but its main purpose was practical vocational training in the comparatively new realm of commercial horticulture.

What she learned there did indeed change her life, and gave her the impetus and direction for a new career. It was not in the way of horticulture, however, but of psychoanalysis, and eventually as a leading practitioner of the occult!

2

THE DWELLER ON THE THRESHOLD

Studley Horticultural College for Women had been a forward looking enterprise when set up at the turn of the century by the benevolence of the Countess of Warwick. It sought to provide training in the burgeoning business of horticulture and to provide an alternative means of livelihood for young ladies, whose career opportunities in those days were severely limited. In 1903 she bought Studley Castle in Warwickshire to house it, an early nineteenth century construction adjoining an old castle dating from the late 16th or early 17th century.

However, the college was going through a difficult time. After a promising start in its early years, the aristocratic subvention ceased in 1908, and the college fell into financial and organisational crisis. Eventually its trustees, warden, and many senior staff resigned.

All this occurred just before Violet Firth arrived, for the summer term 1911, and her time coincided with the regime of a new and formidable warden who had been appointed to turn things round, three years before.

Dr. Lillias Hamilton, at any rate by irreverent student accounts looked rather odd. A woman of uncertain age with a shapeless dress and a ginger wig above which a bunch of her own hair protruded through a hole in the top. However she was an experienced administrator, if in some strange walks of life, and a woman of considerable will power and ability.

After training as a nurse at Liverpool Infirmary, she had gone on to qualify as a doctor in 1890, no mean feat for a woman in Victorian times. She then went to India and established a considerable private practice for herself in Calcutta and was appointed physician in charge of the Dufferin Hospital in 1893. Then, taking advantage of a short lived international treaty, she left to become court physician to the Amir of Afghanistan in 1894. Three years later she was ordered to leave, as she liked to say "on the orders of Queen Victoria," but it was really a case of a resurgence of Afghan independence, reinforced by a wave of fanaticism by the tribes along the North West frontier. This led to extensive British military operations and tribal skirmishes that were never finally resolved until the establishment of the North-West Frontier Province in 1901.

Apart from being a cockpit for international politics the post was also so exposed to court intrigue that her food had always to be tested for poison. Such were the stories she liked to tell her "gels", perhaps with the usual exaggeration of travellers' tales. This was much the time of Rudyard Kipling's tales of the Raj, and she may also have picked up a certain amount of esoteric knowledge besides a toughness in dealing with "lesser breeds without the law", be they tribesmen, eunuchs, or the staff and students at Studley College.

After her return to England she pursued a successful consultancy practice in London and pursued another adventure in South Africa where she started a farm in the Transvaal that was later carried on by her brother. She also wrote a couple of books, "A Vizier's Daughter" and "A Nurse's Bequest", before being taken on as Warden of Studley. Here drastic problems required drastic remedies and these Dr. Hamilton was able to provide.

Making the most of her medical qualification Studley was discreetly advertised as being suitable for girls or women who suffered nervous or psychological problems. No doubt most of the girls were normal enough, simply going through the pains of adolescence in an era when adolescence was hardly even recognised. Apart from the horticultural instruction they lived a closely regulated regime of healthy open-air exercise with responsibility for their own little plots of land as well as corporate work.

Dr. Hamilton no doubt had a difficult task on her hands. She had to make a viable commercial enterprise out of what had probably become a bureaucratic and complacent institution in its years of aristocratic patronage. She had a large staff to pay and a market garden business to render profitable on the back of an educational hostel for adolescent girls. All this was situated in a run down castle with forty acres of gardens, two hundred and fifty acres of farmland and extensive lawns and woodland.

In coping with all this she developed a reputation for a short temper as well as a managerial style that could be savage at times. She must have realised she needed to wield a hatchet to some of the staff to turn the place round financially, and wield it she did with a will. In days when there was little legislation to protect employees' rights she could still be so abrupt in sacking staff as to lay herself open to possible litigation. In the space of five weeks she sacked eleven men, three boys and four women, with the promise of more to go.

She was, however, capable of dispensing great charm as well as inspiring respect and even awe, and Violet Firth's time at the college was on the whole a happy and constructive one throughout her two year course.

She had a sardonic sense of humour and the alleged remedial aspect of the place was not lost upon her. One new girl received a characteristic welcome as she walked up the drive: "Oh my name's Firth. Are you mad? Don't you get on at home? Or have you been crossed in love?"

Poor Evelyn Heathfield, only eighteen, going on fifteen, hardly knew how to reply to a reception like this. As far as she knew she had just come to learn how to be a gardener. Sixty years later the memory of this welcome and the girl with a crooked smile was still vivid, which says a lot for the charisma of her newfound friend.

Violet Firth also had a reputation as a "kindly" practical joker. One remembered incident was stealing a look into the Warden's bedside mug to see if it really contained false teeth or, as was widely rumoured, a glass eye. It turned out to be teeth, but the two good eyes of the Warden caught her at it, peering above the sheets with an acerbic "Good morning Miss Firth!"

She also developed her literary flair, and collaborated in writing plays for the annual celebration of the Warden's birthday, a red-letter day in the February of each year. The first, in 1912, "Now and Then, a Contrast", by N. Brunton and V. Firth, was in two acts and showed Studley Castle as it might have been in 1812 when women sewed and were horrified at anything not regarded "proper". The second act was in the form of a dream by one of the 1812 daughters and a prevision of what the place would be like a hundred

year's hence. There was plenty of scope for light-hearted satire
here on the staff and senior students of 1912. In 1913, in
collaboration with a Miss Pearson, the play was a spoof pantomime,
"The Babes in the Castle" with further caricatures of senior students
and staff.

As a student Violet showed a gift for working in the poultry section.
The leghorn fowls were profitable and prolific layers but needed
careful tending. At the beginning of the January term of 1913, having
completed her time as a student, she was therefore taken onto the
staff. She seems to have distinguished herself in a somewhat
original way, as the Warden's notice of her appointment reads:

> You will see by our staff list that Miss Firth is back in charge of
> the poultry section. It would read like a detective story if I told
> you the details of how she found out that we were being robbed,
> and how she laid plans to discover the thief. She did discover
> him and he is gone. We are not sure, however, that there was not
> more than one. Be that as it may, our special private detective is
> not likely to allow such a state of affairs to recur.

It was a post, however, that she did not fill for long, and it would
seem that her penchant for being a "special private detective" soon
got her into very hot water. As she recounts in her book "Psychic
Self Defence", it would also appear that the Warden had special
talents in the techniques of interrogation.

That is to say, when the Warden needed supporting evidence to
sack or downgrade a member of staff, she would fix her chosen
witness in the eye with a concentrated gaze, tell them her version of
what had happened, and demand and expect their unqualified
agreement.

Violet had experienced something of these methods on a couple
of occasions. The first time resulted in something of an impasse
because she had kept a diary of events, which was directly at variance
with what the Warden wanted her to say. This did not prevent a
long and painful interview, after which she felt dazed and exhausted
and collapsed on her bed in her clothes and slept for a solid fifteen
hours.

On the second occasion there was no conflicting diary and she
found herself tamely agreeing to everything that was alleged, even
though she did not believe it to be true. What made matters worse

was that the accusations concerned her immediate superior, and may well have provided the opening for her on the staff as head of the poultry section.

Again she slept the sleep of nervous exhaustion, only this time, as she left the office, she felt that her feet were somehow not where they should be. It was as if the carpet were ballooning underneath her, a symptom that she later diagnosed as etheric extrusion, although medical science might still prefer to label it hysteria.

Soon after her elevation to the staff she discovered a scheme of the Warden's to lift financial pressure from the college by tapping the assets of some of the wealthier students. This may have been perfectly legal but it seemed to the idealistic Violet to sail somewhat close to the wind. A recent attempt had apparently backfired and led to a student's withdrawal from the college.

She now had reason to believe that a similar approach was going to be made to an amiable but mentally retarded old woman they all called Auntie Barclay. This offended all Violet Firth's principles and she took it upon herself to pack the old lady off to her relatives while the Warden was away.

Inevitably this act of disloyalty was discovered, and she was privately warned by the College Secretary to be prepared for trouble. Not wishing to wait until she was manoeuvred into a situation where she could be dismissed without a reference, she decided to take the initiative and seize the first reasonable excuse to provide her own good reasons for leaving. With the Warden's irascible temper this did not take long to find.

Full of righteous self-confidence, she packed her bags overnight and bounced into the Warden's office next morning to announce that she was leaving. She had, however, been warned by a fellow student that it might be better for her just to slip away without an emotional confrontation. So it proved to be.

Not entering into any argument, nor with any sign of being set aback, the Warden fixed the girl before her with a concentrated gaze and stated as a matter of incontrovertible fact:

"Very well, leave if you must, but first you must admit that you are incompetent."

Violet denied this with a show of youthful bravado. If this were the case why had she not been dismissed? And anyway, was she not a product of the Warden's own training?

This riposte elicited nothing but a repetition of the statement
and the maintenance of the fixed gaze:

"You are incompetent, and you know it. You have no self-
confidence, and you have got to admit it."

No matter what the girl before her said, the one sided litany
continued:

"You are incompetent, and you know it. You have no self-
confidence, and you have got to admit it."

And so it continued, remorselessly, over and over again:

"You are incompetent, and you know it. You have no self-
confidence, and you have got to admit it."

Rooted to the spot in the authoritarian ambience of the Warden's
office, this most junior member of staff met, hundreds of times,
with:

"You are incompetent, and you know it. You have no self-
confidence, and you have got to admit it."

And so on, and on, and on, and on, for four long hours, from ten
o'clock in the morning until two o'clock in the afternoon.

It continued until the bullied girl found the phenomena of hysteria
creeping up on her. She sensed two walls of darkness creeping up
upon her, from behind, one on either side. She felt that if that dark
tunnel engulfed her she would be broken, and her will and her
consciousness would be wiped out.

Still the repetition continued. It may seem very strange for a
college Warden to spend half her working day in bullying a defecting
member of her staff, but it seems that envenomed spite lent her the
will and energy to carry on this one-sided vendetta.

"You are incompetent, and you know it. You have no self-
confidence, and you have got to admit it."

And so, in the end, admit it Violet did. She thought that by this
she could trick her tormentor into giving up the obsessive attack
before she was really defeated. It seemed to her that voices from on
high came to her with this advice, but this higher intervention was
more likely to have been a dissociation of consciousness. In the
event, she gave in to what was demanded, kneeling upon the floor
in abject surrender, begging forgiveness, promising to stay at her
post and never ever to do anything to upset her employer again.

Victory complete, and purring complacently, the Warden allowed
the cowed girl to return to her room, where she collapsed once again

fully clothed upon her bed and lay unconscious for thirty hours.

The housekeeper next morning, who brought her round by shaking and cold water, discovered her. She remained however in a state of nervous collapse until eventually her parents were called. It perhaps caused the Warden some embarrassment to have to explain how their daughter came to be in such a condition, but she had of course the ultimate defence that they, just as we, have only the girl's allegations to prove it. What is more she could also say that it might be just an unforeseen development of the nervous condition that first persuaded them to send their daughter to the college.

It is something of an irony of fate that the victim of this psychic aggression should turn out to be one of the leading occultists of her generation.

It was, however, this first-hand demonstration of the power of magnetic suggestion that projected Violet Firth, the future Dion Fortune, into a study of psychology in its deeper aspects.

On a more fanciful turn of speculation, one might wonder what ancient grudge, what karmic net, what obscure initiatory test, what first step upon the path of destiny, might have brought the two of them together in this life like this? It is worthy of the plot of a fantasy novel, to see the bizarre figure of the Warden, rather like an old Atlantean priestess in attitude and demeanour, in a twentieth century re-enactment of a confrontation with some junior priestess in Atlantis.

A similar confrontation would indeed later occur, only upon the astral plane, between Dion Fortune and Moina MacGregor Mathers.

In fairness to Lillias Hamilton, we have one side of the story only, as recounted by Dion Fortune in "Psychic Self-Defence" and supplemented by the researches of Janine Chapman in "The Quest for Dion Fortune". Her obituary in "The Times" describes an ambivalent character. On the one hand her *"deep and generous understanding of human nature, her gay courage, her unconquerable zest for life, brought even those who might be differing from her under the spell of her persuasive charm."* On the other hand *"she could not suffer self-conscious fools gladly"* and *"To her work spelled salvation, and however great the demands she made on others – and she asked of them the utmost they could give, and generally got it – yet she 'laboured more abundantly than they all'..."*

Lillias Hamilton was obviously in many ways a most remarkable woman and one who might well be deserving of a biography of her own. In 1915 she left the college in the care of her sister to go out to the Balkans where she took charge of a hospital in Montenegro until driven out in the general retreat through Serbia. Back at Studley she continued as Warden until the year before her death, on 6th January 1925, (coincidentally the same date as Dion Fortune's demise, twentyone years later.)

Whether or not she ever made a serious study of occultism, she has been credited with writing a book with an intriguing title in this respect, "The Powers that Walk in Darkness", but it seems never to have been published.

Certainly she had come from a hard school during her sojourn in the East, particularly when she was Court Physician to Abdur Rahman, Amir of Afghanistan. As she wrote in her novel "A Vizier's Daughter", which was based upon her experiences there:

If my readers complain that there is no brightness, no happiness in my book, that it is a story without one ray of hope, I can but reply "Then I have succeeded but too well in my task of drawing a fair picture of life as it is in Afghanistan." There is no such thing as joy there. There is no such thing as peace, or comfort, or rest or ease. There is never a moment when anyone is sure he is not the subject of some plot or intrigue. There is no amusement, no relaxation; the people don't know how to enjoy themselves.

Indeed one punishment meted out to a harem girl who spoke out of turn to her superiors was to have her tongue cut out. In comparison to life styles such as this the young Violet Firth might well consider that she had been let off lightly for a similar misdemeanour!

In any case, leaving Studley College in April 1913 was the beginning of her years of esoteric apprenticeship. In this respect the dragon figure of the Warden might well be seen to have played the part of the traditional Dweller on the Threshold.

As to the effect upon the College, the following issue of College Notes simply recorded:

As usual there are some changes. Miss Dupree is no longer housekeeper, though still at College in another capacity, and Miss Firth has left the Poultry Department.

3

THE MEDICO-PSYCHOLOGICAL CLINIC

For months after this spiritual, mental and emotional drubbing Violet Firth's main concern was to recover from being a nervous wreck; to learn how stop her mind racing round and round, circling about the traumatic experience of the breaking of her will.

By the remedy of doing page after page of simple sums from a school arithmetic book she gradually gained more control of her mind and her life, although she was still prone to nervous exhaustion and general lassitude, where once there had been a vital energetic personality.

She found no answer in Christian Science and looked around for other ways to deal with problems of the mind. This led to the study of psychology and in particular to its latest advances in the field of psychoanalysis. This was no theoretical interest either. She enrolled as a student at the Medico-Psychological Clinic in Brunswick Square, that was founded in June 1914, and whose objects were:

i) *The treatment by medical and psychological means of functional nervous diseases and of functional disorders accompanying organic diseases.*
ii) *The advancement of this branch of Medical Science.*
iii) *The extension in the community of knowledge of the laws of Mental Hygiene.*

It soon became apparent in the operations of the clinic that most of the patients needed psychological re-education as much as medical treatment, for many of the nervous conditions they were called upon to treat were a result of faulty attitudes that patients had with regard to their problems and the ignorance of the laws governing emotions and behaviour. The training of a body of staff to carry out this re-educational therapy thus became an objective of the Clinic, and in July 1915 a parallel organisation was founded, called the Society for the Study of Orthopsychics, a name coined by one of the financial backers of the project, the novelist May Sinclair, some of whose later fiction had a distinct occult slant. ("The Tree of Heaven" 1917, "Uncanny Stories" 1923, "Far End" 1926.) The Society occupied part of the Clinic's premises in Brunswick Square, with facilities for a students' kitchen and common room and a lecture room. Violet Firth became one of these students.

The three-year course included a personal psychoanalysis together with lectures on the general principles of science, biology, psychology, philosophy, anthropology and comparative religion and mythology. After presentation of a thesis they were awarded a final certificate of proficiency.

Violet Firth must have shown considerable promise and ability for although she did not complete the course, she was allowed to supervise the work of other students, and even to give a series of public lectures on the basic elements of psychology. These were eventually published under the title "The Machinery of the Mind" with a foreword by A.G.Tansley, author of a major psychological textbook and Fellow of the Royal Society.

Students were assigned patients by the medical staff of the Clinic, who retained general supervision of the case while the process of re-educating the patient went on.

The type of re-education that was required is revealed in a later report of the activities of the Clinic and Society. It included what is now called occupational therapy, but more importantly what is nowadays called counselling, to help patients to cope with a variety of nervous symptoms.

The symptoms complained of are often of the sort which the lay mind is accustomed to regard as outside the province of medical aid, such as a secret mental worry, an apparently unfounded anxiety or depression, inability to take interest in the ordinary affairs of life, a morbid fear which is recognised to be absurd, a

secret habit which is struggled against, an unnatural impulse
which cannot be controlled.

Many persons whose lives are burdened by such symptoms
suffer in silence rather than reveal them to their most intimate
friends, or even to their physicians; either because they are afraid
of being laughed at, or because they do not realise that there
exists a department of medical science which has devoted years
of research to the investigation and treatment of these distressing
complaints.

The type of counselling that Violet Firth conducted at this time,
between 1914 and 1916, is revealed in a book that was published
ten years later as "The Problem of Purity". It is obvious that most
of the clientele who came to her were seeking some means of coming
to terms with their sexual urges in a repressive society. The text
may read a little strangely now, in a secular society where it often
seems taken for granted that sexual gratification, of whatever kind,
is the ultimate goal of existence. It reveals a glimpse however of the
psychological attitudes of 1916, when sexual urges were linked to
feelings of guilt, whatever the social circumstances. When even
contraception was regarded as taboo, and considerable stigma
attached to the woman who had "fallen". It is difficult now to
appreciate just how crippling and intractable the conflicts in the
hearts and minds of people at that time must have been.

In the course of her book she reveals that she by no means
accepted the psychoanalytic theories of Freud. Indeed she considered
that although Freud taught that all cases start with a sexual problem,
after a course of psychoanalysis most of the patients end up with
one! In her experience, the liberation of the sexual instinct tended to
lead to unlimited self-abuse.

Accordingly, she tried to instil a sense of the sacredness of sex
into those who came to her, to analyse its true physiological causes,
and to come to terms with it by means of controlling the imagination.

The opening paragraphs of foreword and introduction in her
book describe her aims and intended readership:

In this book I am trying to do for my readers what I have so often
done for patients who have come to me for psychotherapy. It is
really a course of treatments for sex control, and the earlier chapters,
which deal with standpoint and motive, should be carefully read

and re-read because they are intended to produce a frame of mind in the reader, just as I would do if he or she came to me as a patient.

Many books have been written which explain the facts of sex in simple language; many others which make appeals for social purity; and some few, of varying value, which deal with the problems of married life; but, so far as I know, none have attempted to deal in a really practical manner with the difficulties of celibacy, and to follow an appeal for control of the sex instinct by practical suggestions as to the method of attaining that much-to-be-desired end.

Whilst the approach may be based upon her psychotherapeutic practice of 1914-16, the book of 1927 (the last to appear under her own name of Violet M. Firth) contains some interesting visualisation exercises that are occult in origin even if the word is never used. They anticipate what Israel Regardie was later to reveal in "The Art of True Healing" (1937) and "The Middle Pillar" (1938) as a technique known as the Fountain Breath, derived from teachings of the Golden Dawn. If Moina MacGregor Mathers had taken exception to "The Problem of Purity" rather than to "The Esoteric Philosophy of Love and Marriage" one would have been less surprised, but it is unlikely that she ever read it as it was published close to the end of her life.

In this system as here described, a fountain of force is visualised as rising, manipulated from the base of the spine, not into the generative organs, but up the spinal column into the centres of the head.

As soon as it enters the brain it must be directed to the intellectual centres in the forehead, and you must picture yourself as having a third eye in the centre of the forehead, like the giants of old, and with that third eye you must imagine yourself to be looking out on the world from a great altitude, as if from an aeroplane, so that you see it with a bird's eye view, remote from yourself. Next you must choose some philanthropic movement that is of national service; you must then make a little mental picture of the work of that organisation being carried on, and you must project the energy you have dragged up from the base of your spine in a radiant stream on to that little mental picture, and then imagine yourself taking part in the work and willing the energy you are sending to be a driving force behind it.

This is pure occultism but would not have been part of Violet Firth's original psychotherapeutic practice, for she knew nothing of occultism then.

However, it seems as if her subconscious mind, even at that early stage, was pushing her towards a source of esoteric teaching. In preference to the student kitchen at Brunswick Square she spent her lunch hours at a centre run by the Theosophical Society that was close to her place of work and ran a good canteen.

Unrealised by herself at this time, she was a natural psychic, which is probably why she had been so profoundly shattered by the brow beating methods of the Warden at the college.

One day, more in a spirit of condescension than enquiry, she sat in on a lecture on mental telepathy. The lecturer proposed a simple practical experiment. She would concentrate upon an object and invite those present to see if they could pick up her thoughts. Into Violet's head came the image of a bunch of delphiniums. To her surprise, the lecturer announced that that was what she had been "projecting".

She was inclined to write this off as coincidence, but was further taken aback when the experiment was repeated. This time she saw a bunch of the flowers known as "red hot pokers". Once more she was correct. Again she realised that somehow she had read someone else's projected thought forms.

She just might have allowed all this to pass off as an interesting mental diversion but she was then brought face to face with even more startling evidence of the hidden powers of the mind. It came out of a strange case that one of her students at the clinic had brought to her.

Certain physical phenomena were occurring in the vicinity of a young man who was being treated by her student. Doors were flung open from no apparent cause, just after dogs within the immediate neighbourhood had set up an outcry. The student who was trying to treat the young man felt considerably out of her depth, particularly when her supervisor Violet Firth seemed unable to offer advice.

Accordingly, she decided to call in the help of a man who had recently returned from South Africa, an Irishman named Moriarty, of considerable charismatic presence, who was said to know a great deal about occult phenomena.

They all assembled at the flat, and upon witnessing the doors fly open again, with the accompanying barking of local dogs, Moriarty declared that an invisible presence had entered the room. The lights were lowered and a dull glow could indeed be discerned in a corner, it also induced a tingling sensation if a hand were put in its vicinity.

Moriarty pursued this phenomena by force of will, cornered it in the bathroom, pinned it inside a magic circle and despatched it by a process of absorption into his own aura, the repercussion of which knocked him unconscious.

The end result however was successful. It transpired that the young man occasionally felt himself possessed by some kind of presence but did not like to say so for fear of being thought mad. His condition immediately improved. So also, did that of a cousin of his, a young officer who had recently been returned, ostensibly shell shocked, from the Western Front, where after a successful cover-up by his influential family, he had narrowly avoided court martial for necrophilia.

It transpired that the two young men were in the midst of a homosexual relationship, and the sexual games the two young men played included the bed-ridden officer biting his young cousin in the neck to draw blood.

Moriarty's explanation was that the root of the trouble was the earth-bound soul of an Eastern European soldier. With knowledge of certain magical techniques associated with Transylvania, he had been maintaining a parasitic ghostly existence by feeding off others in this way.

This sudden confrontation with the deeper powers of the mind came as a great shock to Violet Firth. It confirmed a growing realisation that, although psychotherapy produced some insights into the human mind, it often fell far short of bringing real and lasting alleviation to its patients. In cases like this, admittedly rare, even diagnosis fell far short of an appreciation of the realities involved.

She later described the case in the chapter on Vampirism in "Psychic Self Defence" and wrote it up as fiction for the story "Blood-Lust" in "The Secrets of Dr. Taverner". The deviated sexual elements of the case demonstrate the truth of her assertion that some of the stories had to be written down rather than written up, before they were fit for popular consumption. The strong impression it had on her also led her to use much of the case for her first novel, "The Demon Lover", some years later.

More immediately the incident brought about a crisis of conscience as to the nature of her true vocation. Although she later maintained a great interest in psychotherapy, particularly the work of Jung, she retained no illusions as to her reasons for abandoning her psychotherapeutic practice.

I had come to the point when I felt I could no longer carry on my work as a medical analyst owing to the poor percentage of success that attended our efforts. (1922)

At the time when I first came into contact with occultism I was a student of psychoanalysis, which I had hoped to make my living as well as my life work. I had achieved some standing among my fellow workers, but was gradually being brought face to face with the fact that I had very little success in alleviating human misery, and this was a thing for which I was sincerely concerned; it made me genuinely unhappy when I saw cases drag on and patients spend their little all in the hope of a cure of which I knew there was no prospect. (1925)

I have seen a great deal of the inside workings of psychotherapy and if the truth were told, it would have to be admitted that it is the least promising branch of therapeutics. (1937)

It was also sparked by the awakening of awareness to the inner side of things.

... in the meditation class I had not only had a personal experience of thought transference, but some power had touched me that produced a profound spiritual upheaval; I looked at my psycho-spiritual work straight in the face, and knew that I could no longer go on with it, threw in my post and joined the ranks of the Land Army.

The time was 1916, and in an attempt to replace young agricultural labourers who had gone off to the war, the Women's Land Army had recently been formed. Violet decided that, as an immediate solution to her spiritual crisis, she could devote herself to the national war effort, and "do her bit" on the land.

4

THE LONE VIGIL
AND THE VISION OF DESTINY

There followed a hard year on a farm near Bishop's Stortford on the borders of Hertfordshire and Essex. She found conditions severe but the experience gave her the background for one of her later novels. Monk's Farm, the village of Thorley, the pub called "The Green Man" and Tilty Abbey all made their reappearance in "The Goat-Foot God".

She had now regained much of her confidence. From a middle class background in a class-conscious age she naturally fell into a median position between those who owned the farm and those who laboured upon it. She felt this experience between two social worlds helped in the writing of another of her early books "The Psychology of the Servant Problem". It was not published until nine years later, in 1925, but reveals something of the situation in which she found herself from 1916 to 1919.

> I cannot claim actually to have worked as a domestic in other people's houses, but during the war I had three years on the land, in which time I was made to realise the servant's point of view, for the simple reason that, working as a lady gardener, I was virtually in the position of a servant under private employers, and knew the servant's position from personal experience.
>
> Moreover (and it may be that I was lacking in proper pride), when I found that my interests were identical with those of the servants, I made common cause with the kitchen; and because I was also a servant, and had to come in at the back door, I got to know the minds and feelings of the girls I met during those three years in a way that I could never have done had I descended upon them from an above-stairs Olympus, however democratic my intentions might have been.

*The point of view of one who really "takes a job" in order to
earn a living is quite different from that of one who, in more or
less of a disguise, penetrates into working-class conditions in
order to see "how the poor live."*

Subtitled "A Study in Social Relationships" some of its chapter
headings reveal the stand she took, which was that servants had
their own self respect which should be observed, and they would
respond far better to employers by being treated more as fellow
human beings.

III   ANALYSIS OF THE CHIEF CAUSES
OF THE SERVANT PROBLEM

1. Class Distinctions
2. Two Standards of Living under One Roof
3. The Group-tone of the Servant Caste
4. Long Hours and Lack of Freedom

Some of the subsequent reviews indicate something of the rigid
class structures that were taken for granted in those days, and of
the religious party to take the most reactionary attitude.

*"... as she is of the employer class her contribution to the subject
should be of interest to both sides." Times Literary Supplement.*

*"In these matters we think Miss Firth allows her sympathies to
run away with her." Church Times.*

As far as the management were concerned however, it seems she
constituted quite a problem herself. Her strong idealism, belief in
direct action, and sense of fair play came to the fore as once they
had at Studley. This time she retained the initiative. When wages
were being paid late, tired of evasions and excuses, she stood with
the keys of the establishment poised over the sewage tank, and
threatened to drop them in unless the money was forthcoming. The
story is apocryphal, but it would be small wonder if some such
incident did not spur her transfer to a post with less inflammatory
potential.

A lonely laboratory post was found for her in a scientific
establishment. There was no risk here of her taking the part of

downtrodden fellow workers, for there were none – she virtually had the place to herself.

Her appointed task was watching over bacterial cultures, pursuing research into the soya bean. In a period of wartime blockade of an island nation, finding alternative sources of nutrition was important, and at the beginning of 1917 the Board of Agriculture established a Food Production Department to organise the greater production of food at home, under whose auspices it appears that Violet now worked.

The protracted isolation gave her, moreover, the opportunity to undertake some private experiments of her own, which gave very promising results. Indeed she made the major discovery of how to manufacture cheese out of vegetable casein, that is to say, from soya milk.

It was, as far as she knew, the first time anyone had succeeded in producing a non-animal protein of this type. It was a vegetarian alternative that might revolutionise the meat eating habits of the world. It could remove the burden of humanity from the animal kingdom. With her father's help she might even turn it to commercial advantage, with a company for the production of humane foods.

Indeed in 1925 she did publish a book about it: "The Soya Bean – an Appeal to Humanitarians", promoting the work of The Garden City Pure Food Co., Ltd., Letchworth, which was manufacturing pure vegetarian foods from the soya bean, and in November 1924 an advertisement in "The Occult Review" announced that the sole distributing agents for their plain and malted soya milk and cream, pure vegetarian butter substitute, and soya flour for bread and cakes, besides various other foods, were Firth, Weir & Co., Ltd., of Westminster Bridge Road, which was her parents' address just before they moved to Letchworth.

The boredom and isolation of her post also had another effect. It began to develop her natural psychic faculties. In the loneliness of the great empty building, what had seemed in the past simply to be a vivid imagination, now began to develop coherence as a series of astral visions. Vivid dream-like pictures rose before her inward eye with more than the force of normal imagination.

Her psychological studies enabled her to retain a sense of objectivity in the face of what was happening. Her experiences were similar to the symptoms of schizophrenia, or what was then called dementia praecox, but she was sufficiently aware of the mechanisms of the mind to realise that this was not incipient insanity.

Nonetheless, it set her thinking hard, and led her back to the Theosophical Society library in Tavistock Square. Here she found a stimulus in the writings of Annie Besant, the former assistant of Madame Blavatsky and now the President of the Society. In "The Ancient Wisdom" she read of the brotherhood of the Great White Lodge and of a hierarchy of adepts who watch over the evolution of humanity.

One passage in particular struck her with great force, just as a similar call, in the Rosicrucian manifestos two hundred years before, had enflamed a whole generation of esoteric seekers and has appealed to many ever since:

Still they teach eager pupils, showing the Path and guiding the disciple's steps; still they may be reached by all who seek them, bearing in their hands the sacrificial fire of love, of devotion, of unselfish longing to know in order to serve; still they carry out the ancient discipline, still unveil the ancient Mysteries.

The effect of this passage on Violet Firth was mantric; it ran through her head like a tune. Her whole nature became concentrated into a one-pointed desire – the desire to find the Masters. It dominated her conscious will. They had only to make themselves known and she would be willing to comply with whatever they asked.

She moved all day in a dream, performing her duties automatically. The Masters were her first waking thought in the morning, and her last thought as she fell asleep at night. Even her dreams were coloured by this same desire. She remained in this state for ten whole days and then on the tenth night had a vivid dream.

She found herself going down a long passageway, with many doors opening onto it. At the end was a place she recognised - the reading room of the library in Tavistock Square. The passage had been dark but the reading room was full of sunshine.

She stood for a moment in the golden rays that shone through the window, and then the whole side of the room opened out. She was caught up through space and transported to a plateau among great snowy mountains. She knew they were the Himalayas, and then she found herself kneeling at the feet of two great spiritual beings.

One was clad in a purple robe and the other in dark indigo blue. The first gave the impression of intense and all-embracing compassion, the second of tremendous intellectual power. The first she felt to be appropriately called the Most Holy, the second the Most Wise. So she remained in their presence for some time, remembering nothing, save that she should cultivate more reverence for that which was holy.

Then she felt a conscious change and in her dream was returned to the room in the library. Eventually she awoke, unsure whether it had indeed been a dream, a vision or an actual experience. An abiding sense remained however. She had been accepted as a pupil. Not by the Most Wise but, somewhat to her chagrin, by the Master of Compassion.

During the next three days she began to recover memories akin to those that she had had as a child. Of initiation in Atlantis, and an almost unbroken record of lives in temple service, apart from a recent incarnation when, after a most adventurous life, she had been hanged as a pirate at Bristol. Along with this came an intuitive grasp of the basic teachings of occultism.

Now she began actively to seek more formal instruction in these things. The stage of the Seeker had arrived.

5

THE FIRST TEACHER
THEODORE MORIARTY

Despite the impact of Mrs. Besant's book Violet Firth did not go to the Theosophical Society for practical instruction. She had seen some practical occultism at first hand and it is only natural if her thoughts turned to its source – Dr. Theodore Moriarty - who had acted so resourcefully in the strange case of the "vampire". She later described him as the first of her teachers and "an adept if ever there was one!"

He was of Irish origin, born on July 27th 1873 in Dublin, the son of a captain in the Royal Navy, the Irish Republic still being under the British crown at that time. According to the scraps of biography he told his students, he ran away to sea and joined the merchant navy. However one of the ship's officers interested him in philosophy so he returned to Dublin to study and from thence went on to Heidelberg, where it was assumed he had obtained a doctorate, although not in medicine.

He fell prey to tuberculosis at the age of twentyfour, a not uncommon illness in those days, and told to seek a dryer climate, emigrated to South Africa. There he worked on surveying roads before enlisting in the Customs service. He married, had two children, and developed an anthropological interest in local tribes, particularly the primitive Bushmen. He also became a Freemason and co-authored, with another prominent mason, Thomas N. Cranstoun-Day, two specialist books on the subject, "The Freemason's Vade Mecum" and "Notes on Masonic Etiquette and Jurisprudence"

He must also have studied occultism very seriously, for by the time he returned to England, during the war, he had begun to gain a reputation as an esoteric teacher, with students even in America. He taught a system of "Universal Theosophy" which had much in common with Theosophy but with a distinctively western bias, presumably all his own.

Three sisters helped him when he arrived in England, daughters of Francis Allen JP, of Swaffham in Norfolk. They provided him, each in their way, with facilities for his classes.

The first was Elsie Reeves, the widow of a surgeon, who provided residential accommodation for courses at The Orchard, in Eversley, a village in Hampshire, at whose church Charles Kingsley had once been vicar. In those days it was situated in the midst of wild heath land and in "Psychic Self Defence" Dion Fortune describes how visitors were met at the station by a horse and ancient fly. It is the location for some of the events associated with the strange "Miss L." including the strange duel with carving knife and saucepan of boiling vegetables for weapons.

There we find descriptions of Moriarty drawing pentagrams over door lintels as psychic barriers to control an unstable and recalcitrant student, an act that in the circumstances may have owed a lot to induced suggestion for its effectiveness.

The second sister was Ursula Allen-Williams, the wife of an army officer, who provided Moriarty with a large shed for lectures at the bottom of her garden in the west end of London, at Inverness Terrace - one street away, coincidentally, from Queensborough Terrace, where Dion Fortune would later have her London headquarters.

The third sister was Gwen Stafford-Allen, who allowed Moriarty to run his Science, Arts and Craft Society from her home, the Grange, in Bishops Stortford, not far from where Violet Firth spent her first year with the Women's Land Army.

The Grange was also a home for unwanted babies, run by Mrs Stafford-Allen with the help of two doctors and nursing staff under the auspices of the County Council. Here also Dr. Moriarty's Society offered an extensive course of esoteric study, including practical exercises and written examinations.

It is an amalgam of these three centres that forms the "nursing home" run by the fictional Dr. Taverner, who is in turn loosely based upon Theodore Moriarty. The stories ran as a series in the

"Royal" magazine between February and July 1922 and were the first fictional efforts of Violet Firth using her pen name of Dion Fortune. What Moriarty made of it all is not recorded but the author was considerably impressed when Leo Bates, the magazine's illustrator, although never having seen the man, drafted a very passable likeness of him.

In the stories the incident of the vampire story leads the field, under the title of "Blood Lust". It is of course considerably written up for purposes of popular fiction, although in another sense, having the less salubrious circumstances written down. The other stories provide dramatic scenarios for telepathy, induced autosuggestion, karmic debts, and influences of past incarnations, elemental beings, seedy occult groups, and a goodly ration of fictional skulduggery.

The introductory paragraph leading in to the first story reveals much of the intended readership of the magazine.

Do you throw a pinch of salt over your left shoulder? Do you avoid passing under a ladder? Do you mind if a hare runs across your path? Why?

You pretend to despise superstitions, but something beyond your intelligence, some instinct, compels you to obey them. The instinct remains since the days when your ancestors worshipped forgotten gods in forest groves, when the shriek of the human sacrifice propitiated the Evil Ones.

We dwell in a mechanical civilisation, but the strange men of the East know the secrets of the soul. They know that all our science is childish beside the things of the spirit.

Dr. Taverner, the hero of these amazing stories, was a physician of souls. He possessed the secret lore of the centuries, the key of past lives, an entry to the spirit world. He restored the soul-sick, and purged many of strange sins committed while the body slept and the spirit wandered amid its own element.

The creator of Dr. Taverner has studied psychic matters deeply. These stories are based on the very latest discoveries. They are a new note in fiction, the most thrilling and sensational stories yet published.

How much the real Moriarty and the fictional Dr. Taverner have in common is a matter for conjecture. Dr. Taverner could go into trance and this was also one of Moriarty's abilities. In "Psychic Self Defence" the process is described:

The adept, who was head of the occult college to which I have previously referred, and from whom I received my first training in occultism, was able to perform this operation, and I have many times seen him do it. He would go into a deep trance, after a few convulsive movements, somewhat like a slow tetany, and would then lose about two-thirds of his weight. I have many times helped to lift him, or even lifted him single-handed, when he was in this state, and he weighed no more than a child. A man can fake many things, but he cannot fake his weight. I have lifted him single-handed from the floor on to a sofa when in this state. It is quite true that, being rigid as a board, he was much easier to handle than the ordinary limp, unconscious human form; but there is a certain ratio between the weight of a grown man and the strength of a woman of average physique.

One of the Taverner stories, "The Power House" reveals the hero as skilled in ceremonial ritual. Moriarty was also keen on it, and the principle of co-masonry, that is to say, Masonic ritual open to women as well as men. Whether or not he obtained official sanction for it, he opened a lodge in Sinclair Road, Hammersmith, where such rituals were performed.

A record survives of the list of ritual officers for 1919/20. This was probably the first year of its operation, for eight members, including Violet Firth, are mentioned as "accolades". That is to say, they were appointed from the very beginning to form a team and not initiated in the normal way, as all later members would have to be. In this ritual team the Adeptus was Theodore Moriarty; most, if not all, of the officers were female, and the office of Junior Warden was filled by V.M.Firth.

She did not appear in the list of officers for the following year, probably because she had transferred her allegiance to the Hermetic Order of the Golden Dawn. However, her great friend Netta Fornario is named as Outer Guardian and the group seems to have made excellent strides for there had been thirteen initiations and an affiliation within the year.

Also, although Violet Firth, the Dion Fortune shortly to be, passed on to other teachers, and became a teacher in her own right, the influence of Moriarty persisted in many ways throughout her occult career, including the interest in Atlantis, in esoteric healing, in systems of cosmology, in the techniques of trance, and the bed rock of symbolic ritual.

She paid him a sincere compliment in the Introduction to the later publication of the Dr. Taverner stories as a book:

"Dr. Taverner" will no doubt be recognised by some of my readers; his mysterious nursing home was an actual fact, and infinitely stranger than any fiction could possibly be. To "Dr. Taverner" I owe the greatest debt of my life; without "Dr. Taverner" there would have been no "Dion Fortune", and to him I offer the tribute of these pages.

6
B. P. Wadia - an Oriental Interlude

Immediately after the war Violet Firth was still fancy free as far as esoteric affiliations were concerned. As well as her links with Moriarty and his group and her impending initiation into the Hermetic Order of the Golden Dawn she became involved for a time with the work of a visiting Indian occultist – B. P. Wadia. The association was short lived but significant enough in its way to point up some conclusions as to the working of the occult world.

B. P. Wadia was born in 1881, the eldest son of a successful Bombay businessman. He became an enthusiastic member of the Theosophical Society in 1904 and in 1907 went to work at its headquarters at Adyar, Madras. He became closely involved in the Indian Home Rule movement and for a time was interned by the British along with Annie Besant and George Arundale.

He was strongly politically conscious and started the first labour union known in India. In 1919 he came to Europe to attend a conference on the trade union movement and while in England took the opportunity to form a group to assist Westerners to make contact with the Himalayan Masters who had been behind the launching of the Theosophical Society.

Violet Firth joined this group, and vouched for the genuineness of some kind of contact, although she became a little uneasy as to just what it was, and eventually found herself at odds with Mr. Wadia. His interest in political activities and esotericism inclined him to try to influence the turn of events by meditation upon the group soul of the British nation. According to his lights this was in a very bad way and needed redemption and regeneration, which he intended to supply.

Violet Firth, however, could not quite understand how anyone could genuinely help the British group soul who appeared to dislike it so much. To her mind, he was a man of intense spiritual pride whose root idea was that the West should acknowledge the spiritual supremacy of the East and takes its spiritual inspiration from India. However elevated the expression of his spiritual ideals she felt he was trying to feed in an influence alien and hostile to her race and nation.

Taking stock of things she realised she was the only English person present in the group and Wadia, sensitive to her misgivings, suggested she withdraw from the group, which she found herself very willing to do.

However, as far as she was concerned things did not rest here. Although many people, including her friends, believed in the good faith of Wadia and the work he was doing, she remained very uneasy.

This disquiet came to a focus some days later, when sitting with a friend as dusk was approaching, they both became aware of an antagonistic presence in the room. To her own vision it took on the appearance of Mr. Wadia in an egg shaped sphere of misty yellow light.

She told her friend to wait outside and then projected a pentagram at it, as no doubt taught by Moriarty. The appearance shattered and disappeared to the accompaniment of a loud crack, which turned out to be a split in the panel of the door.

It was another of those bizarre synchronicities that occur from time to time in the practice of occultism, for which no logical explanation can be provided. Suffice to say that the projection of pentagrams, even accompanied by words of power, does not usually have such drastic effect upon the door furniture.

The incident served to concentrate her mind, and she decided to call for help upon the inner. It is revealing that at this time she had no conscious inner contacts of her own, apart from a general kind of beneficent presence that seemed to be of help in times of personal need. She therefore just put her head out of the window, figuratively speaking, and appealed to whoever or whatever might hear her to come to her aid. It would seem therefore that if Moriarty had any inner contacts of his own he kept them very much to himself, rather than reveal them to students.

Somewhat to her surprise she did received an answer. It came in terms of a voice within her head, which said: "You are to go to Colonel Fuller".

This was an instruction she did not fancy, and was very willing to put down to an aberration of her subconscious mind. She had met this gentleman once before and was conscious of him as a very formidable presence. He was quite well known in the occult world, having, in 1907, as Captain Fuller, published a long dissertation "The Star in the West", ostensibly "A Critical Essay upon the Works of Aleister Crowley" that was in effect an effusive panegyric of the Great Beast. In the course of time he rose to the rank of general, and was regarded as an expert on tank warfare, and was also an enthusiast of extreme right wing politics.

Violet Firth replied to her inner voice that she would need a sign before she bearded this lion in his den. The reply came that he would be at her next lecture. She was somewhat relieved to hear this, as it seemed to let her off the hook. She knew that the Colonel's regiment had been ordered abroad and presumed that he had gone with them. Nevertheless the voice was adamant that he would be there.

To her surprise, at her next lecture, Colonel Fuller duly appeared. Not only that, when she approached him he said that he had been expecting her to do so.

It turned out that one evening some time before, his two dogs had become greatly disturbed over something that was not there, and at the same time he received a strong inner impression that she would be asking him for help and that he should give it. So strong was this impression that he asked a mutual friend to write to ask how she was getting on, but not realising the connection, she had answered noncommittally.

Having heard her story he told her to leave things in his hands, and it so transpired that Mr. Wadia left the country a few days later. So things rested for about five months and then she heard her inner voice again. It told her to go to another eminent person and tell him the story she had told to Colonel Fuller. She felt much the same reluctance at the instruction as before, but was told the way would be made plain. Soon afterwards an old friend whom she only saw occasionally offered to take her to meet him.

She did not reveal the identity of this old friend, or of the eminent person, save to say that he was an advanced occultist. However, taken in conjunction with the time that all this occurred, we might well take an educated guess as to whom they were. In 1919 she was initiated into the Alpha et Omega Temple of the Stella Matutina – originally the Hermetic Order of the Golden Dawn. Her old friend whom she saw only from time to time, but who was obviously aware of what went on in the occult world was no doubt Maiya Curtis-Webb, as her introductor to the Order. The eminent person would thus have been the head of the Alpha et Omega Temple, the novelist J. W. Brodie-Innes. She certainly met Brodie-Innes and retained a great respect for him, in later years referring to him as *"an advanced esotericist and scholar in these things"* and as *"the late Brodie-Innes... whose pupil at one time I had the privilege to be."*

At the appointed meeting, when she duly delivered the message, her friend remarked how curious it was that Wadia had returned to the country only a couple of days before.

There is no conclusion to this story as recounted in "Psychic Self Defence" some ten years later. It ends with the remark that *"unless we are prepared to pull the long arm of coincidence out of its socket, we must conclude that some directing intelligence was at work."* However, we are not necessarily dealing with a psychic game of cops and robbers, of deliberate psychic attacks, and white magic and black.

B.P.Wadia was a respected member of the Indian section of the Theosophical Society for a period of eighteen years, during ten of which he visited overseas sections in America, Belgium, Canada, Denmark, England, France, Holland, Norway, Scotland, Sweden and Switzerland. In 1922 he resigned from the General Council of the Theosophical Society at Adyar because he felt that the Society had strayed away from its original teaching of the Masters given through H.P.Blavatsky. He then joined the United Lodge of Theosophists, a worldwide international network that had been founded in 1909 for much the same reason and purpose.

It is something of an irony that in this respect he was allied to a cause espoused by Dion Fortune a few years later, in opposition to the latter day Theosophical Society's promulgation of a movement announcing the coming of a new world teacher, to wit Krishnamurti.

Whether or not the experience of the hostile presence amounted to a deliberate occult attack is an assertion that has to be taken with a certain degree of caution, for although it was apparently perceived by two people, it was identified by only one of them. The psychic impression of the Indian guru could well have been pictorialised feelings of grievance upon Dion Fortune's part. On the other hand, should he, for his part, have been harbouring feelings of resentment, exacerbated by years of racial prejudice and political subjection, then these, unconsciously projected, could well have been picked up by a natural psychic.

In short, we have to be very careful before we jump to conclusions about deliberate psychic attack, which, along with occult secrecy, tended to be a favoured obsession with occultists of that era. Indeed, in this case, we have to ask what would the motivation have been? The troublesome member had already been ejected from the group.

The tides and currents of the Unseen are never easily catalogued and defined, as later ably demonstrated by Dion Fortune in her novel "The Goat-foot God", where we can not be sure whether we are dealing with personal delusions of the hero, reincarnationary memories, a straight forward haunting, or any combination of two or all three.

There are national and racial elements in the Unseen worlds, the archetypes of which can be very powerful, even in secular circles. They are the motivating force behind fanaticism and martyrdom for a national or political cause, as well as the natural feelings of patriotism or clan or family loyalties. Thus B. P. Wadia and Violet Firth may well have found themselves at the colliding edge of what might be described as two inner plane tectonic plates. They were occult representatives of two nations and cultures in ideological conflict. In such circumstances the occult scene may not be a comfortable place to be, for greater powers may well be tapped than might be intended, or that would be normally available to the individual.

In circumstances such as this these powers can be like opposing terminals of a highly charged battery. If they are short circuited, energies may be unleashed that are well capable of building or shattering astral images, even synchronously splitting the panel of a door. Indeed, the psychophysical effect might be regarded as a lightning conductor, shorting the supercharged energy safely to the ground.

In the last analysis of course, history has approved the justice of Mr. Wadia's cause, although the politics would have been nowhere so clear-cut, and would have aroused very deep feelings, in 1919. At least he lived to see it. He passed away in 1958 and Indian independence came in 1947.

7

INITIATION INTO THE
ALPHA ET OMEGA TEMPLE

In 1919 Violet Mary Firth was initiated into the Alpha and Omega Temple of the Hermetic Order of the Golden Dawn. It was, she later said, a feeling of "coming home" to where she belonged. At the same time it healed the leak in her aura that had caused her occasional nervous depletion since the incident at Studley.

It was now that she took on the Mystery Name, or aspirational motto, of Deo Non Fortuna – God not Luck - which also happened to be the motto on the Firth coat of arms, adopted by her grandfather John Firth. When she began writing on occult subjects she chose the slight variation of Dion Fortune as a pen name.

Strictly speaking it is a misnomer to speak of the Golden Dawn at this time. Three members of the Societas Rosicruciana in Anglia had founded it as the Hermetic Order of the Golden Dawn in 1888; a learned body open to high grade Masons. The esoteric basis for the Order was said to be derived from some manuscripts in cipher of German Rosicrucian origin that gave details of ritual initiations. These came into the hands of Dr. William Wynn Westcott, who asked his colleague Samuel Liddell Mathers to translate them and try to put them into working order.

Mathers, still in his early thirties, was of no fixed profession and dedicated his life, so far as he could, to researching occult subjects in the British Museum. 1887 was an important year for him, for he had just completed his first book "The Kabbalah Unveiled" which was published with a dedication to his friend and mentor Anna Kingsford. He was also on the point of marrying Mina Bergson, an art student at the Slade, sister of the famous philosopher Henri Bergson. She was also a close friend of Annie Horniman, the tea heiress, whom she had met at the Slade, and who funded the work of the two of them for some years. Mathers, who was proud of his Scottish ancestry, added the name MacGregor to his name, and on her marriage Mina Bergson changed her name to Moina as it had a more Celtic ring.

He now had the task of translating and editing the cipher manuscripts, which some people say do not exist. However Dion Fortune certainly believed in their existence for she knew people whom she trusted who said they had seen them.

Whatever the facts of the matter both Mathers and his bride were psychically gifted, and much of the power and more advanced teachings of the Hermetic Order of the Golden Dawn came from them albeit built upon a structure that had been received from elsewhere. This was particularly relevant to the 2nd Order, which was comprised of adepti, that is to say, those who had gone through the 1st Order initiations.

It is arguable however, that many initiates were allowed to pass through them far too quickly, particularly as they contained powerful contacts. Aleister Crowley, for example, who joined the Order in November 1898 as a young man of 23 had become an Adeptus Minor in fourteen months. He may have been intellectually bright but there are many other necessary qualities that need to be tested within the lower degrees of an occult fraternity that is working with power.

Shortly after founding the Isis Urania Temple of the Golden Dawn in London, the Mathers left for Paris and had considerable success in publicly staging the Rites of Isis at the French International Exhibition of 1889. Thus they anticipated Dion Fortune's similar enterprise at the Belfry in London by almost half a century. They then set up a Parisian branch of the Golden Dawn, the Ahathoor Temple, in December 1893, which attracted the membership of some leading French occultists, including Dr Gérard Encausse, better known as "Papus" founder of a reconstituted Martinist Order.

This same year they chartered the Scottish novelist Brodie-Innes to found the Amen-Ra Temple in Edinburgh, (an addition to two other provincial temples that had been founded in 1888, the Osiris in Weston-super-Mare and Horus in Bradford.) In the 1890's three American temples were also chartered, in Boston, Philadelphia and Chicago.

However, all was not well back in London, where the too readily invoked and ill controlled powers began to break loose, causing all kinds of dissent and distrust. Problems began with Annie Horniman whom Mathers felt obliged to expel in 1896, a major financial blow to him as she still provided subvention. Then Dr Wynn Westcott, a senior colleague and surviving founder of the Order was warned off by the authorities who felt involvement in a magical order unacceptable in a London coroner. He continued to perform a role discretely however.

Then came a major schism in 1900 when a number of 2nd Order adepts broke away. Shortly afterward a major scandal broke. In a highly publicised criminal trial a pair of confidence tricksters who claimed to be members of the Golden Dawn were convicted for raping a 16-year-old girl.

The Golden Dawn name, which had been desecrated in this way, was therefore abandoned by Mathers who changed the Order's name to the Alpha et Omega temple. The adepti who had tried to oust Mathers from the Isis Urania Temple chose to become the Hermetic Society of the Morgenrothe and then the Stella Matutina (Amoun temple) under Dr R.W.Felkin and W.B.Yeats.

Felkin, before he finally emigrated to New Zealand in 1916, chartered three Stella Matutina temples in England, of which the Hermes Temple in Bristol will concern us later. Yeats resigned and went his own way.

A second Alpha et Omega "northern" temple was founded in Edinburgh under Brodie-Innes in 1913, which also developed a London branch, in which Maiya Curtis-Webb played a leading role. It was into this that Violet Firth was initiated.

Soon afterwards, Moina MacGregor Mathers returned to London, after the death of her husband in Paris in November 1918 and took over the London branch from Brodie-Innes, which effectively became the third or "southern" Alpha et Omega temple.

The newly initiated Sr. D.N.F. did not at first appear to be a very impressive student but nor was she greatly impressed by the training that was offered her.

This was not a matter of disrespect for the powers behind the Order nor for the magical and psychic abilities of its founders. Her view was that if MacGregor Mathers was the original author of the Golden Dawn system he was one of the world's greatest men, but having seen the Order in operation she did not think he was that. Of the system itself, she wrote:

The effect of the ceremonies and methods taught by MacGregor Mathers was to produce the most remarkable psychic experiences and extensions of consciousness in those who had any psychic capacity at all; the methods and aim of these processes were intelligently taught in the higher grades in certain sections of this Order, and it was possible for those so instructed to produce the results at will, and the effect of repeated experiments was cumulative. They obtained, in fact, by psychic methods, the same results other people achieved by the use of such drugs as hashish and mescal, and without the disastrous after-effects that result from "loosening the girders of the mind" by physical means.

In the light of the experience thus gained, the ancient Mysteries became comprehensible, and the possibilities of psychic work thus unfolded were simply limitless.

She went on to point out, however, that students varied enormously in their capacity to make use of this opportunity. Some were simply futile, others merely scholars, frightened out of their wits of obtaining any practical results, although others became genuine adepts with signs following, including Aleister Crowley.

Certain aspects of the system she found too eclectic and synthetic, and in "Principles of Hermetic Philosophy", written towards the end of her life, she gave a practical example:

I have dismal recollections of consecrating the Lotus Wand to all twelve Signs of the Zodiac in a single operation. They kept on neutralising each other, and at the end of the operation one felt like the Irishman who tried to take his pigs to market, each tied to a separate string. People to whom magic is a vain observance may be contented with such methods, but for my part I never saw that Lotus Wand again, and never wanted to.

Whatever the merits of the system, a great deal also depended upon the administration of it, and these she found somewhat wanting in the Alpha et Omega temple, as she trenchantly observed some twenty years after her initiation.

The Order suffered severely during the First World War, and Mathers himself died in Paris from influenza during the epidemic. When I came in touch with his organisation, it was manned mainly by widows and grey-bearded ancients, and did not appear to be a very promising field of occult endeavour.

But I had had considerable experience of practical occultism before I made its acquaintance, and I immediately recognised power of a degree and kind I had never met before, and had not the slightest doubt but that I was on the trail of the genuine tradition, despite its inadequate exposition. For some reason best known to them, the elucidations and interpretations had been withdrawn into the innermost Inner by the secret chiefs, who simply sat upon them like broody hens on china eggs. The organisation had broken up into a number of disjecta membra, and everybody regarded everybody else with suspicion as not being of the true orthodoxy.

I, for my part, took no part in the human pettiness of the mundane plane, but worked at the system, and the system yielded fruits.

These fruits concerned the ability to make contact with powers behind the outer organisation. She later said that on looking back, for at least three years before her initiation, she had been working on the contacts of the Order into which she was now physically received. This takes us back to 1916 and the throwing over of her psychotherapeutic career.

She also remarked that on two subsequent occasions when the physical links had been broken they were eventually restored. These restorations would have been with Hope Hughes of the Hermes Temple of the Stella Matutina in 1930, after Moina MacGregor Mathers had expelled her from the Alpha et Omega; and then Maiya Tranchell-Hayes in 1940, after Hope Hughes had considered her support of Israel Regardie, as a renegade from her temple, reprehensible. Of this, more later.

8

TRANCE EXPERIMENTS
WITH MAIYA CURTIS-WEBB

Whatever the shortcomings she found in the Alpha et Omega training the new Soror found a support and guidance from the old family friend Maiya Curtis-Webb, who was present at a series of early experiments in trance mediumship between January and March of 1921.

Trance mediumship was no part of the regular curriculum of the Golden Dawn, and it is a technique that Dion Fortune would seem to have learned, at any rate in its rudiments, from Theodore Moriarty. It may well have been in Bishops Stortford that the incident took place described in "Psychic Self Defence" when she assembled a scratch team to do a bit of adventuring upon the astral and ended up doing acrobatics round the room before a terrified bunch of beginners.

In the first recorded instance of a properly controlled and conducted trance we find, on 11th January 1921, Maiya Curtis-Webb and an unknown man seated beside Dion Fortune, while she lies in trance dictating messages from an inner plane contact. The man might well have been Dr. Curtis-Webb, which could have stimulated the medical bias of some of the material. Dion Fortune is reported to have said, in later years, that Dr. Taverner was also, in some respects, based upon the husband of Maiya Curtis-Webb.

The communicator refers to himself at one point as the Master of Medicine, and the transcript begins, without preliminaries, in quite hair-raising fashion:

Suggestion may be used upon the ductless glands in dementia praecox in order to stimulate them to activity. It should be given under deep hypnosis if one can get it. It may be obtained by ordinary methods, by hypnotising through normal sleep, by the use of hypnoidal drugs such as a whiff of ether...

The words lie on the fringes of medical science and whether any medical or psychotherapeutic practitioners carried on in this fashion, using ether as an aid to hypnosis, and experimenting on the endocrine glands of schizophrenics, is a matter for conjecture. At least it seems no worse than convulsive electric shock treatment.

These early communications are in the nature of apprentice work when compared to the standards of fluency and coherency in Dion Fortune's later mediumship. Much that they cover in rudimentary fashion is later dealt with more systematically and in far greater detail.

As well as the medical snippets there is a short analysis of the seven planes of consciousness and passing references to Atlantis, as well as dark hints about occult attacks, a subject that seemed to excite great interest in those days.

There are also some interesting comments upon the techniques of trance communication that are being used.

Two people are required, in addition to the medium, one of each sex. The un-named male present is also acting as scribe, noting down all that is said. Maiya Curtis-Webb's function is referred to as the "bar" – a kind of guardian, watcher and mistress of ceremonies. By her knowledge of practical occultism she is expected to be a defence against the intrusion of lying or evil spirits.

The medium is described as the lower terminal in a circuit of communication that draws down force from a higher level. The inner plane communicator is the higher terminal who transmits his thoughts down into manifestation. The "bar" acts in-between.

At the start of the work, the medium, or lower terminal, withdraws from phenomenal consciousness, passes into sleep and thence into trance. The moment that sleep gives place to trance is indicated by a sound in the throat that marks "the closing down of the thyroid." Passing through sleep before going into trance seems a rather odd sequence, and the change of state of the thyroid gland would hardly be made by the gland itself, but might well be a resultant involuntary action of the larynx.

When the medium passes into an objective condition on the inner planes she raises her hands to call down the power. This is the moment that contact has to be made upon the physical plane. Their hands are joined to form a triangle, the male to the left of the medium, the female to the right.

Then when the medium crosses her hands upon her breast, in the sign of the Good Shepherd, they will know that contact has been made with the communicator, and the work can proceed.

Trance is described as of two kinds: the trance of perception and the trance of communication. In the trance of perception the medium closes down the physical sense organs, passes into a subjective state, and then becomes objective upon a higher plane.

In the trance of communication the medium passes subjectively to the appointed level, steps aside, and the communicating being makes contact with the subject's nerve endings, thus assuming control.

A being of sufficient calibre can bring through knowledge of the past and will have the power to function upon all planes, as well as having direct perception of the inner side of nature, the plane of causation, and the capacity to act as a channel for the transmission of power.

The same process can also occur with the medium's own Individuality or Higher Self. Indeed, as time goes on, given the right conditions, the Individuality will function more and more, eventually coming through in full waking consciousness. This can lead to the perfect synthesis of the whole consciousness, enabling the superconscious to manifest - which is the meaning of Initiation.

They were counselled to guard against premature psychism. That is to say, when the medium, having passed to a subjective condition, constructs a fantasy. This could be a great source of confusion, caused by emotional involvement on the part of the medium. No one can pass to the higher levels unless they are desireless, for desire holds the focus of consciousness to the level of repressed wishes. These wishes are then expressed in the form of an audible daydream passing off as a communication.

All communications should be examined in the cool light of the morning, and sifted by the test of Freudian symbolism and expressions of wish fulfilment by the medium's subconscious, the prime source of error.

During the next three days, if free association is employed, much additional information could be extracted from the subconscious mind of the medium, for much more is given than can be brought through at the time of the trance.

There also seemed to be problems of communication at the level of the inner plane communicator. In one script he refers to the medium as *"this on the floor"* almost in terms of her being an object.

Immediately after this, however, we have a spate of dark hints and flattering praises:

> *This entity has been trained and will be guided; you must help to bring it through. You have been trained for this purpose; you were bred for this purpose; all three were bred for this purpose. It is the South American line of the Sun Temples – the Maya line – the Atlantean Initiation.*

This kind of message one would normally associate with the worst kind of pseudo-occultism – high-handedness on the inner planes and egoic massage on the outer. However, in the record of the years that follow we have the basis for a more considered judgement as to the validity of these claims.

9

FREDERICK BLIGH BOND
AND THE GLASTONBURY SCRIPT

There is no further record of meetings after 15th March 1921 but work of this nature obviously went on. It would seem to have come to some kind of culmination that coincided with the Autumnal Equinox of 1921 and it took place at Glastonbury.

Maiya Curtis-Webb is no longer recorded as being present but we do have, along with Miss F., the medium, a Mrs. F. That is to say, Mrs. Firth, the medium's mother. The male member of the triangle on this occasion was a man whose name had become famously associated with Glastonbury, Frederick Bligh Bond.

As an architect and antiquary the Somerset Archaeological Society had appointed him, in 1907, to direct excavations of the Abbey ruins. He also happened to have a strong interest in psychical research and, without telling anybody, enlisted the aid of a medium, John Allen Bartlett, to aid him in his researches and guide him where to dig. With the help of automatic writing they drew up plans which led directly to the discovery of both the St Mary's Chapel and the Edgar Chapel.

No mention was made of the psychic means that had been used until 1918, when Frederick Bligh Bond revealed the fact in a book called "The Gate of Remembrance". As a result of this, and the fact that ownership of the abbey ruins had passed to the Church of England, official reaction set in and he was effectively barred from any further involvement with the abbey.

We do not know when his path crossed that of Violet Firth but she had become enamoured of Glastonbury herself. Much of the evocations of the atmosphere of the place that later appear in "Avalon of the Heart" have their origin at this time. She describes attending a performance of Rutland Boughton's "The Immortal Hour" there, which would have been the Glastonbury Festival performance of 1920.

When in Glastonbury she often used to stay at the guesthouse and art and craft centre run by Alice Buckton at Chalice Well. As part of the peace celebrations of 1919 Frederick Bligh Bond had designed and donated the wrought iron *vesica piscis* that adorns the well-cover to this day. He shared with Alice Buckton a belief in the Watchers of Avalon, an inner plane company of monks and other beings that are said to watch over the spiritual destiny of England.

At some stage Dion Fortune, or Miss V. M. Firth as she was still more generally known, made her mediumistic faculties known and at the Autumnal Equinox of 1921 a meeting was held with Frederick Bligh Bond present to try to make contact with the Watchers of Avalon. The results of this were looked upon as of some importance by those concerned, and it was carefully typed up and privately distributed under a formal heading.

Transcript of a Communication received in Trance through the mediumship of Miss F...at Glastonbury 9.30 p.m. on the night of the Autumnal Equinox September 25th 1921

Present: Mrs F... Miss F... and F.B.Bond. The trance was preceded by a few minutes meditation on the subject of the Watchers as Merchant-mariners of the old time and bringers of the New Philosophy of Glastonbury with the symbolism of the Temple.

The medium placed her hands in three successive attitudes uttering at the same time the words:

> *The Sign of the Builders;*
> *The Sign of those who sailed East and West;*
> *The Sign of the Good Shepherd.*
> *Joseph of Arimathea was a name – not a person – but a function, or office. There was much coming and going, not one single mission only, and the work was established in connection with the Druidical Orders; and was largely Druidical in its nature. It had a Druidical side.*

Question by F.B.B.   *Is it a fact as stated that the Druidical worship was very similar to the Norse?*

Answer   *The inner side of all religions is similar. This coming and going had been from time immemorial, and both in and out of the body on the part of the illumined. Travel was not so difficult in those days as we are apt to think, for the early voyagers had not the fears of the later. The Phoenicians held the secrets of the Tyrian Mysteries, and the Jewish were closely allied to the Tyrian.*

Having blocked off Bligh Bond's irrelevant questioning the communicator went on to say that there used to be a College of Illuminati here at Glastonbury, which had been a great centre of the Druid faith. Members of this College used to come and go in the ships of the tin trade in order to take their higher degrees on the Isle of the Holy Thorn, now Wearyall Hill and the site of Joseph of Arimathea's thorn tree, but the thorn tradition dated from before the Christian era.

There were many holy centres about Europe and Asia and men would journey from one to another in search of the special wisdom of each. Here, on the Isle of the Holy Thorn, was the best of the Sun worship and Serpent worship of the Northern Tribes, Gaul, and the coasts of Spain, protected by the marshes, for the purpose of prayer and meditation. Among the Abbey stones might be found stone of a different sort, harder, greyer, and of another formation, hewn from what had once been an ancient circle.

In early Christian times the true power lay in the wattle church, which was circular, a form not customary in Christendom, for the ancient power that was built here remained, That which was noble in the pagan was carried on into the Christian times. The original Christian impulse, which contained a heretical element from orthodoxy, had likewise gathered into itself that which was noble in the pagan Sun worship in the Syrian lands from whence it came. Hence the Sun Worship of the East met the Sun Worship of the North, and these conjoined gave stability.

Hence there is here an unbroken line of descent of mystic power connecting directly with the elemental powers of the soil, in which are the roots of the soul of the race. That is to say, of those who inhabit the land.

The earliest form of worship was of the Elemental Powers, whereby man planted in his soul the consciousness of them, by these means becoming partly self-conscious. Then the great Being who had previously taught the race returned again and curbed the Elements, which showed signs of taking control, and made the Cross of Nature into the Crucifix, whereby man sacrifices the natural to attain the human state.

We are now in the era of the Human – which might be called the middle kingdom, in which the human and the Divine interpenetrate, just as at the beginning of the era the human and the Elemental interpenetrated.

The brethren of Joseph of Arimathea were reputed to be twelve in number, just as Jesus had twelve brethren. These twelve were degrees, not men; twelve grades of initiation ruled by a thirteenth who was not of this plane but of the Executive Order of the plane above.

Therefore there has never ceased to be an open Lodge at Glastonbury. The succession has never failed; there has never been darkness there. The Tor has never lacked its Hermit. There has always been an Upper Chamber within the bounds of the circle of the marshes, where one soul in solitude meditated upon the Mysteries. Thus was maintained a focus in the flesh whereby the necessary contact could be made upon the other side.

Those who have functioned in this way have kept the channels open by their concentrated thought, leaving merely the thinnest film, like a psychic parchment, lest the power behind should break through into a world all unprepared, leading to martyrdom, not magic. This symbolic parchment has an osmotic action. Thus at Glastonbury the contact has never been broken.

Now the true Church was the Wattle Church and it is symbolic that in this summer of 1921 they had dug down to its foundations. The stone Church was built when the powers had passed men's minds, and the symbolism alone remained.

The builders knew the measurements; the meaning of pillar, arch, and triforium; they knew how to orientate, and where to place the symbols, but, in Jerusalem, the secrets had been lost.

The structure of stone represents the interplay of force. The concept in the mind of the architect is based upon the actual interplay and is thus nearer the truth than the resultant structure in stone. The church, temple, or other symbolic building is an attempt at Microcosm. The architect, conceiving the Macrocosm, attempts to reproduce it in stone.

The principles of Cosmic architecture are the same as the principles of ecclesiastical architecture, and great truths are conveyed, though blindly, in the proportions of the structure. But the greatest truths and the profoundest teachings and the truest morality are contained in the architect's failures for when he grasps beyond the scope of stone to express his ideas he is reaching towards the Absolute. Passing beyond the sphere of translation, he touches that which he cannot bring back in his hand.

Hence the dome that falls is often built by the aid of a greater mathematics than the dome that stands. It will be observed that, as greater concepts have imbued the minds of men, so have materials become known which could do that which could not be done before.

Upon all these points much more could be said, but they pass beyond the scope of a single communication.

Here the trance communication ended. It marked Violet Mary Firth's arrival as a medium of some quality.

10
THE OCCULTIST AS PSYCHOLOGIST

Frederick Bligh Bond was appointed to an editorial post at the College of Psychic Science in 1922 and he commissioned a long article from his mediumistic friend to appear in its Transactions under the title of: "Psychology and Occultism". The author was named as V.M.Firth and it marked a transitional phase between Violet Firth as psychologist and Dion Fortune as occultist.

These two elements were always present within her, but as she later remarked she began by trying to explain occultism in terms of psychology but ended by having to explain psychology in terms of occultism. In this early article she strove to tread the tightrope of the way in between and persuade occultists and psychologists to abandon their mutual suspicion and enter some meaningful dialogue.

She divided occult phenomena into five divisions:

1. The physical phenomena of the séance room - table turning, spirit rapping, levitation, moving of objects, materialisation mediumship, and even poltergeist phenomena. This is largely the province of psychical researchers with their various instruments and tests, as well as a vast amount of spiritualist circles, particularly in the 19th century, with amateur or professional mediums.

2. Unconscious transmission or translation of messages in techniques such as speaking in trance, or automatic writing

when the writer is not conscious of what is being written at the time – the technique used by Bligh Bond's friend when investigating the Glastonbury Abbey site. Bligh Bond often used to read a book to his friend to distract his mind while the writing went on.

3. Direct conscious perception such as telepathy and psychometry, clairvoyance or clairaudience. Automatic writing in this sense would be when the writer is writing down words that appear spontaneously in the head – not far distant from creative writing or psychoanalytic free fantasy. Or the describing of spontaneous images that appear in the visualising faculty of the imagination.

4. The action of individuals without a physical body, that is to say the humans who have passed beyond this life or various spirits from angels to demons and fairies or those humans in life who have the power to withdraw consciousness from the physical vehicle, in what is sometimes called astral or etheric projection, according to level.

5. Theories of reincarnation and karma.

Orthodox thought tended to sweep the whole of this away as fraud and delusion, not worth investigating, but which occultists, (including herself, upon personal experience) claim to exist. The point she wished to make that the occult theories, robbed of their esoteric verbiage, could be translated acceptably into psychological terms.

The 1st Class to her mind represents the point of contact between mind and matter. That a substance, either visible or invisible, exudes from the medium and frequently also from the sitters which is capable of being moulded by thought and then used as the basis for certain phenomena. This means that it can be moulded by the thoughts of the living as well as the dead, so that what is experienced within the séance room may not necessarily represent the presence of the departed at all, but the expectations and emotionally charged wish fulfilment hopes and memories of the bereaved.

She also thought that these ethers, being a vehicle for the life forces, if influenced by the mind of a gifted healer, could prove a *modus operandi* of mental healing and faith cures.

The 2nd Class, of automatic writing and trance speaking might well be the permitting of beings upon another plane of consciousness to act upon the medium's physical vehicle but might equally be a secondary personality of the medium, including perhaps one of a superior calibre to the normal personality with easy access to a great subconscious memory storehouse to draw upon.

She drew attention to seven "hypnoidal levels" corresponding to the planes described in occult theory.

i)   the etheric plane of spirit rapping phenomena;
ii)   the lower astral, the level of extremely undesirable manifestations;
iii) the upper astral, the commonest level of mediumship, of communications that are neither strikingly bad nor good, and seldom of much intelligence;
iv)   the lower mental, whereon the trained occultist usually begins to function, with communications of a much higher type containing interesting and valuable information;
v)   the upper mental, a level of abstract thought and a very high degree of intelligence not often contacted save by a high order of occultist, and only then by invitation of a being upon that plane;
vi)   the lower spiritual, seldom contacted, a level of cosmic awareness, which will make an indelible mark upon anyone who should have the privilege to touch it.

In the midst of all this there is the fact however that phenomena can be perfectly genuine examples of subjective conditions with no connection with other planes of existence or beings thereon. The long training of the occultist is to teach those who desire to experience these states how to recognise when results are subconscious and subjective or superconscious and objective.

It also frequently happens that a perfectly genuine medium may remain at a subjective state particularly sensitive to the minds of the sitters and also any mental currents that may be in the environment. Alternatively, a secondary personality left over from childhood may start to function. The situation here will be that the pool of subconscious memories may be motivated not only by the wishes and volition of the medium but by those of the sitters as well.

From this comes the rubric to judge communications entirely by their content, rather than their claimed source, with all the light that psychoanalytical techniques can throw upon the matter.

The 3rd Class is based upon the hypothesis of telepathy, upon which the bulk of occult phenomena are built up, and the consequences are very far reaching.

Orthodox psychology has always repudiated the assumption root and branch and when confronted with many well authenticated cases has preferred hypotheses in terms of subconscious seeing, hearing and remembering which seem even more far fetched than the occult hypotheses they deny.

Admitting thought transference or telepathy to be true however might give a clue to many obscure derangements, not least in the psychopathology of family life where the influence asserted by parent upon child, particularly an only child or a favourite child, could be in fact a most unwholesome rapport. The same condition can exist between friends, business connections and employer and employee.

In her psychotherapeutic practice wherever she had been called to deal with a problem of pathological resentment of authority or discipline, or inability to get on with others, an explanation of the theory of thought transference and advice on how to defend against it could very quickly solve the problem.

On the objective kind of telepathy that is sought in psychometry, the detection of ideas associated with an object or place, a whole theory of the nature of thought and being is involved. Whilst she believed that genuine psychometry does exist in a large percentage of cases it is more likely to be the action of subconscious phantasy mechanisms, and perfect good faith is not necessarily incompatible with error of this nature.

As for large scale reading of "akashic" records as in seeking to reconstruct past scenes in the world's history, such as Scott-Elliott's "Atlantis" or Rudolf Steiner's "Atlantis and Lemuria", before the subject should be dismissed with ignominy she simply wished to say that it was in entire accord with Jung's concept of a racial unconscious to which we all have access and upon which much of our behaviour is based.

With regard to Class 4, she wished to point out that the hypothesis of discarnate spirits and the survival of bodily death was not at all at variance with the doctrine to which all Christians nominally subscribe. If the idea that there are souls without bodies is added to that of telepathy then surely they are also able to communicate. In this connection, it may well be possible that suggestion and "rapport" could be set up between discarnate beings and the living and this could also play a part in certain forms of psychopathology.

Here the phenomenon of the Thought-form is also a matter to take into consideration, and upon this and thought transference the widespread phenomena of Christian Science and other forms of mental healing was based.

Class 5 and the doctrines of reincarnation and karma raise an extremely important point in terms of psychology. Are we to construct the psychology of personality upon the hypothesis of a single life or of the reincarnated expression of an evolving soul?

Science explains all innate disposition of a child in terms of heredity, but in her experience this was not enough, for a person's life often seems to be appropriate to his or her character. That is to say, if there is a weakness, the environment will conspire to play upon it, not once, but repeatedly as if presenting tests or a lesson to be learned. She had remarked upon this in the life histories of cases that had passed through her hands, whether as patients undergoing medical treatment or as those wishing to be analysed for the sake of self improvement. The logical result of this was that the karmic record of a case was the key to the present day character. Whilst it might be too much to expect at the present time that clairvoyance should be as important to the psychologist as the microscope is to the biologist, in her experience the more successful psychotherapists had a streak of psychism in them.

Her final view in the whole spectrum of psychology and occultism was quite unequivocal, and harked back to her own experience and decision to abandon her practice:

I believe that psychology is steadily being forced towards the occult standpoint, and that the present generation will see the theories of thought transference and reincarnation incorporated among the body of orthodox scientific doctrines. How anyone who works upon the human mind can escape his or her significance is a mystery. I only know that to me they came as a flash of light upon the darkness. I had felt as if I stood in the centre of a small circle of illumination cast by scientific knowledge, and that the darkness of the unknown pressed in upon every side. A number of threads were placed in my hands, and I was bidden to unravel them, but the ends thereof disappeared into the darkness, and those threads were human lives. I had come to the point when I felt I could no longer carry on my work as a medical analyst owing to the poor percentage of success that attended our efforts, when the doctrines of occultism were brought to my notice. Immediately on this realisation, the circle of light was widened, and I could trace the run of the threads; I could see whence they came and whither they were tending, and from the segment could calculate the circle.

She therefore commended the occult doctrines to psychologists, not as natural laws but as working hypotheses, and taking them in that spirit see where the facts led them. No one who investigated the matter could doubt the existence of the phenomena, and it was only those who had never seen them who repudiated them.

— PART TWO —

THE FOUNDATION YEARS – 1922-26

11

C.T.LOVEDAY AND THE COMPANY OF AVALON

Did she but know it, Violet Firth's formative years were over, and the foundation years of the work of Dion Fortune were about to commence. The student being ready, it was the time for those who were to help her to appear. She did not have long to wait.

Some time in the first half of 1922 Charles Thomas Loveday, an executive in London Tramways, accepted an invitation from a friend to pay a flying visit to Glastonbury. He had served in the Royal Flying Corps during the war, was an accomplished musician and also keen on the new science of radio, or "wireless" as it was then known. He made his own wireless set to listen to early broadcasts, and even when thermionic valves were introduced to radio receivers insisted upon using the old quartz crystal sets for the purer quality of sound. He was also a motorcycle enthusiast and owned a large Harley-Davidson motorcycle combination. It was riding in the sidecar of this machine that may have inspired Dion Fortune to write so evocatively of the Great West Road as they later motored between London and Glastonbury.

A neat precise executive type of man, he earned the nickname of "His Nibs" amongst the group of friends that formed around them both. He was already married, although not too happily, for a deed of separation was drawn up between him and his wife on 24th February 1923.

Although this came a few months after his first having met Violet Firth no romantic attachment seems to have formed between the two of them. He was some sixteen years her senior, having been born in Forest Hill, London, on 31st October 1874. His affectionate and friendly nature seems to have been channelled largely in the direction of Christian mysticism, although he was at one point, some years later, admonished by the inner plane powers for appearing to be too friendly to young ladies within the group. The emphasis however was upon naïve innocence on his part that could be misinterpreted. He later chose the magical motto of Amor Vincit Omnia – love conquers all – and as he rose in the ranks of the future Fraternity took on the archetypal name of Anselm of Avalon, after the great bishop of Glastonbury.

Nonetheless the meeting of Violet Firth and Charles Loveday, if not a case of love at first sight, was certainly one of instant recognition and realisation of a common destiny.

They were visiting Chalice Well, quite by chance. It was a moonlit night, and they entered the courtyard together from opposite sides. They struck up a conversation, and from then on their destinies in this life became closely linked. Loveday was at her side, or in the background, providing material and moral support for the rest of their lives. He did not long survive her, and his remains lie close to hers in the municipal cemetery at Glastonbury.

He later wrote a brief account of the beginnings of their work together and the key point, as he saw it, was an inner plane contact made with a group known as the Company of Avalon. This inner group, it should be said, was not unfamiliar to other Glastonbury dwellers, such as Frederick Bligh Bond, Alice Buckton and Kitty Tudor Pole.

The message they received, at 9.15 p.m. on August 5th 1922 through Violet Firth's mediumship, came ostensibly from a former priest, who gave the name of Arnolfus, and reiterated the gist of what had been received in the presence of Bligh Bond at the previous Autumnal Equinox.

When the Church first came here it was a place of power, and there was peace in the midst. The worship of the Sun passed over into the worship of the Son. The younger of the Druids came into the Christian faith; the older did not oppose, for this was ever a

*place of peace. For, think ye, it was a stronghold of the old faith.
How could a small band of pilgrims, men of peace, not of war,
have landed and built and dwelt, if those who held the island had
not permitted, and welcomed, and given as a gift the land on
which the church stood. The old faith gave the land, and the new
faith raised the building, and the young men came in, so that
there were men who were priests of both faiths. For at heart both
faiths are one, and the Druids held a tradition of the coming of
the wise men from the East; they were heralded by signs and
portents, and when they came were known and welcomed.
Therefore here you get the unbroken tradition of the Sacred Fire;
there was not conquering, there was reception, and the old faith
carried on. And here you have a line of force that strikes its roots
in the earth.*

He emphasised that every country has a head centre and a heart
centre, and in Britain these were represented by London and
Glastonbury respectively. It was thus in line with these sentiments
that they found themselves later with a headquarters in London and
a pilgrimage retreat at Glastonbury.

Arnolfus went on to emphasise the significance of the work that
was afoot.

With the ending of the Great War another age had come, bringing
in the powers of the spirit, and the old centres would awaken,
re-open and vivify. Here the nature forces, the Earth forces, and the
so-called lower forces of man's nature were friendly, not inimical,
because they had been attuned by pagan priests of old handing over
by acknowledged right of accession to the priests of the new age.

There had once been the building of the abbey but now an
unseen edifice was being built upon the same site, with invisible
walls, strong in spirit, raised by a great company of just men made
perfect who loved and served the spirit and faith of England. They
sought to meet those in the flesh who still served and remembered
the ancient glory that was Glastonbury.

The following day they received a similar message from one
who announced himself as Bishop Anselm. He emphasised again
the unique quality of Glastonbury as a place where there had never
been a break in the tradition of worship, from one epoch to another.
From the Elemental to the spiritual powers of the Grail there was a
complete run through of spiritual power. It was, in short, a place of

spiritual regeneration – as befits its ancient description as "the holyest erthe in England." It was represented as a native church, not a foreign one, wherein the people of this land could receive a down pouring of the Holy Spirit typified by the symbol of the Grail. There was here, something which could be found nowhere else in Christendom save at Jerusalem, the unbroken line of a national spirit partaking of the initiations of every age of the world's history. Avalon had never lacked a seer.

So much for history. What came now was a concentration of power, focussed by great men who had prayed, and still prayed – hence the power. In any attempt to pierce the veil between the planes three have always done the work, and this would be the case now. Later, others would be called to the work, but must be accepted with caution.

They should so live and order their thoughts that a channel might be kept open, for a channel was needed, and the communication ended in ringing terms in a contact obviously of great power:

Therefore with principalities and powers, angels and archangels, and the greater mysteries, bless we, preserve we, protect we those who serve.

[a different voice]
The greeting of the Company of Avalon to the brethren.

[Anselm again]
Remember, in the greater church you have power, the church of the great multitude who have crossed the bright ferry to the blessed fields of the dead. These ever pray, and await the return of all souls to the fold.

Eleven days later, on 17th August, they received more specific intimations of the power that was to be channelled through symbolic images at Glastonbury.

You have had those who told you of the past, I will tell you of the future. We are met here together for the down pouring of the power. The Chalice is above the Tor. This is the hour of the power of the Chalice. Those who look can see it as a crystal cup through which shows the ruby of the Blood, sailing across the night sky above the tower. Let all look who can see the vision, for now again there is power as of old time, and that power is upon us.

This I would have you learn – the secret of the power. You have had the gift of wisdom to prepare the way, just as John the Baptist prepared the way for his Master, so you must now have the power, and the power of the Chalice I can give you. And made strong by the wine you can approach the source of the power for yourselves. For power is the keynote, and power ye must possess, and by faith ye approach the power. Know that it is there – the power of the Risen Lord.

All Christendom has worshipped Christ crucified, we worship the living Christ, and in His power do we come, as with His messengers of old, each one sent by the living Master. And it is the living Bread that we offer to you, not a stone. It is the lifeblood, not merely the pressed juice of the grape that we present, and that fills the chalice. To each one that comes in faith shall power be given. For we preach not only the Christ of Galilee and Calvary, but the Christ of the Easter morning, the Christ who is amongst us though unseen, and who is the companion of the heart of every man.

These be living waters rising from an everlasting wellspring, drink ye of them. The power of the Unmanifest must be made manifest, and there be ways and means by which this can be done. There be some, who have the open eye to perceive, but others there are who can only understand with the heart; therefore must ye who can see be eyes for the blind. Now have we a place of power wherein it is easy to contact power, avail ye yourselves of it. Greeting.

These communications, with their penchant for the quasi-archaism of the 2nd person singular, seem a direct line from that which had been received the previous Autumnal Equinox in the presence of Frederick Bligh Bond. There was however a gradual change coming over the work. This subtle change was in the role and type of communicators upon the inner side.

It seems that they were being passed on from the mystical Company of Avalon, with its mission of a national spiritual influx into the church; towards a somewhat more Hermetically oriented hierarchy.

The young Violet Mary Firth aged 15 or 16, as featured in *The Girl's Realm*.

Above: Violet Firth as a student aged 20 or 21 at Studley Horticultural College.

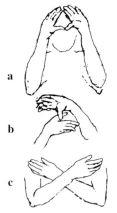

Left: Hand signs used in trance sessions with Frederick Bligh Bond in 1922.
a) the Sign of the Builders
b) the Sign of those who sailed East to West
c) the Sign of the Good Shepherd.

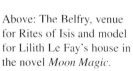

Above: The Belfry, venue
for Rites of Isis and model
for Lilith Le Fay's house in
the novel *Moon Magic*.

Above right: Violet Firth as
a student at Studley
Horticultural College,
c.1910.

Right: Dr. and Mrs. Penry
Evans, probably soon after
their marriage in 1927.

Above: C.T. Loveday with Miss G.P. Lathbury beside him and Katherine Barlow at the far right, at Glastonbury in the 1930s.

Soya Beans

The SOYA BEAN is unequalled as a human food, owing to the high percentage of PROTEINS and FATS, and the low percentage of STARCH, whilst the amount of VITAMINES in the SOYA BEAN makes it one of the MOST VALUABLE Foods, especially for Vegetarians and Food Reformers.

THE GARDEN CITY PURE FOOD CO., LTD., Letchworth,

are now manufacturing

PURE VEGETARIAN FOODS

from the

SOYA BEAN

at their Garden City Works.

SOYA MILK and CREAM
(Plain and Malted).

Pure Vegetarian BUTTER
Substitute.

SOYA FLOUR for bread, cakes, etc.

Various other Foods.

Full particulars from Sole Distributing Agents:—

FIRTH, WEIR & CO., LTD.,
Dept. C,

95 Westminster Bridge Road,
London, S.E.1

Tel.:—HOP 345.

Left: Promotion of products of the soya bean in *The Occult Review* for November 1924; the name of the "sole distributing agents" indicates her parents' interest in the scheme.

12

THE COMING OF THE MASTERS

A meeting on 28th September 1922 marked the beginning of the transition. The triangle consisted of Dion Fortune, (still referred to as VMF), C.T.Loveday and "E.P.", commonly referred to as "Edie". This is no doubt short for Edith, but her surname has slipped from history.

> *Place your hands within the chalice that you may feel the power. We are now building up a new group for the work that is to go forward. It is easy to build because we are already prepared with what has been formed. We are now pouring power into the room. It will be well when it is finished.*
>
> *There has been a combination of forces at work as there always are. These act as obstructions when the great spiritual force is flowing. These forces work through whatever channel they can find, especially through those who invoke them. They bring men power exceeding their own natural powers.*
>
> *But through all difficulties and dangers the work must go on, calling upon the name of the Masters. And be assured of this, there can be no harm done in spite of the ebb, storm, flow and wreckage of what is personal. Trust the Masters upon the bigger issues.*

From here on they began to receive a systematic series of teachings about the seven planes of the universe and their psychological equivalent, which in effect was an expansion upon much that is to be found in Violet Firth's article on Psychology and Occultism.

There was no indication as to the identity of those who were putting this information through. Indeed there seems certain fluidity in this respect, and the suggestion of a team rather than a single communicator - as in a postscript of October 4th:

When the course is completed we will take questions on it. Much that is not clear now will be clear then. You may have to change teachers; I am not the same as the other lecturer, as you may have guessed. You get to know us after a bit.

This turn of phrase suggests one who would shortly reveal himself by name, as David Carstairs. He came through with a more specific personal revelation very soon afterwards, in answer to a direct question:

Do I know the name Carstairs? Ought to. Signed cheques with it. My father was a cycle manufacturer in Coventry. I couldn't get on with office work. I was in the Cycle Corps. Of course I am pretty close to the Earth. Haven't been over very long. That is why I was put on this job. Makes it easier. The others have been dead a long time. Lucky to get this job, wasn't I?

The meeting of 15th November 1922 started off with rather heavy formality:

I give you the greeting of a Master in Christ. Tonight the lecture will be upon the subject of immortality.

At the conclusion of this Carstairs looked in for a few minutes to say:

Hello, thought I'd look in. That was Erskine the lawyer. He tells you what is right and what is wrong. The Greek will tell you how to do both. I will tell you the consequences. The Greek deals with more scientific matters.

You wrote up my remarks pretty accurately. I am often with you in the office. If you are in doubt just let your consciousness go. I will help you out.

You are quite right to read other books, they act as a countercheck.

Further elucidation about the mysterious Greek came at the end of November. In the meantime, the openings became more formal and the name "Lord Erskine" appears at the top of the transcript of each meeting. Typical of his style is the salutation of 24th November:

Greeting my brethren, in the Name of the Lord and Giver of Life the Most Holy.

You have done well, my children, and there is a blessing. You have taken down that which we have desired to communicate with admirable clearness. As has been said by our younger brother, your duty and privilege will be to present this matter in assimilable form to the uninitiated, but that will take a little time. It has first to sink well into your minds that this end may be achieved.

I will now, as promised, consider with you any points that may seem to you to be lacking in clearness. What are these points, my son?

Taking him at his word Loveday asked no fewer than sixteen questions on various aspects of the material they had so far received. At the end of this, after thanks had been expressed, Carstairs made his usual farewell appearance, to say:

Yes, I am here. You gave the old chap a gruelling tonight. Hasn't had such a gruelling since he was at college. Appealed to me two or three times to help him out, you won't see him again.

Carstairs seems to have had the function of what in spiritualist circles would be called a "control". That is to say, one upon the inner side who organises those who wish to communicate with the medium. This is certainly implied here, although it is only the senior teachers who seem to get a look in. He also evidently had a role as protector and guard as suggested by his closing invocation.

There are others waiting – queues of them – I stand at the door taking tickets. "All seasons please!" I am staying on with you for a bit.

Before I go, let us rededicate ourselves to the Master, and give thanks together to Our Lady for the love and protection she has given us, and to the Holy Michael – Saint and Angel – for defending us from the attacks of the dark forces. Amen.

However this was far from the last they had heard from "Lord Erskine", who continued working with Dion Fortune for the rest of her working life.

Carstairs' earlier mention of a Greek communicator came to fruition on November 30th, when he announced that an important new message was about to begin and they should make sure they recorded it.

It was the first arrival of the Greek master, who gave an address outlining the progress of the soul through the processes of initiation. After it, Carstairs reappeared to give a few breezy remarks about the abilities of the other teachers, in terms of the theory of the planes that had been the gist of much of the recent teaching.

Well, how are you getting on with the new teacher? He is finished for tonight. He does not find it easy to do yet. He has been over a long time. He was a Greek. Yes, the one mentioned before. He is working from a pretty high plane, and the result is that the vibrations get a bit faint. Not like me; just next door. He may be a bit scrappy. It will want sorting out. He is fond of aphorisms.

Lord Erskine was unusually good. He was used to public speaking. This man is more used to dealing with pupils by question and answer, as they did in Greece. He would get on the step of some public building, and young men would come and ask how many eggs made five, and he would tell them. He was later than Pythagoras. He got put to death, was a bit too much for them.

He finds it hard to keep a contact at all. He has to come down a plane, as we have to go up one. He isn't working from his own plane, but from the one below, and to do that he has to construct a vehicle, two moves, as it were. He is on the 5th plane; so is Lord Erskine. This one is not so good in coming down. I work from the plane on which I live – the 4th – they use me because I can get through easily.

You have a 4th plane medium. Most are of the 3rd plane. This one can be got on to the 5th if necessary, which is very rare. If you hoist her on to the 5th plane a 6th plane Master can come down, and this is how Initiations are done.

Now at one time it was as much fuss to get her on to the 4th plane as it is now to the 5th. But now she can come and go as she likes on the 4th, but we have to hoist her on to the 5th.

You are ahead of your schedule on this work. We did not expect to start on this till after Christmas, but all goes very smoothly. It is quite unusual to work a medium as much as this.

Most of the teaching so far received was written up and subsequently published as "The Esoteric Philosophy of Love and Marriage". It is in many ways a transitional book, combining elementary esoteric theory with Violet Firth's earlier concerns with social and sexual problems as a psychotherapist. It was also a period when both communicators and medium were learning the ropes of communication as they went.

Some streetwise modern occultists have declared this early work risible, but a high-powered contemporary occultist, Moina MacGregor Mathers, was aghast at what she felt it revealed. When published it almost caused Soror D.N.F. to be expelled from the Alpha et Omega for betraying higher knowledge reserved only for initiates, until it was pointed out that the initiate concerned was not of sufficiently high grade to have had access to this teaching.

It has been alleged that there was no such teaching within the Order to cause such a furore, but in a letter to Dion Fortune in August 1938, Paul Foster Case, writing to congratulate her on her work "The Mystical Qabalah" mentioned in passing that in his view what disrupted the Golden Dawn was "its worship of Mrs. Grundy." He gave as an example a reprimand he had received from Moina MacGregor Mathers when he was Praemonstrator of the Thoth-Hermes Temple in New York City in 1920, in which she wrote:

I hear that the Sex Theory subject has been under discussion in Thoth-Hermes Temple. I regret that anything on the sex question should have entered into the Temple at this stage for we only begin to touch upon sex matters directly in quite higher grades. In fact we only give a complete explanation of this subject in that grade where the Adept has been proven to be so equilibrated and spiritualised that he is complete lord of his passional self.

What is obvious with the benefit of hindsight is that Dion Fortune had, during this period forged her own inner contacts with Secret Chiefs that were at least on a par with much that had been achieved in the inner recesses of the Golden Dawn.

13

THE IDENTITY OF THE MASTERS

By the end of 1922, the principal triumvirate of Masters who worked through Dion Fortune's mediumship had made themselves known. David Carstairs, Lord Thomas Erskine and "the Greek", otherwise known as Socrates.

They may seem an unlikely trio, but as far as practical occultism is concerned, the only way to keep a contact flowing is to take it at face value. As in the theatre, for the magic to work, there must be what Coleridge called "a willing suspension of disbelief."

As the better type of communicators insist on saying, it is the quality of the communication that counts rather than any assumed authority behind it. This is quite obvious in regard to the vapid meanderings that are often "channelled" from exalted names, be they St. Paul, Merlin or Sanat Kumara.

As Dion Fortune was fond of saying with regard to any material that she had received by these means, let it be regarded at least as an experiment in practical psychology. If, in the last analysis it should be that the source is the subconscious mind, or the Higher Self of the medium, or the real identity claimed or some other teaching intelligence using it as a convenient mouthpiece, then so be it. Let the experiment run its course and see what value comes out of it.

Thus she took at face value the identity of her various contacts and questioned the results later. It was felt wise not to reveal these identifications indiscriminately to the outside world for, as Carstairs remarked, it never makes you popular to boast about your influential friends or rich relations. However, with the passage of time it probably does no harm to describe them now as their names have in any case passed more or less into the public domain.

Some doubt has been placed upon the very existence of the first contact, David Carstairs, for no army records confirm his existence.

However, possibly in accordance with some obscure occult law that says that nothing shall ever be certain in this game, it is possible he enlisted under another name, for according to his story he was an adopted child. He revealed as much in conversation with Dion Fortune's friend, Netta Fornario, in February 1924.

Did I ever tell you my story? You got some bits.

I was nobody in particular. Pater honest, but not poor. I was eldest of five. Three boys, two girls. I didn't do well in business. That annoyed the Pater. He wondered whether it was cheaper to pay me a salary or a pension. I wanted the salary. You see I got my eye on a girl. I should have retired earlier otherwise. Like most of us, we find girls a problem. I was puzzled because I got T.B. Had it in my knee and hip, but got over it. In splints till I was eight.

Thought she would have me. Asked the Pater what he thought of it. Told him I was thinking of getting spliced, was it alright? You and Mother are all sound, I was the only crock in the family.

Pater turned pea green, said "Afraid it isn't alright. The four aren't your brothers and sisters. Your mother died two weeks after you were born, of T.B. I'd cut my throat before I'd do the same thing again." So I cut it.

Then I took up the Boy Scouts. If I couldn't have a family in one way I thought I'd have one in another. Then it started in my lungs again, and Pater said he'd pension me.

He did not seem keen, however, that they make contact with his family, which they offered to try to do at this time.

No, nothing personal, I have no personality. Things in the Midlands are best left. I am obliged all the same. There was enough trouble over me in life, I don't want to poke my nose in, no one has asked after me. You cannot wait for people when evolution is on the march; have to keep up with your regiment.

Contacts with this perennial young soldier continued to be made for many years afterward. In 1950, after a long gap, he turned up to give a couple of talks through the mediumship of Margaret Lumley Brown, revealing that he had recently been taking an interest in the after death state of executed war criminals. In 1979/80 he made consistent contact with a close associate of mine in connection with Sandhurst military academy, and the ideals of young men who took up a career in the army. More recently in 1996/98, his character and story inspired a play by Rebecca Mazonowicz, "This Wretched Splendour", which had productions at the Playhouse Theatre, Cheltenham and the Grace Theatre, Battersea in 1997 and 1998. To those in the know it was a very powerful experience and it impressed a number of others too. A leading critic of the day, Michael Billington, observed in the Guardian: *The standard first world" war play is still R.C. Sherriffs Journey's End, but [this] knocks it into a cocked hat. "*

It was the culmination of an extended series of contacts, which involved visits to Ypres, and other battle sites of the Western Front on the occasion of the 80th anniversary of the Battle of the Somme. Much of this has been described in "An Introduction to Ritual Magic", and whether or not Carstairs "really exists" he is certainly capable of making his presence felt to those who are rightly attuned to him.

Lord Thomas Erskine (1750 – 1823) is largely forgotten outside of those interested in legal history. He was the third and youngest son of a relatively impoverished Scottish peer, the 10th Earl of Buchan. His family lived in an apartment in Edinburgh and because a university education could not be afforded he enlisted as a midshipman at the age of 14 on the frigate Tartar and was stationed in the West Indies.

When his father died, four years later, he used his patrimony to leave the navy and buy a commission in the army in the 1st Scots Royals. He married at the age of 20 and was posted to the island of Minorca for two years where he whiled away the time studying literature and learned most of Shakespeare, Dryden and Pope by heart.

In 1772 he was on leave in London and because of his aristocratic connections and easy manner gained an entry into polite society. He appears briefly in Boswell's "Life of Johnson", who records on Monday April 6th 1772:

I dined with him [Johnson] at Sir Alexander Macdonald's, where was a young officer in the regimentals of the Scots Royal, who talked with a vivacity, fluency, and precision so uncommon, that he attracted particular attention. He proved to be the Honourable Thomas Erskine.

Soon afterwards he made a big impression upon Lord Mansfield, the Lord Chief Justice, who encouraged him to give up the army and study law. In spite of the financial constraints of a growing family he managed to complete his studies at Lincolns Inn and Trinity College, Cambridge and was called to the bar in 1778.

His success was immediate and unprecedented. He was retained as a junior defending counsel in a celebrated case for criminal libel which showed every signs of being lost, until, casting aside protocol, he leaped to his feet on the last day and won the case with a brilliant speech. His reputation was made overnight and henceforth he was overwhelmed with briefs.

In a dazzling legal career he was made Kings Council at the early age of 33 when he also entered Parliament as M.P. for Portsmouth. He was appointed Attorney General to the Prince of Wales and became the highest paid counsel in the history of the English bar.

His sympathy with the French Revolution led to him to undertake the defence of many political prosecutions under the draconian laws for "conspiracy" and "seditious libel" that had been introduced by Pitt's Tory government. He defended Tom Paine, the author of "The Rights of Man" and a succession of other reformers such as Hardy, Tooke, Thelwall and Holcraft. The young poet Samuel Taylor Coleridge included him in the first of a series of twelve sonnets upon eminent men, published in the "Morning Chronicle" on December 1st, 1794.

TO THE HONOURABLE MR. ERSKINE

When British Freedom for an happier land
Spread her broad wings, that flutter'd with affright,
ERSKINE! thy voice she heard, and paus'd her flight
Sublime of hope, for dreadless thou didst stand
(Thy censer glowing with the hallow'd flame)
A hireless Priest before the insulted shrine,
And at her altar pour the stream divine
Of unmatch'd eloquence. Therefore thy name
Her sons shall venerate , and cheer thy breast
With blessings heaven-ward breath'd. And when the doom
Of Nature bids thee die, beyond the tomb
Thy light shall shine: as sunk beneath the West
Though the great Summer Sun eludes our gaze,
Still burns wide Heaven with his distended blaze.

In Fox's short Whig administration of 1806 he was raised to the English peerage as Baron Erskine of Restormel and appointed Lord Chancellor. Those who despised his success and his politics (that is to say the supporters of the Tory party and William Pitt the younger) lampooned him as "Sir Ego", a caricature of conceit. However, Coleridge's lines of his possibly continuing to shine from beyond the grave seems to have come to a more than symbolic fruition if Dion Fortune's contact is a valid one.

After his short lived Chancellorship he retired into private life as a man about town and caused something of a stir in 1821 when, at the age of 71, he eloped to Gretna Green to marry his housekeeper. The reason for this stratagem was because his sons by his first wife, fearful for their patrimony, wanted to have him confined as insane rather than see him marry again.

He was not a great Parliamentarian and is remarkable only for supporting one of the earliest Bills for the prevention of cruelty to animals. He also published pamphlets on army abuses, the war with France and one in favour of the Greeks, and a political romance "Armata", which has been described as an imitation of Thomas More's "Utopia".

This parallel with Thomas More, another Chancellor, is of speculative interest in the light of later belief that the Tudor statesman was a former incarnation of Erskine's. However, this connection was not made during Dion Fortune's lifetime but was first made by Margaret Lumley Brown in March 1958. As far as Dion Fortune was concerned her principle contact was always Thomas Erskine, referred to in most of the records as "Lord E." until 1940, after which he was only referred to as Magus Innominatus, by his own request, to outsiders.

Perhaps it is the claimed identity of Socrates that is likely to cause most problems of credibility, the famous Greek philosopher and inspirer of Plato, whose death took place in 399 B.C. We may as well at this point quote his address of self introduction when he first came through Dion Fortune's mediumship on December 5th 1922.

Greeting my children. It is not easy for me to speak to you. In the first place it is 1800 years [sic, later altered to "over 2000" by a correcting hand] *as you reckon time since I used these modes of thought, and conditions have changed so that they are almost unrecognisable. Then I have never used the language in which the ideas are expressed, and therefore have to impress them as glyphs, or pictures, which are translated with the help of our young friend who assists me, so I am really working through two relays or mediums. Moreover, I am not accustomed to the method of teaching by lecture, but of discussion, whereby the readiness of the pupil determines the nature of the teaching.*

I was a wandering philosopher, and lived in abject poverty, coming daily from my hovel to teach in the Portico, and the young men of the city of Athens came to me and we discussed life and death, and the gods and the future, and it was my privilege to direct them towards the Path even as I had been directed by my teacher, and for this they slew me as a corrupter of youth, and thereby did I win to the Path itself.

I came not back again, but worked in all grades in the worlds you call unseen, training and teaching the Illuminati, and have continued so doing ever since. Hence do I know the grades and work upon this side of things, but not upon your side. But my young friend who has just come over knows well the Path by which the soul comes to enlightenment. Therefore between us can we teach you the way of initiation as far as the portal of the Greater Mysteries. Beyond that, you must tread the Path yourself before teaching concerning it can be given you, for each grade is guarded by a ceremony and an obligation, without which you penetrate at your peril.

Now my children, I never lectured, but if you will gather round me as my boys used to do, on the steps of the Portico, I will tell you concerning these things. In those days I had a dear disciple who took down my words and gave them to the world, and by his writings alone am I known, for I was not learned as men reckon learning, even in those days, and today I would be reckoned an ignorant and superstitious old man, but I lived the life, and I was privileged to know the inner nature of things.

Now my children, we are all upon the Path; some are nearer the goal than others, and we all seek the same thing, but some have seen it more clearly than others, not because their eyes are keener, but because the Path mounts higher as you advance, and the higher the point of vision, the wider the horizon, and although I cannot see clearly the effects on your plane, I can see clearly the causes on the inner plane, for upon the plane of causes do I work.

Now as much as you may be taught by an old man who was not even reckoned wise in his day, I will teach you, for we are all seekers, and we all serve.

Now my children, this is like old times, when I gathered my boys about me in the sun and the dust on the steps of the Portico. And as we talked of eternal things, while the things that did not matter passed us by, men called it foolishness, but the gods thought otherwise; and when I died I was caught up to the Upper Heaven, and I went on teaching because I loved it.

Now my children, it is my task to talk to you concerning the Path that leads to illumination, which you all seek. What would you like to know about it?

Little need be said about Socrates that has not already been mentioned above. He was a model citizen of ancient Athens, given to philosophical discourse that would have been lost to the world if not recorded by his pupil Plato.

He fulfilled all his duties as a citizen, serving in the army and in the legislative assembly, where he distinguished himself by refusing to bow to the clamour of the mob to condemn nine defeated naval commanders to death without due process of law. On another occasion, under the rule of the Thirty Tyrants he refused to bring in an innocent man for execution. He was eventually condemned upon a charge of corrupting youth with his ideas, but rather than make an expedient escape to exile as was largely intended, he insisted on dying, as he had lived, in accordance with the law. His final hours are recorded in Plato's "The Last Days of Socrates".

These are the principal agencies behind Dion Fortune's mediumship. Whether their identities be taken at face value, or regarded as convenient stage names for archetypal models, or complexes from the medium's subconscious, can only be speculative theories. Much the same thoughts exercised Frederick Bligh Bond with regard to communications from members of the Company of Avalon.

However, Bond found help in his archaeological investigations by believing what they said, and Dion Fortune formed a Fraternity that has had a major impact upon the Western Esoteric Tradition. Something of the detail of how they did this, and what they said to achieve it, is revealed in the chapters that follow.

The Greek was often in contact in the early days of the Fraternity, encouraging members to try to make their own contacts with those upon the inner planes.

Have you yet become familiar with the inner planes? Use the picture method. Try and see us. It makes us so much more real, and when we are real to you we can talk to you so much more easily. It is by building a form on the astral that we contact you. That form has hitherto been built by the consciousness of the transmitter, but if you could build composite forms with the group consciousness you would obtain more definite results, and when each one of you has become accustomed to building a picture in consciousness in group meditation, and of hearing the sound of the voice, you would soon find that you are able to build that form in solitary meditation and hear the voice in your inner consciousness; and the more to whom we can speak, the stronger will the group be.

You will have many problems to solve in the course of your work, but one thing you must always guard, and that is your belief in the Masters, for without that you can do nothing. It is your contacts with them that are the source of your powers as a group, but it is highly desirable that each one of you shall learn to hear for yourselves the voices within, and for that purpose we shall work upon you and visit you individually, and you must try and hear us. You must listen for us and reach out towards us. Visualise us one by one, and call upon us and try to hear the answer. Thus shall you make the contacts for yourselves. For we are real. We are what we claim to be, and the proof lies in the power. If you doubt that power, invoke it and watch it work. When you come to these meetings come in faith, for it is your faith that makes the communication possible, and without it we cannot come through.

Reach back also into your past lives and try to remember seeing the scenes and yourself as moving among them. This is a valuable exercise in waking the higher faculties. You must become to dare greatly, and to trust your own psychism. The images rise dimly at first and are elusive, but not illusory. Learn to look at the fleeting images as they form and disappear and with practice you will be able to hold them steady. Remember that it is the imagination that is trained. It is with the imagination, that is to say, the power of visualising that the form is built in astral matter, which we use as material for contacting you.

Whenever you think of the Masters, you touch them, you lay the hand of your soul upon them. Think of the Master by his colour. It is very necessary for the work that the Masters should be with those who may be an open channel for communication;

*therefore we shall often come and talk to you about simple things,
and about your life, so that we may get to know each other.*

This is a far cry from the tendency to elevate the Masters to being
remote cosmic beings. It is also unusual to find positive encouragement
to try to recover past incarnationary memories – although it is
recovering memories for oneself that is encouraged, rather than
seeking out someone else's clairvoyance.

The reference to a Master's colour refers to teaching current at
the time of associating different spiritual rays with different colours
of the spectrum.

The Red end of the spectrum corresponded to the development
of the individual and the Purple end with the development of group
mind of the many, while the Green Ray of beauty mid-way between
them formed the connecting link.

During some of the vicissitudes that the early group had to
contend with Erskine also pointed out that in giving them advice he
laid no claim to being an infallible oracle of divine wisdom.

*I will now give you certain counsel, but in so giving I would
make this clear – that I do not speak out of omniscience, but am
even as yourselves, but more experienced. It is not a question of
difference in kind, but in degree. Moreover, I function upon the
plane of causation, and can perceive causes operating that are
beyond your cognisance. I have therefore access to more data
than you have; but I have not access to all. We will therefore take
counsel together to the best of our understanding. But I would
counsel you that you do not credit me with omniscience lest you
be disappointed.*

It was Erskine who also gave the pragmatic advice about the Masters
that is often quoted, albeit in slightly edited form from the original:

*The Masters as you know them, and the Hall of Initiation, are all
imagination. I did not say the Masters were imagination. I said
the Masters, as you know them; and I imagine myself, and you
imagine me, and between us we make a simulacrum on the astral
which enables us to get in touch with each other. What I am you
cannot realise, and it is a waste of time to try to do so, but you
can imagine me on the astral, and I can contact you through
your imagination, and although your mental picture is not real
or actual, the results of it are real and actual.*

The Masters, as they are supposed to be in popular would-be esoteric thought, are pure fiction. Learn to write novels on the astral because it is by creating a true-to-type thought form that you get in touch with that which transcends thought; and as long as you are a concrete consciousness you will have to use the astral to touch the abstract, and it is the laws of the astral thought form that are taught in occult science.

14

THE COSMIC DOCTRINE

Socrates turned in with a very complex talk on 3rd January 1923 and Carstairs said immediately afterwards:

You have had a pretty stiff time tonight. He is trying to make you understand different dimensions. It takes a fearful lot of force to get that stuff through. You had a sort of "trunk call". We worked it from this end. You are highly favoured. You can't keep this stuff up for long at a time.

All the work up to this time had been done by means of a triangle, as in the initial work with Maiya Curtis-Webb. Now however it was Dion Fortune, with C.T.Loveday and "E.P.", commonly known as Edie. Edie disappears from the record at this time but Carstairs said that as they had established such a harmonious working relationship they could carry on with just the two of them.

Weekly meetings continued in contact principally with the Greek, mostly on a discussion of the seven rays. All this might be termed "proto-Cosmic Doctrine" material. It was complex and to a certain degree disjointed, and most of what was received was expressed better later on. They realised they were being primed for some important work that lay ahead.

One communicator, simply called "an Agent of the Lords of Karma" on 28th March 1923 warned Loveday what to expect:

This Easter will prove a turning point in more ways than one. You will see a new life opening up before you, and new work.

Your first duty will be to equip yourself for the new work that will open up ahead of you. You must be equipped upon the outer and the inner planes, both working together.

Your first duty after Easter will be study by the means with which you are acquainted. Study forms the prime duty until you

*are both equipped to give that to the world, which is coming
through you. Study is more important than original work. Through
long years of study and experience your partner fitted herself to
give out teaching on the esoteric psychology of sex. Long years
of study and preparation will be required of you both for the
work that lies ahead.*

*Upon the physical plane, order, discipline and security are
requisite. While you study on the inner planes you must build up
conditions on the outer plane until the time is ripe for the greater
work. In the way of discipline your partner has much to learn,
but is improving. On the Path of Knowledge there is much for
both of you to learn, and it shall be your joy to learn it.*

*Conditions are being put in order for the work to go forward.
Ties are being adjusted, and the financial position is being made
secure. All things are being harmoniously worked out.*

*There is much work ahead, a great work to be done for which
conditions are being made.*

*You will always work in obscurity, but your influence will be
felt further than you yet dream. Means are being provided to this
end. Have no fear; you will be protected, even as you have been
protected. Do not fear the censorious eye, you are safe.*

*You will follow the study marked out for you. You will be in
the hands of certain teachers. Trust them, but trust no one with
confidences.*

In the years that followed, this statement turned out to be
accurately prophetic. It was confirmed a week later by one called
"An Initiate of the Order" who gave general instruction on what
constitutes the work of an Esoteric Order. The following extract
might be noted, for it has a bearing on their relationship to the
Alpha et Omega Temple of the former Golden Dawn and the inner
Order that might lay behind it.

*The visible aspect of an Order: its lodge, its regalia, its
manuscripts, its tradition, its officers, its ritual, and its
members, is but the physical body of the Order. The ensouling
force is in the Unseen; and the ensouling force, though it may be
withdrawn, should the body fall into decay, can reincarnate in a
new foundation.*

In light of subsequent events relating to Moina MacGregor Mathers
in 1927, Hope Hughes in 1930 and Maiya Tranchell-Hayes
(formerly Curtis-Webb) in 1940, to say nothing of Israel Regardie

in the intervening years, there is much within this statement that
bears consideration.

The more immediate hints and portents came to fruition, at least
in part, on 30th July. The Greek arrived and began to dictate the first
chapter of what was to become known as "The Cosmic Doctrine".

This work has been compared to Moriarty's "Aphorisms of
Creation and Cosmic Principles" which his senior students
succeeded in compiling from lecture notes at much the same time.
A number of terms and concepts are common to both works, which
Violet Firth may well have heard when attending the lectures of her
first teacher. Indeed, following the instruction they had recently
received to turn their minds to study, it is natural to assume that
this would have included lecture notes she herself had made whilst
working with Moriarty.

There is a considerable sea change however in the way that
Moriarty's terms are used. It is as if they are verbal or ideational
bricks in consciousness, which higher intelligences are using to
build a completely different edifice. Moriarty's aphorisms in turn
bear a strong resemblance to "The Stanzas of Dzyan" in Blavatsky's
"The Secret Doctrine" before taking off into his own realisations.
So it would seem that we are seeing the successive building in
succeeding generations of an extended body of doctrine based upon
a common inner tradition.

As it happens Moriarty died from angina pectoris on 18th
August 1923 in a hotel in Kings Lynn. It is therefore unlikely that
he had anything to do with the transmission of "The Cosmic
Doctrine" from the inner planes. Section One, entitled "The
Evolution of the Cosmos", was dictated by the Greek over six
meetings between 30th July and 30th August 1923.

Then there was a break until 9th December when a new and
different communicator took over, who was simply called "The
Psychologist". He dictated twelve chapters in twelve sessions on
"The Evolution of the Logos and his Regents", concluding on 17th
January 1924.

Of this new communicator, the Psychologist, the Greek
remarked:

> We are progressing very satisfactorily. We were privileged – very
> privileged – to obtain the last communicator. The most difficult

*part of the work is now over. You had a history so far. We shall
not be able to continue a straight line of historical narrative
any more. We shall have to deal with different branches.*

These different branches came through at various times during 1924
and early 1925. An unnamed new teacher took over on 16th January
1924 and continued through to 25th May, giving them the sections
on "Influences under which the Evolution of Humanity is
Conducted."

The remainder of the work, consisting of teaching on various
Cosmic Laws was commenced on 10th November 1924 by yet
another new teacher, referred to as "The Young Greek". Carstairs
arrived to announce him:

*You have got a new man tonight – another Greek. A younger
one. He is doing all the "influences". He works through two
relays – another and me. It is a higher plane than you have had
yet. You get a kind of imprint, you get the impress of a mind and
that produces its equivalent as near as possible. We get a
remarkably good transmission. They generally have to try their
hands. He has done a good deal of it. You should have heard the
other Greek fiddling with the controls!*

On 9th December another member of the inner team arrived to say:

*In the preceding lectures you have received an enumeration of
certain Cosmic principles. In the set of lectures, which are now
being given you, you are shown the application of these principles
in the mundane sphere.*

*I have not lectured to you before. The previous lecture was
given by a man who was a teacher before I was an initiate.*

On this night and on 14th December he gave them teaching on the
Law of Limitation and it is apparent that there was a small group
present, for questions were invited. By way of illustrating the
working of the Law of Limitation he explained that bringing an
abstract spiritual principle down into manifestation is a form of
limitation, and this includes the process of communication from
inner plane teachers such as himself. This throws further light on
the matter of identities used for the purpose of communication.

*When great spiritual truths are to be communicated to finite
consciousness they have to be transmitted through the medium*

of a personality, which shall exemplify the teaching given. That is why the teachers who communicate with you always give you a sense of the last personality in which they were incarnated, because this forms the link with the physical plane for them. What they are now is quite different to what they were then, and what that is you cannot grasp.

It has, therefore, to be transmitted to you through two relays, one on this side and one on your side. The entity who desires to communicate visualises himself as he was in his last incarnation, and impresses that picture on the consciousness of the person who is to transmit the communication. That is why the medium always impersonates the communicator. This will explain many things if you think it out. It explains the voice, it explains the vocabulary and mannerisms, but it does not explain the power you feel in the room; that is the emanation of the entity itself. And remember entity can speak to ego if ego can hear.

Each one who is present on these occasions should endeavour to concentrate and to hear the vibrations of the entity. They will then be in the same position as the medium. They should not seek to hear a voice, because in all cases the voice is the product of a point of limited consciousness, but they should endeavour to feel the vibrations of the entity, which is about the medium.

Do not concentrate on the medium, concentrate on the entity, and the ideas it is unfolding, or concentrate with us in your consciousness as well and this opens the way to receive the direct teaching yourselves. Never lose the opportunity of making the acquaintance of the person who communicates, because it will familiarise you with the unseen.

I shall no doubt come to you fairly frequently, because I shall have instruction to give you on the phase of the work that is opening up before you. Continue as you are doing.

They had by now succeeded in acquiring a permanent headquarters for their work with a sanctuary set apart from day to day disturbance. The communicator went on to stress the importance of this.

The more you come out into manifestation, the deeper must be the isolation between whiles. You must maintain very carefully the sanctity and isolation of this home. It is for that reason that you are isolating your Sanctuary, and great power will concentrate there. Keep the lights dim there, and allow nothing to disturb it. Lodge work will reinforce it. You can conserve in the Sanctuary the atmosphere of the Lodge, for the East and the

Altar will always be in the Sanctuary. You will have great power generated there.

It is well for you to accustom yourselves to this means of communication. It is perfectly normal. I am just as much alive as you are. You must learn to accustom yourselves to the idea that man is consciousness, not a vehicle, and then there will be nothing strange to you in the idea of contacting consciousness. It is one of the chief bases of occult work that the imagination takes the initial step. Faith is the basis of all things. If you have faith, determination, and courage, you can achieve anything. It depends on no one but you.

There is more power in meditating in silence, but you should invoke aloud. By invoking aloud you give rise to certain vibrations, which have an important effect because they have their correlation with the subtler planes. You invoke aloud in order to bring through from the subtler planes to the physical, but when you meditate you aim to go to the subtler planes.

It is so much easier to go on to the subtler planes than you realise. First you imagine yourself to be there, and then you will yourself to be there. People usually reverse the process. It is necessary to make the form before you pour in the force. You do it now to a greater extent than you realise – you are functioning on two planes, you have more vision than you bring through to conscious consciousness.

The work of "The Cosmic Doctrine" was finally completed on 25th February 1925. On 1st March the Greek master congratulated them all.

It is a long time since we have met. I find myself somewhat unskilled.

The work was completed in other hands than mine, but not by another mind. The mind of the Master continues to inform his tradition. The conclusion of the work was no doubt a great satisfaction to you, and even a greater satisfaction to us. You have had very steady contacts.

The dictation of an entire system in such a manner as you received is a unique achievement. Such teaching is usually conveyed piecemeal to consciousness and therein sorted out with more or less addition of extraneous matter, preconceived opinions and limitation of type. In this case the communication was rendered verbatim, and though not in all respects complete, is

accurate so far as it goes and will no doubt receive elaboration
in due course.
This will no doubt provide you with material for some time to
come. You will not immediately exhaust its possibilities.

In conversation with Loveday immediately afterwards he hoped that
it would be published, as it would form a stepping-stone for future
work. It was indeed produced in duplicated form for study by senior
students in the coming years, and C.T.Loveday gave public lectures
based upon it, but it was not until 1949 that it achieved wider
publication, in a slightly edited version with a certain amount of
additional material. An unedited text, with Loveday's contemporary
diagrams, was eventually published by the Society of the Inner Light
in 1995, and by Samuel Weiser in 2000.

15

THE INFORMAL GROUP

In pursuing the reception of "The Cosmic Doctrine" we have somewhat anticipated ourselves, for a very great deal else was happening to Dion Fortune and her group during 1924.

Although they had been meeting regularly for trance work they had no permanent place of their own as a focus for the work.

When in Glastonbury they would have stayed at Alice Buckton's guest house at Chalice Well, and they also hired an old farmhouse nearby in Chilkwell Street. It was here that Dion Fortune experienced her celebrated vision of a salamander after a fiery accident with an oil lamp.

Some trance work also took place in Letchworth between 1923 and 1925 in connection with her parents' projects, although the inner plane contacts were somewhat indeterminate, being described as "a Communicator from Glastonbury(?)" or "Another Communicator", although at the end Carstairs might turn up to answer a few questions. Letchworth was regarded as a type of spiritual centre, coming under the protection of St. Alban, and working through Christian socialist ideals and the early Labour party. As one script has it:

> *The veil there is as thin on a group level as it is on a church level at Glastonbury. The church and churchyard around it is as much a centre in its way as Glastonbury Abbey and the Tor are in their way. It is not on the same spiritual level as Glastonbury, but it is a true centre of its own level and has to do with the soul's development.*

Despite their lack of a permanent base they seemed to accept a few pupils on the Masters' behalf. There is an interesting interview at this time with Dion Fortune's old friend Netta Fornario on the occasion that David Carstairs spoke about his former home life, as previously quoted. This was part of some introductory chat about Netta Fornario's dramatic and literary interests, for she was also active as a writer using the pen name Mack Tyler.

The main point of the meeting though was whether she could be taken on as a student along with her boy friend, who, somewhat to mutual embarrassment, happened to be already married to another.

The interview that followed throws an interesting light on the trance personalities of both Carstairs and Erskine. Carstairs seemed quite shocked, and remonstrated forcibly with the man for becoming so involved with two women at once.

> *What did you reckon you were driving at when you started this affair? When you announced yourself and came out of your burrow. You reckoned you'd work with her, is that it? Why couldn't you work without talking to her? When you announced yourself, what were the terms of the proposition?*
>
> *It is not a crime to love, but sometimes it is a crime to tell. If you can't say "Marry me, and I'll make you happy" all you can say is "Love me, and I'll make you miserable."*
>
> *You wouldn't have done it with my sister. If you can make good of it you can redeem it but you are going to pay up in suffering for speaking.*
>
> *What I say to you, as man to man, is "Those things aren't done." You don't need to raise the dead to be told that.*

Following upon this barbed response, Lord Erskine turned up, to take a much cooler line, in part as lawyer, in part as inner plane adept, in part as spiritual director, in part principled, in part expedient, in part avuncular. In the text that follows, only Erskine's words were recorded, but interjections and responses from the young man and Netta Fornario can be surmised.

> *Greeting my son. Yes, I am Lord Erskine.*
>
> *So you brought us two new pupils. Well my children, what is all this about? In my day I was a law officer of the Crown, what is it that you wish to ask me about?*
>
> *You can disentangle your affairs with two things – boldness and patience. You, my daughter, are normally bold. My son, you are normally patient. Let the bold one practice patience and the patient one boldness.*

You desire to serve the Masters, I think. The Masters need those who can stand up before them, and before the world, and interpret them to the world by speech and by their lives.

I gather, my son that you have made a bargain that you have reason to regret. What were the terms of the bargain? What did you offer? What did she offer? Has she given what she offered? What did she offer? When people make contracts we expect that and no more.

Did she say she loved you? What did she refuse that she had promised? Did she ever promise them?

My son, if you look at the terms of that bargain, you will perceive that you made a very bad agreement. Though irksome, it was the agreement to which you put your hand.

Did you expect a happy marriage? Then, my son, you have been disappointed in your expectations. You put your hand to a contract, my son, which you had not read through, and you have paid the price. There are yet the costs of the action, my son, for release from a contract contrary to the public interest.

You are entitled to institute nullity proceedings. I do not perceive any danger. Wherein does danger lie?

I should advise you to start nullity proceedings. I think it questionable whether you would obtain a decree, but I would advise you to start nullity proceedings.

You desire to partake in this work that is afoot. Before you can do that it is necessary to balance your account and settle all outstanding debts. This should demand your attention. Until you have met your liabilities, my son, and are satisfied that you are morally solvent I should advise you to place this young lady beyond the reach of harm.

[Firmly] *I am a lawyer, not a parson. I am not interested in your soul. I repeat my advice that you should safeguard this young lady's reputation. You will admit that that advice is not uncalled for. May I suggest that you act towards her as a man of honour, so that you can show your face among men of character.*

[To her] *Until he can safeguard you from attack; until he has arranged a satisfactory quittance to the unsatisfactory bargain. Legal marriage is not necessary; you have no occasion for marriage. But you must ensure the work and the teaching. If you were guilty the work would be judged, and you would bring discredit upon that which you have sought to benefit.*

[To him] *I should advise you to take the necessary steps to limit your liabilities with your wife until freedom is completed.*

My son, if you handle this matter wisely you can, I have no doubt, make an amicable settlement, which shall leave you free for the work. I may tell you this, you would not be able to obtain a divorce. You have no grounds for divorce.

I should counsel the greatest discretion, my children. If you cannot stand a few months' separation, can you stand the test of a life long partnership?

In my opinion there is no possibility of divorce unless you disgrace yourself; but a bargain, having proved unsatisfactory, a separation might be satisfactorily arranged. This would be a suitable conclusion to an injudicious bargain.

I should suggest that, acting upon legal advice, you make a definite offer in writing. That you should negotiate through your legal adviser in the matter. But I would urge most strongly that you should not bring disgrace upon this young lady, or allow her to soil her repute.

Lack of thought will not substitute lack of wish. She would be free from the danger of being dragged into Court. My children, when you can enjoy each other's society as harmlessly, you can enjoy it as freely.

[evidently in answer to a question as to whether they could write to each other]
You may, but be careful as to signatures. Send unsigned letters of which the envelopes are destroyed. Envelopes bear postmarks.

Set the heart on the highest, my children, and realise that the lowest is not for you. If you elect to follow the Path, and serve the Masters, you elect to forego the pleasures of the personality. Before the door of the temple stands the altar of sacrifice. In this work, upon its higher aspects, the forces that a man and woman use for their mutual pleasure are sacrificed to lift the burden of humanity. It is a dedication, as the priesthood is a dedication; and at the end of a life of dedication there is no further need to reincarnate. You would enter the Light as one, my children.

Of the abstract affections one gives all and asks nothing. You have let this slip too far, and if it goes further then it will be broken. Conditions can be remedied, however, without disturbance. Meet as friends meet, but not as lovers, because you are not lovers, you are servants.

Do you meet any other men of your acquaintance twice a week? At lectures one meets freely, but remember, my daughter, you must safeguard your honour. You can meet as friends, as you used to meet, but not give occasion to censorious talk.

Remember, my daughter, that your reputation is the basis of your service. If you sacrifice your reputation you sacrifice your usefulness.

Wherever there is true love there is no wish to harm the beloved. You will not ask such a sacrifice of him in vain.

It is the Path, by which many have gone, my children, and by which many will go, and if you tread it aright it will be easier for those who come after you. You have both suffered, and there are many who suffer as you suffer. If you suffer aright, my children, there will be less suffering for others.

What does your karma matter? If you clear this you will not reincarnate. If you think that either I or any other Master will cause a death you are mistaken. We shall not offer you the pleasures of the senses. We shall not free you to gratify them. We offer the pleasures of the spirit.

My children, it is the way of the Cross. Perhaps you will fall beneath the Cross, but they will raise you again. At the end there is the Crucifixion. Do you know what follows on the Crucifixion? You are sent into Hell first, where you preach to the spirits in prison; and when you have done this, there is the Resurrection. Easter morning follows the night of Good Friday, and after the Resurrection there is the Ascension; and after the Ascension eternal redemption.

Therefore, my children, by treading the way of the Cross, and by the Crucifixion of the Self, you will rise to Redemption. The Path, which you tread with bleeding footsteps, you smooth for those who come after you. If, by the bearing of this burden you achieve the summit, the burden will never be so heavy for those who come after you. This is the sacrifice of the great Love.

Another interesting interview was recorded in March 1923 between Carstairs and Lillian Reeves, who had been a member of Moriarty's 1920/21 team, had later worked with Dion Fortune and Loveday in a somewhat desultory manner, until she left, as much pushed as resigning. It is worth quoting for the points it makes about personal contacts and the role of the church:

I will give you a big tip. Make your thought form, and ask for it to be ensouled. Visualise it. That gets your contact. For instance, you go to Mass; you see with the eye of imagination what ought to be; at the invocation of the angels, imagine the church full of them; at the consecration imagine the power coming through the east window – see the dove come and settle on the bread and wine – and as you picture it see it suddenly "flick" alive. It is a very difficult thing to build a thought form from the unmanifested planes, but it is easy to get it ensouled when it is well built on the manifested planes.

Visualise a form, and so make a form in astral matter, that's your trick. See it all in pictures, and then see your pictures become real.

You lost some good things in leaving the Church. People are not sufficiently tolerant. You lost a lot worth picking up again. Nothing is all bad, otherwise it couldn't remain in existence.

There are many aspects and types of nature, or ministers, and particular places. You can get something out of anything; a case of what suits your temperament. You had an overdose of Church. You have had to put it aside and get your poise.

Catholic work is 3ʳᵈ Plane work – the plane of the emotions. The 3ʳᵈ and 6ᵗʰ Planes are closely allied. That's why the quickest way to get to the 6ᵗʰ is through the 3ʳᵈ. If, however, you wish to retain steady contact on the 6ᵗʰ, you must go by way of the 4ᵗʰ and 5ᵗʰ.

Your work is essentially a 3ʳᵈ Plane work, but balance it with the 4ᵗʰ and 5ᵗʰ, and inspire it with the 6ᵗʰ.

The Planes work in pairs: the 6ᵗʰ and the 3ʳᵈ; the 5ᵗʰ and the 4ᵗʰ, and the 7ᵗʰ and 2ⁿᵈ.

You will find the big and the low often run together. Only the 7ᵗʰ can control the 2ⁿᵈ. Where there is spirituality there is always sex.

Now, for practice, visualise me.

Answer: Fair, not tall, blue eyes, nice face, etc.

Yes, you'd find me in a crowd.

16

THE HOUSE OF THE ORDER

In April 1924 Loveday was told that a London headquarters for the group would shortly be obtained into which they could move at the Autumnal equinox. The contact was simply recorded as being "a 5th Plane Master", who went on to make some remarks on the mechanics of inner plane communication and some of its problems.

He defined two types of mediumship, the automatic and the inspirational. In the automatic type the medium was completely dissociated from the body, with the nerve endings of the organs of speech acted upon directly by the communicator.

In the inspirational type of mediumship however, which they were using, the medium's personality remained intact, only the conscious mind being dissociated, and the communicator worked with the complexes of the medium's subconscious mind.

All such complexes that were integrated with the personality were at the communicator's disposal but if the medium had any dissociated complexes, they failed to come under his control and were the falsifying elements in any communication.

The communicator also drew attention to the need for a high quality group surrounding the medium, for the subconscious mind is naturally telepathic and therefore receives impressions from the sitters as well as the communicator.

This is of no great consequence in matters of which the sitters have no knowledge and to which they have no emotional reactions. The results will be accurate.

However, where the sitters do have knowledge, the subconscious mind of the medium can avail itself of this knowledge to extend the range of ideas at the disposal of the communicator. This can be a great advantage, and even essential in communications requiring specialist knowledge. A later example of this was the series of contacts with the Master of Medicine, which required a qualified medical practitioner to be present for communication to be fully effective.

If however members of the group have strong feelings about the subject, they will flow like currents of air about the circle, and it will depend upon the power of the communicator as to whether he can maintain his ascendancy over the medium or not. It can seem as if several people were trying to speak at once through the medium and the loudest voice will make itself heard, distorting the communication.

Carstairs arrived on 4th June to confirm that the matter of the London headquarters at Queensborough Terrace was virtually accomplished. It came to them apparently as a result of a legacy in Loveday's favour but Carstairs gave Erskine full credit for it.

He wangled the house business, as he said he would. Things like this take place on the inner planes about three months before they manifest on the physical plane. We had moved already on the inner planes, and the focus of attention was there. That is why it is not possible here to get into deep trance. Trance will become deeper when things have settled down again. VMF must be kept from mundane affairs, she cannot do both.

This period of uncertainty and expectancy had indeed had the effect of closing down the "Cosmic Doctrine" communications between January and November of 1924.

By the end of August 1924 they were able to hold meetings in the new house and by the beginning of October had installed their first bed-sitting room tenants to help pay their way. In what seems something of a bizarre procedure those so admitted were introduced to Lord Erskine through the mediumship of their entranced landlady. No doubt those concerned were familiar with esoteric teachings but nonetheless they evidently found the situation somewhat unnerving.

Erskine tried to reassure them:

Greeting, my children. This is no doubt a new experience for you. There is no occasion for alarm, you will grow increasingly familiar with the fact that a man's body is the least part of a man. That which is essential, however, is the mind, and the mind persists. The soul is not answered by the actions of the body but of the mind.

No doubt you wonder why you have been summoned tonight. It is for the purpose of making your acquaintance. All things must have a beginning, and this we trust will be the beginning of many things and of much work that we shall perform together...

You have penetrated, my children, deeper into the arcanum than you realise, and you must not be surprised when you find the power of the arcanum about you. There is nothing you need fear. They are powers of good – regenerative powers – great spiritual potencies...

You have been summoned residents in this house in order that your dedicated service may be given effect to. It is your function to maintain the conditions of the mundane plane for the performance of this work. As you are no doubt aware, the work has to be performed by a group upon the inner plane and a group upon the mundane plane, and the intermediary between the two...

As time goes on you will become increasingly familiar with those of us, your brethren, who are not blessed, or shall we say encumbered, with physical bodies. We are all about you, coming and going, just as any other members of your group. It is only because you have not the senses to perceive us that we pass unnoticed. Under special conditions we are able to render ourselves perceptible to the denser senses, and by this means we familiarise you with the concept of the unseen worlds close about you.

Believe me, there is nothing strange in the concept of unseen presences, though there may be something strange in the methods of manifestation which have to be used at present, but as your consciousness develops, as it will in this atmosphere and under these conditions, you will become increasingly less dependent on such unnatural modes of manifestation as we have temporarily to make use of. The veil between the seen and unseen grows steadily thinner with the progress of evolution and under certain conditions, and in certain places, the veil may be drawn aside. It is intended that this place should furnish these conditions.

After which impressive introduction one can only guess the effect of Carstairs' breezy hail and farewell:

Hello, I feel kind of left over. I feel like the beer after the champagne. It seems to me that after you have dined at the Ritz you don't want to drop in at a coffee stall on your way home, so I won't keep you.

17

RECONSTRUCTION OF THE LODGE

Although the disturbance of finding accommodation had effectively closed down the deeper forms of trance communication, it did not stop Dion Fortune from getting on with other things.

When Theodore Moriarty died in August of 1923, it is reported that Dion Fortune somewhat shocked his followers by inviting them to accept her as their leader. The invitation of this junior member was forthrightly declined but it seems that nonetheless she was quite prepared to take the lead in continuing his ritual work, whether or not the others chose to follow her. The implication is that it would otherwise have been abandoned.

Thus on 20th August 1924 she started a formal ritual group along similar lines to the one led by Theodore Moriarty. The notes of the meeting are headed "Reconstruction of the Lodge", with Violet Mary Firth as Adeptus and five accolades making up the ritual team. These were Charles Thomas Loveday, Florence Chamberlain, Violet Gregorowski, Gladys Pauline Lathbury and Elizabeth Chambers, none of whom appear to have been members of Moriarty's group.

By the Vernal Equinox of 1925 they had formally initiated three new members. One of these was concerned about already being a Mason, but was reassured by Lord Erskine in a long address of March 29th that he had not betrayed his allegiance in joining this group but had merely "changed his lodge". This indicates the type of ritual that was being used, which is confirmed by the nature of Erskine's address.

He provided a potted history of Freemasonry since 1717 together with a more traditional history going back not only to the Temple of Solomon and the Tyrian school associated with Hiram, but even to the ancient days of Atlantis.

The Great Work, of which Freemasonry was in part derived, had its origins upon the inner planes, although because the consciousness of those upon the outer plane was generally somewhat limited, progress often had to be made by means of schism. The ultimate loyalty however, was to "the Grand Lodge which is in the Highest" – an allegiance to principles and not to personalities. Principles expressed under another physical plane jurisdiction remain the same principles.

The Lesser Mystery Degrees of Masonry were given their present form in 1717 but they existed long before that date. The tradition of their origin in Solomon's Temple is largely symbolic although with a sub-stratum of historical fact, as is the way with all allegorical histories.

The Temples were the repositories of the Secret Wisdom, with its sources from high spiritual beings upon the inner planes, but craftsmen and artificers were required in the building of these edifices who perforce had to be acquainted with a certain amount of symbolic knowledge. There thus grew up around each Temple a body of lay brethren, and in order to bind them to secrecy certain oaths were administered. Thus was formed the embryo of the Lesser Mysteries, of those who possessed secret symbols, even if they were not fully aware of their interpretation.

In ancient days of Atlantis promotion never took place from the Lesser to the Greater Mysteries for the priesthood were part of a Sacred Clan specially bred for the purpose, whereas those of the Lesser Mysteries had been drawn from the populace. The only way to progress from Lesser to Greater Mysteries would have been through physical death and appropriate reincarnation into the Sacred Clan.

When King Solomon desired to reorganise the ancient Jewish mysteries he sent to the Tyrian School for an initiator who brought with him a school of artificers familiar with the necessary symbolic knowledge to perform their craft, and they were then known in Jerusalem as the Clan of the Craftsmen or the Sacred College. Various Jewish subordinates were admitted into this clan, which led to an insurrection when some of these desired admission into the Greater Mysteries. This was denied them but in the end the Tyrian artificers were returned to their homes and the work was completed by Jewish craftsmen. The Temple services were duly inaugurated and conducted by the Levites.

A considerable body of men remained, however, who by means of the experiences they had undergone and the symbols they had handled, had attained a degree of enlightenment, and were counted as neither priests nor populace. They banded themselves into the first Building Guilds and wandered wherever their work was required, all over the known world, with their wives and families and the tools and implements of their trade borne on the back of asses and driving herds of goats. With their knowledge of the arts of applied geometry they left the mark of their training on all the edifices they erected, but conserved their knowledge of the building arts as tribal secrets. They were the forerunners of the medieval trade guilds.

It was the custom of these patriarchal guilds or fraternities to employ solemn worship whose ritual they derived from the days of the Temple building. Each edifice was ritually consecrated at its commencement and dedicated at its completion. In the dedication they aimed at the propitiation of Earth Spirits of the site, a practice that still survives in placing coins of the realm under a foundation stone. This is the remote relic of the great invocations by which the Tyrian adept consecrated each corner of his Temple.

The medieval Building Guilds, substituting saints for Elemental spirits, continued the tradition, using a symbolism which they did not understand and employing arts and crafts of whose esoteric significance they were ignorant. The line of the Greater Mysteries however had never died out and the tradition stretched down the ages despite the persecutions of the Church.

At the turn of the 17th and 18th centuries of our era the Secret Science received a great impetus owing to the activities of certain men of outstanding character, and many students desired instruction in these arts. When the Adepti concerned desired to organise the training of such aspirants Lesser Mystery rituals were required, which however had become extinct. Therefore, seeking to construct rituals suitable for the initiation of candidates they cast about for such relics of old rituals as might be extant. They had not more affinity with the Building Guilds than with the Guilds of any other trade but the superstitious practices of the Building Guilds were found to contain remnants of the ancient Craft Mysteries, and therefore it is that the abstract truths of the Lesser Mysteries of the western nations are expressed in the formulae of masons' technicalities.

It follows from this that the validity of a Lesser Mystery ritual depends entirely upon being operated by those who have been initiated into the powers of the Greater Mysteries. And it is also important to note that only three Craft Degrees of Freemasonry were instituted by the Adepti and higher Masonic Degrees that have subsequently grown up are but attempts on the part of the populace to aspire to the Sacred Clan. It is necessary to be "twice born" – born of the Spirit as well as of the flesh – to enter the Greater Mysteries, although human evolution having moved on, it is no longer necessary to face physical death and rebirth. The actual transition, requiring an Unreserved Dedication to the Work, is however no less significant and irreversible.

Another consequence of the advance of human evolution was the need for the development of the feminine aspect and thus to allow women to benefit by Masonic initiations. Those who ruled the Order from within wished this to happen but those who ruled from without persisted in holding the gates shut, at any rate in England. Among the French Masons, however, there were a larger proportion of occultists, and these, acting under instructions, gave a Charter for the admission of women.

Certain difficulties arose however. Masonry was designed to act as an introductory school to the Western Mysteries, and Women's Masonry was at first used under Eastern contacts (by Annie Besant), for which it was unsuited.

Another attempt was made at founding a mixed Lodge, and the Anglo-Saxon race being too unreceptive and hide bound by prejudice, the task was given to a Celt. That is to say, to S.L.MacGregor Mathers, in 1888.

Later, a Celt was used again, Theodore Moriarty receiving and acting upon a mandate in 1919, which worked for a time before the force broke bounds, the mandate was withdrawn and the Lodge closed.

Now another attempt was being made, and to counteract the instability of the Celtic stock, the Nordic stock was being utilised. It is to be noted that Dion Fortune had been a member of both organisations acting under previous mandate.

The three graded rituals, which they were now in the process of founding, had, as their ultimate function, to be an introductory school to the Greater Mysteries. As the work developed, they were given specific advice on various aspects of ritual, based upon general Masonic principles but with the introduction of various additions and variants of symbolism to make it uniquely their own.

The ritual group admitted four initiates in 1925, another six in 1926 and ten more in 1927, and a 2nd Degree was opened on 23rd November 1926.

Of these, Edgar Homan, the Freemason, was one of the first initiated, in March 1925, and became the first Secretary of the group. Of the 1927 entry, one was Violet Firth's future husband, Dr Penry Evans and another her father, Arthur Firth. One of the original accolades, Elizabeth Chambers, was also a cousin of hers.

Having established themselves in their London headquarters they were informed after the Vernal Equinox of 1925 of the necessary development of the work of the group. The aim had to be to have everything in the house running automatically and smoothly; order, system and harmony being the basis upon which the higher work could be based.

They were enjoined to make full use of the opportunities and contacts being made available to them. There was apparently a tendency among some of them to cling to the theory and eschew any responsibility in practice.

You are a little afraid of the powers placed in your hands. You accept the theory but make little use of its implications. On the few occasions when you have invoked the Masters in group meditation have you had any occasion to be dissatisfied with the results? Then why do you not do it more frequently? There is much more power at your disposal than you avail yourselves of.

Loveday was also warned that the work would undergo considerable change and development as they opened up the higher degrees, and that he would have to understand certain matters rather more clearly than he did at the present. That he had not yet fully realised the scope and significance of the work upon which they were embarked.

It penetrates deeper into the hidden side of things, and extends less far into the outer world than you have fully understood. You must realise clearly that the aim of the work is to train for initiation, not to convert the world.

Erskine concluded with a no nonsense and no excuses injunction:

So far as the question of mundane support goes, it shall be always adequate to those needs, and can always be invoked through group meditation. Instead of fearing the limitations, and limiting the work on that account, gather together, realise the need, and invoke, and the need will be met.

It is entirely needless for you ever to be delayed or hampered for lack of funds. You have only to use the methods of invocation to bring through all you require.

— PART THREE —

FORGING THE FRATERNITY -
1926-1928

18

CHALICE ORCHARD
AND THE CHANT OF THE ELEMENTS

During 1924 they had also managed to acquire a plot of land, an old orchard, at the foot of Glastonbury Tor. With the erection of a war-surplus army officers' mess hut it gave them a base in the heart centre of the land, as Glastonbury had been described to them two years before.

In course of time a veranda was built on the main hut and other chalets erected, together with a sanctuary for the performance of ritual and meditative work, as part of a complex comprising retreat, guesthouse and pilgrimage centre. It also became an important place of retreat for Dion Fortune in the early 1930's when she was preparing her magnum opus "The Mystical Qabalah".

The importance of Glastonbury to her is encapsulated in a little book called "Avalon of the Heart", published by the general interest publisher Robert Mueller in 1934 and culled from a series of essays about Glastonbury that had appeared in "The Inner Light" magazine.

Although obviously written off the top of her head, for they contain a number of factual inaccuracies, they were obviously also written straight from the heart. "The Road to Avalon" evokes memories of the Great West Road, now replaced by the M4 motorway, but still existent as the A4 main road, down which she must have travelled on a few occasions in the sidecar of Thomas Loveday's motorcycle combination. It contains evocations of the Avalon of

Merlin, the Avalon of the Graal, the Avalon of the Keltic Saints, the legend of the Holy Thorn and Wearyall Hill, the Abbey and Glastonbury of the Monks, the Tor, even Avalon and Atlantis. The importance of Chalice Orchard for her is signalled by a speculative remark she made in a magazine article of 1937, where in spite of having a house in London for a headquarters, she writes:

> *When I look at the ruins of the temple of the great Fraternities of the past, I sometimes wonder whether the Inner Light will leave behind it any more imposing structures than the wooden huts at Glastonbury, or whether we shall have there our only memorial.*

In acquiring this plot of land and setting their huts upon it they had built upon a place of power, and at Whitsun in 1926 they experienced exactly what that meant. Upon Glastonbury Tor they received an influx of Elemental powers that profoundly moved them at the time and significantly affected the future direction of their work.

They had apparently a little while before been celebrating a ritual invoking the Element of Air when, walking upon the Tor, they were suddenly taken up with a feeling of ecstasy which set them whirling spontaneously in an impromptu dance. Then they saw a friend rushing across the fields below, who raced up the hill to join in their revelry.

It is tempting to wonder if this athletic newcomer was Thomas Penry Evans, who had been lodging at Queensborough Terrace for the past year with his sister, and who within a year became Dion Fortune's husband.

Another possible companion in the revel might well have been Mary Bligh Bond, (Frederick Bligh Bond's daughter), an artist capable of very powerful elemental paintings, who designed the cover for Dion Fortune's first novel "The Demon Lover" in 1927, and whose novel "Avernus" of 1924 was a spine chilling evocation of Atlantis.

In the whirling dance a repetitive chant seemed to beat through into consciousness, which they rendered into words, a kind of affirmative ritual, often used in later years as a means of stimulating Elemental contact and vitality. Its appearance on the printed page may perhaps seem repetitious and devoid of intellectual content, but that is because the Elementals do not work upon the plane of intellect. For its full effect it needs to be chanted out loud with spontaneous movement and perhaps to the accompaniment of light percussive instruments.

The wind and the fire work on the hill -
    The wind and the fire work on the hill -
       The wind and the fire work on the hill —
Evoke ye the wind and the fire.

The wind and the fire work on the hill -
    The wind and the fire work on the hill -
       The wind and the fire work on the hill —
Trust ye the wind and the fire.

The wind and the fire work on the hill -
    Hail to the wind and the fire.
Draw that vitality into you —
    Learn to work with the Nature forces.

The wind and the fire work on the hill —
    Hail to the wind and the fire.
       Sun and air. Sun and air. Sun and air.

Earth and water are friendly and kind —
    Earth and water are friendly and kind —
       Earth and water are friendly and kind —
The sun and the fire work on the hill —
Hail to the sun and the fire.

Fire will not burn you —
    Water will not drown you —
       Wind will not overwhelm you —
          The rocks will not fall upon you.

But Fire shall be to you
    as a friend and companion,
       and a comforter in sorrow and loneliness.
So that from the flame you may draw comfort
    and comradeship for your soul.

And the Wind shall be to you as a comrade and a messenger,
    And the Water a friend and protector,

And the Earth a refuge and a strong defence
and sustainer.

Greeting in the Name and Power of the Tor.
Greeting and welcome within the Gates.
The Gates are open - Pass ye through.
Let those who can see, see the vision of the opening of the
mountain.

The place is guarded.
A ring of fire is about you,
and the freedom of the hill is yours.

By day and by night is it guarded with a force that shall keep
off all enemies -
The force of the Fire of the Tor.

For this is a hill of Fire
And the forces of Fire are about you
And the protection of Fire is upon you.

Do not think about the Nature forces, feel with them.
They have not minds – you cannot touch them with the
mind.
Feel with them –
Move with them –
Sing with them –
Do not be afraid of them.

You need them,
For they are on the Power side of things,
And without the Elemental Forces, you have no
Power.

You have no Power to give expression to your desires unless it be
the will of the Lords of the Elements, for they hold the Gates, and
the Gates open to admit to the Inner World, and you can go in by
the grace of the Lords of the Elements.

They are your friends if you can rule your own Elemental
nature. They share with you the holiness of Elemental Nature.
Control and force must be balanced –

They love not weakness –
They scorn it.
You must make them respect you,
And you must respect them.
You must love them,
And they will love you.

Those who love the Elements, and those whom the Lords of the
Elements respect and trust, shall be entrusted with the Force of
the Elements.

And the Power of the Elements shall be as a flame among men.
As a rushing tide –
As a mighty wind –
And as still as the rocks.

You shall sweep things aside as a Fire if the Lords of the
Elements ride with you.
The Kings of the Powers of the Air shall ride with you.
And the stability of the depths of the Earth shall
guard you.
Where our friends are there is purity and power. Where the
waters sweep out to the endless horizon, spaceless and timeless
for ever, there shall be strength.

Where our people are, there is strength and wealth and
wisdom.
As the rocks are rich, as the rocks are strong, so the deep
things are wise.

Wind and Water -
Wind and Water -
Wind and Water.

Water and Earth that makes fruitful –
Water and Earth that makes fruitful –
Water and Earth that makes fruitful.

And you shall never lack the water springs.
You shall have power to call up the water springs and
upon the rain.
The water springs in the Name of Earth and Water –

And the rains in the Name of Water and Wind.

Water and Wind –
    Water and Wind –
        Water and Wind –
            Wind and Water.

Fire and Earth –
    Fire and Earth –
        Fire and Earth.

And the wealth of the Earth for Power to serve the Master.
The Fire shall cleanse –
    The Fire shall enlighten.
And tenderly shall the Water bear you.

Love ye the Elemental things -
    They are very old –
        They are ever young –
Ageless and deathless –
    Eternal –
        Immortal.

From of old, and for ever, rule we our kingdom,
    and we are in the depths of your being.

Awaken and come –
    Awaken and come –
        Awaken and come.

Come from the depths of your Elemental Being and lighten our darkness -
    Come in the name of the White Christ and the Hosts of the Elements.
Come at our bidding and serve with us the One Name above all Names -
    The Lover of men and of the Elemental Peoples –
    'The Great Name –
        of JEHOSHUA – JESUS.

He who said as he descended into the Underworld:
    There shall be no night where my people are –

And the night shall be as day in the light of the eternal
fire –
And there shall be peace where my people are -
The peace of the heights above the winds.
And there shall be purity.

Fire and Air –
Fire and Air –
For Power to serve the Master.

As the Greek explained to them at the time, as they sat in their newly erected hut at the foot of the Tor, they had met a messenger from the Elemental kingdoms, and this was no chance contact but part of their development and education as a group.

In the Elements is power if you dare to use it. And that is a thing we have always tried to teach you, that you must have Elemental power if you are going to do anything. Many people have the best of intentions but they have not got the Elemental power, and therefore their intentions are fruitless. That is why you have been given this house at the very centre of these forces. It is not for nothing that you came to the Tor and have built on the Tor. Not for nothing, believe me.

You will have your devotional aspect in the city. You will have your nature contacts here, but you will have your deeper wisdom contacts where earth and water meet.

He continued:

There is a great expansion coming in your work. Be prepared for that expansion. And the Elemental forces will co-operate with you and give you the aid of their powers.

Learn to do the Chant of the Elements as you have heard it done this evening. Learn to be on terms of friendship with the Lords of the Elements. Always conduct your dealings with Elementals through the Lords of the Elements.

The Lords of the Elements are beings of lofty intelligence – mighty Intelligences. They, like you, are dedicated to the Masters. They will not serve you. Never make the mistake of commanding their obedience, but rather, as brethren, praying their assistance as servants of the One Master.

You have been told that in the Mysteries we serve the Risen Christ. The Crucified Christ is the symbol of the churches, and the Master Jesus, as known to the churches, bade men control and disciplines their elemental natures. That was his mission.

But in the three days between the Crucifixion and the Resurrection, he preached to the spirits in prison, and they were the spirits of the Elements, which had not touched the contacts of Life and Spirit, and to them also he gave the power to become the sons and daughters of God.

Socrates may have been an old pagan, a purveyor of cosmic wisdom, and a friend of the Elemental forces, but he was also by this account, as a Master of the Wisdom, a profoundly committed, if somewhat unorthodox, Christian too.

19

MOINA MACGREGOR MATHERS
AND THE PUNITIVE RAY

During all the foregoing esoteric activity Dion Fortune had still been a member of the Alpha et Omega Temple. It would seem quite understandable, therefore, if its chief adept, Moina MacGregor Mathers, should have become somewhat disturbed by some of the things that this junior initiate seemed to be getting up to.

She had not only started her own ritual group, but also begun to write occult short stories, and also an esoteric textbook allegedly containing secrets of initiation beyond her grade. She also claimed to be an amanuensis for Secret Chiefs who were putting through some kind of doctrine of their own, and on top of this she had found the means to open a headquarters in London and another at a sacred site in Glastonbury. There was also the matter of a series of articles she was writing in the "Occult Review", the main journal of responsible occultism, which cut very close to the bone in criticising alleged abuses in the occult field. These articles were later published in volume form under the title "Sane Occultism".

This was all in stark contrast to Moina MacGregor Mathers' position. She had given the best part of her life to the occult cause to find herself widowed, impoverished and in failing health, and with various schismatic Temples of the Order going their own way.

It is not possible to draw up a systematic sequence of grievances at this late date but the general impression is that despite attempts at reconciliation things were coming to a head as they approached the Vernal Equinox of 1927.

At some point Dion Fortune made the offer that her group might serve as a feeder group for more advanced work in the Golden Dawn. However, she must have privately realised that the practical work she was doing rivalled anything that the Alpha et Omega currently had to offer. Whether or not she made her views known at the time, her assessment was that the glory had departed from it.

In the end Moina MacGregor Mathers expelled her from the Alpha et Omega for not having the right inner sigils in her aura, an accusation, as Dion Fortune pointed out, to which there was no answer. It may indeed have had a certain validity for Dion Fortune was obviously working at some degrees off course from established Alpha et Omega custom and practice. Therefore having an alleged wrong sigil in the aura was simply stating in a pictorial way what may well have seemed psychically objective to Moina MacGregor Mathers' clairvoyance.

Putting matters crudely, the senior adept was in danger of being outgunned by an up-start junior, and this seems to have led to a deliberate confrontation whereby the senior apparently tried to bar the junior from her usual means of access to the inner planes.

Such a reaction in any other context might be regarded as typically "all too human". An example of professional jealousy from which even leaders of esoteric orders were not exempt. Or alternatively a related syndrome that seems to afflict some esoteric teachers, who feel unable to tolerate or release a bright student who has sprouted independent wings.

The incident was described from Dion Fortune's viewpoint, three years later, in "Psychic Self Defence" and is confirmed by entries in the contemporary archives.

The events, as outlined in "Psychic Self Defence", began with a general sense of unease and restlessness, with bursts of uncontrolled psychism, that led to a definite sense of menace and antagonism and picture images of demon faces. There followed a virtual plague of cats upon the physical level, associated with astral simulacra of large felines, which were eventually despatched by normal occult banishing formulae.

Then, at the Vernal Equinox, when Dion Fortune moved out into astral consciousness she saw her adversary, in the full robes of her grade, barring her entry, and forbidding her to make use of the astral pathways. Dion Fortune refused to recognise her authority in this respect and appealed to the Masters.

A battle of wills followed in which she got the worst of it. She had the sensation of being whirled through the air and falling from a great height, to find herself back in her body, not where she had left it, but in a heap in a far corner of a room which was in considerable disarray. By virtue of etheric repercussion her body had somersaulted round the room during the course of the inner struggle.

Somewhat shaken by the experience she realised that if she accepted defeat now her occult career was finished, and in a subsequent attempt, again invoking the Masters, after a short sharp struggle she got through. The fight was over, and she never had any further trouble from this source.

So much for her résumé in "Psychic Self-Defence". The archives record Lord Erskine, on 5th March 1927, reassuring C.T.Loveday and Dr. Evans over some problem that they have recently been having.

You need have no anticipation of trouble tonight, all is quiet. Just a few words of explanation for your guidance. You are dealing with a problem that will recur from time to time. Not that you will get the extreme form you have had on this occasion, but there is always a liability to these conditions in occult work. It is for this reason that it is unsafe to do it except in group formation.

The cause of the depletion is in the etheric body, due to shock, remarkably slight, all things considered....

You are going through a very intricate time at the present moment. It is difficult to say what and when things may happen. The decision of the Equinox counts. ... But you must remember that you are going through an extremely important time. The tides are running very high, and this is not a task to try and cope with single-handed....

Things will steady down in this house when the month is out. You are not yet quite out of the wood.

A few days later, Erskine addressed them again about further disruptions:

You have been wondering at the cause of the disturbances you have been passing through. Part of your difficulty is due to the removal of certain protection you have been accustomed to. But I may tell you this, that the power of a certain person is much over-rated. But big forces are passing through your hands, and you have not yet accustomed yourselves to handling them. They will steady after the equinox.

*As far as the Order forces go it is not so much - in fact it is
not now at all - a case of direct occult attack. That bolt was shot
and failed of its purpose. It is rather that the forces being handled
are exceedingly strong and your leader is not yet accustomed to
coping with them, so that they are slipping through her fingers a
little. But that will steady. Things are moving very satisfactorily.
You will see an important new phase of your work opening up in
the autumn. Things are moving faster than you anticipated. Your
work will open up very much in the near future.*

For his part, Carstairs seemed to imply that they would soon have
their own mandate from the inner plane Order behind the Golden
Dawn, and that what they had had to cope with recently was a blast
of the much vaunted "Punitive Ray" that formed a spectacular part
of the latter's initiation oath.

*You will get on with the Order before the autumn. In fact you are
on with it now. You had a close thing that night. You won't be
missing much if you can handle that. You got off mighty lightly.*
*That Ray was like a bomb. If it doesn't get you at the first
bang it don't repeat. As a matter of fact, when the decision was
taken to go out a second time that problem was solved.*
*You have to move carefully when you begin to handle the
Order forces, and you ought to wait until you get things put right
and the right people are sent along, and watch the times and the
seasons. These things can only be put through if you have got the
nerve. There is a struggle at the gate, but once you are through,
you can shut the gate from the inside.*

All however was not plain sailing on this turbulent Vernal Equinox
tide. There was a problem in getting out onto the astral on 20th
March, which required a powerful invocation from the medium
herself. Nonetheless the contacts failed, and she wandered for an
hour on the astral plane in a state of unrest.

However, the contacts were picked up again the following
afternoon at the time of the Equinox for an address by Lord Erskine.
This repeated much that Socrates had recently said and then moved
on from verbal communication to a direct influx of power, followed
by greetings from various inner plane sources, including the
Company of Avalon, and from Priests of Horus, of the Sun, of Isis,
and an unidentified 6th Plane Power, who opened up a series of
higher contacts for them.

Finally they were met by Socrates, who brought them gently back to normal consciousness:

Greeting. Now, my children, we must return down the planes. You have been high. You must come back steadily and quietly and happily. Come back in the sense of peace – the peace of the three Masters is upon you, and your souls are calm and refreshed within you, and your bodies are harmonised and all is still of the great vibrations that have been awakened. All is peace, my children, peace in the calm of attainment. Peace until we are called to our work. You shall always return from the heights in peace, so that you keep the bond of love unbroken. For where there is love there is peace.

Moina MacGregor Mathers, for her part, was by now largely a spent force. Not in good health, and facing increasingly difficult domestic and financial problems, she went into a rapid decline. Eventually she reached the point of refusing all food and died at St. Mary Abbott's Hospital on July 25th 1928 at the age of 63.

That two of the great women occultists of their respective generations should have ended up feuding in this way is great pity. The cause of the Masters is hardly advanced by two of their followers brawling like fishwives. Of course one problem in situations like this is the high levels of power that drive personalities out of control of their emotions. To outsiders, who may not have experienced putting their fingers round a live high-tension cable, the contortions of those involved may seem somewhat bizarre. However, in subsequent years, rather more has been realised about the effects of these inner plane power levels and by and large attempts have been made to handle differences of direction in the work by other means than self-justification, mutual condemnation, and ill-tempered schism. Nonetheless it is a lesson that each generation has to learn and come to terms with.

A side effect of this dramatic confrontation was a series of scratches on Dion Fortune's body as a consequence of etheric repercussion. This kind of thing can happen very easily, and even Carstairs acting rather clumsily on a previous occasion had caused some bruising.

She went on to remark in "Psychic Self Defence" that her friend

Netta Fornario, recently found dead on a hillside on Iona, had suffered similar injuries. To avoid any implication of accusation by association it should be pointed out that Moina MacGregor Mathers had herself been dead for almost eighteen months before this occurred. And although she may well have been capable enough as a magician to retain an active astral presence after her physical dissolution, it would seem somewhat far fetched speculation to assume she had any connection with Miss Fornario's demise, who had said that she was engaged on a difficult case of healing, and was found naked under a cloak upon a hillside upon which she had cut a cross in the turf.

In any review of the history of the Western Mystery Tradition Mina Bergson, deserves to come high upon the roll of honour. As wife and magical partner of S.L.MacGregor Mathers, maintaining her ideals through times of extreme physical and financial deprivation, to say nothing of libel and slander, she demonstrated an exemplary dedication to her cause. As a pioneer of the modern Western Esoteric Tradition she helped to blaze a trail that those who follow can too easily take for granted. She deserves at least some retrospective acknowledgement – which Mary Greer has gone some way to fulfil in "The Women of the Golden Dawn".

20

THE STAR IN THE EAST
AND THE CHRISTIAN MYSTIC LODGE

The contretemps with Moina MacGregor Mathers was more in the
nature of a domestic squabble as compared to another conflict that
was threatening at this time. This concerned the Theosophical
Society and the movement that had arisen within it known as the
Order of the Star in the East.

Despite the inspiration that Dion Fortune had earlier received
from some of Annie Besant's works, she had made no formal link
with the Theosophical Society. However, at the beginning of 1925
she and Loveday were instructed by Erskine that they should
discretely form one.

*The affairs of a certain Society known to you are in the balance and the
balance is turning. The results will not be seen yet, but the causes which
will produce those results have begun to function. In these you will play
your part, and therefore the advice is repeated – make a light contact in
order that you may be ready when the time comes. Go in, in order that
you may come out. There will be a shifting, a readjusting, recasting,
and finally an amalgamation of certain streams.*

As far back as December 1909 Annie Besant, as President of the
Theosophical Society, had declared the coming of a great spiritual
Teacher and Guide. Together with her colleague C.W.Leadbeater
she promoted the idea that a young Hindu, Jiddu Krishnamurti,
would be the vehicle through whom the Christ, or the Lord Maitreya,
would manifest as he had done two thousand years before through
Jesus of Nazareth.

The movement gained considerable momentum and during the
1920's greatly increased the Society's membership even if at the

expense of some controversy. As we have seen, it was a cause of
B.P.Wadia's resignation and what became known as the "back to
Blavatsky" movement within the Society.

The Anthroposophist Rudolf Steiner went so far as to suggest
that the Masters who had worked behind Blavatsky had been
surreptitiously replaced, and that forces of Indian origin were using
Besant, Leadbeater and Krishnamurti in a political power game
that sought revenge upon an imperialistic and materialistic West.
As a result, the real spiritual forces that were seeking to bring through
a new spiritual impulse to mankind were being diverted and dammed
back.

The Masters working behind Dion Fortune were of a similar
opinion, although they regarded the interloping forces as at root
Mongolian rather than Indian. Erskine confirmed that a new spiritual
light had arisen and was pushing down into human consciousness
as a whole – and should not be diverted into a belief that it was
being channelled into one particular Divine Man as in the original
Christian dispensation.

As a direct result of Erskine's concern Dion Fortune and
C.T.Loveday sought membership of the Christian Mystic Lodge of
the Theosophical Society. A well-known Theosophical writer, Daisy
M. Grove, had formed this in 1919, with the somewhat ambivalent
intention of "interpreting Christianity in terms of Theosophy, and
Theosophy in terms of Christianity".

At the beginning of 1926 Erskine outlined what he expected of
them. They were not to seek controversy but simply to affirm the
orthodox Christian doctrine in the face of attempts to subvert it by
Eastern interpretations.

> *You are part of a larger work and must take your place as a part
> – not a whole. You must neither exceed nor depart from your
> instructions, and your instructions are specific. Your work is
> constructive. The work of destruction is in other hands than yours.
> Your work is positive. Never say in teaching – this and that should
> not be. Hold up the ideal and let it do its own work.*

In November 1926 Erskine warned more specifically of coming
problems relating to the Star in the East and how they should prepare
to meet it.

I can give you some information which may be useful to you, and that is that the opposition that you are encountering will be coming to a head before very long, and your aim should be to play out time and prevent a crisis. The longer you can avoid anything of the nature of a definite division or withdrawal the better. You will find, in the matter of the announced Messiah, that a minor crisis will occur in the Spring, and the whole thing will be over by this time next year. Then your time will begin, but it is very desirable that you should still be within the fold at the time of the crisis rather than that you should be drawn forth. Bow to the storm, it will be no more than a gust of wind. The time is not long now, and as I have told you before, you will receive assistance from an unexpected quarter.

The Greek referred to it again a few days later, in connection with some writing that Loveday was doing.

Do not quarrel with it. Do not criticise or disagree with it for a year. Keep the peace, my son, for a year. Many things are going to happen in that time. It is more important that you should maintain your position within the organisation than that you should reform it. You cannot reform it at present, but you can lose your position. Wait, my son, for time will be on your side. Be not precipitate in the matter. Avoid crises at all costs, even at the cost of yielding points. Time, my son, time.

Never try to work ahead of the tides, otherwise you are like a man dragging his boats up the dry channel of the stream with ropes and rollers. It is hard work and he may break the back of his vessel. Whereas if he waits but for a few hours, the channel will be full of water. Come up with the tide, my son, it saves time in the long run. Learn to wait and watch your time, and do your mental work on the inner planes. The powers of group meditation, my son, are very strong. Develop your group meditation.

And again from Erskine in early March, 1927:

Take no precipitate action, my son, you will find that you will gradually withdraw in a natural way. You do not want to draw attention to yourself or your withdrawal. Keep a link. Just enough for a link. Do not press withdrawal, it will come in due course when the experience has served its purpose. You will not be there indefinitely...

The publications are very important. You need wisdom to guide you. Be not afraid, but be not provocative. Do not precipitate a crisis before this season is ripe, as time will do so much for you and save the reaction.

The whole group at this time was virtually functioning as the Christian Mystic Lodge of the Theosophical Society, with Dion Fortune as its President, and during this time it attracted a growing membership and rapidly increasing circulation of its monthly magazine or "Transactions".

On the inner levels there was great concern about the way the Theosophical Society was going, and the intention was to bring things into the open by placing upon the leading officials the responsibility to state unequivocally whether or not the Society officially repudiated the Christ.

Erskine gave quite detailed instructions on this:

You will remember perhaps two things which were said to you on two different occasions. They have a profound significance.

It was said to you "Be at any moment ready to shake the dust from off your feet". That meant that you were in no way to become dependent upon that organisation.

Secondly, you were told "to stay until turned out".

I would counsel you then, and note I do not direct or order, I merely counsel to the best of my knowledge and belief, I would counsel you that when you encounter direct and official opposition, (opposition, that is to say, which is not a petty personal one, but which is able to make its degree felt officially), that you say to the official opposition: "I am commanded to remain with you until you turn me out. I have no wish to remain. I will not fight to remain. Have I your permission to depart? For I will be very glad to go."

...Head officials would act through the lodge. Head officials are dealing with the matter but are not showing their hand. Counsel has been taken with head officials.

A little later Lord Erskine indicated that the future of the Order of the Star in the East was still not yet clear. However, the duty of whoever remained in the Christian Mystic Lodge was to keep the Sacred Name of Jesus and the Sign of the Cross steadfastly before the eyes of the larger organisation, and these two great potencies would do their own work.

There should therefore be no attempt to embroil them in any attempt to reform the Theosophical Society. Whether it reformed or disintegrated was a matter for its own Masters.

Either the Theosophical Society would take a definite stand and officially repudiate the Master Jesus, or it would officially retain those contacts. If it retained those contacts then they themselves would do the necessary work.

The committee of the Christian Mystic Lodge was recommended to test the point in a carefully worded letter asking a pertinent question that required an unequivocal answer: Yes or No.

"Was there a place in the Society for Jesus Christ, the Son of God, and those who seek initiation through him?"

"What was the position for those Theosophists who still looked to Jesus of Nazareth as their teacher, and wanted no other. Was there a place for them in the Society? Would the Society give reasonable facilities for the development of their work?"

"If the Society did not desire to retain in its membership those who were actively working for Christ, would it care to receive back the Charter of the Christian Mystic Lodge, dedicated to his service?"

With a mind to the talents of Dion Fortune as a publicist Erskine enjoined Loveday:

Either the Society gives a place for the Master Jesus, or it is anti-Christian. Force the issue and give it publicity. Publicity, my son, publicity. Public opinion, with the issue before it, is able to think things out.

It depends simply and solely on the Power of the Name, and act as if contrary opinions did not exist. Do not oppose – ignore.

Throughout the first half of 1927 Dion Fortune began campaigning fiercely in the "Transactions of the Christian Mystic Lodge" a fact which was picked up in the more widely read pages of "The Occult Review", where an Editorial noted that the Christian Mystic Lodge seemed to be *"experiencing an influx of power and a measure of success beyond all expectations, in view of the fact that the existence of the Liberal Catholic Church would appear to make such a Theosophical Lodge superfluous."*

It also quoted a statement of hers in the "Transactions" that seemed rather strange in this context, in which she wrote: *"I was interested to receive (from the Regional Bishop) the information that the Liberal Catholic Church is not concerned with the Master Jesus at all. "*

"The Occult Review" emphasised this last phrase and felt it worthy of noticing also that the Christian Mystic Lodge had announced that it accepted as associates those who wished to join the Lodge only but not the Theosophical Society. It also quoted directly a statement from Dion Fortune that *"For us in the West, the Master of Masters is Jesus of Nazareth. "*

Having well stirred the pot it was probably no surprise to the Editor of "The Occult Review" to receive a letter from Bishop Piggott to say that he was the victim of a misunderstanding:

> *I am represented as giving the information presumably to Miss Dion Fortune that "the Liberal Catholic Church is not concerned with the Master Jesus at all." I have never given any such information to anyone. It is the exact reverse of the real concern of the Liberal Catholic Church. No wonder it seemed to you rather strange that I should have expressed such a view.*

This brought an immediate riposte from C.T.Loveday, writing under the pseudonym of A.V.O., with a sly dig at the theological antecedents of C.W.Leadbeater, formerly a member of the Anglican church until his involvement in Theosophy.

> *With reference to Bishop Pigott's statement in your last month's issue that the Liberal Catholic Church "is very much concerned with the Master Jesus, " can he explain why the Name Jesus is deliberately omitted from the blessing in their liturgy for the Holy Eucharist? (pp. 243 and 262).*
>
> *"May the peace of God which passeth all understanding ... and of His Son (Jesus) Christ Our Lord, etc. "*
>
> *Is it because the ritual, which was designed to perpetuate the memory of the death and suffering of Jesus, has been borrowed to advance the cult of the Lord Maitreya? (One sees His picture prominently displayed in their Church and hears his name frequently used.) Or is it due to the fact that the one who reconstructed the borrowed ritual was discharged from holding office in the Church which exalts the Name Jesus above all other Names?*

Bishop Pigott defended himself as best he might in the next issue of "The Occult Review".

> *Your correspondent A.V.O. asks if I can explain why the name Jesus has been omitted from the blessing in the Liturgy of the Liberal Catholic Church. I do not know why it was omitted; that is to say, I do not know what was in the minds of those who framed the Liturgy when they decided to omit the name Jesus at this point.*
>
> *Many of us in the Liberal Catholic Church recognise a distinction between the Lord Christ, the Founder and Head of the Christian Church, the perfect epiphany and Representative of the Second Person of the Trinity, and the disciple – now the Master – Jesus. Possibly it was to emphasise the high Source of the blessing, that it is the blessing of no less a Being than the Lord Christ Himself, and not for either of the reasons suggested by A.V.O., that the omission was made.*

In this same issue, Dion Fortune weighed in.

> *Sir, In reference to Bishop Pigott's denial that he stated to me that "the Liberal Catholic Church has nothing to do with the Master Jesus," I should like to say to your readers what I said to the members of the Christian Mystic Lodge of which I am president, and in whose Transactions the statement in question was published. Standing in front of the altar in our sanctuary, and speaking in the presence of Our Lord whose Symbol was above me, and whose Name I had just invoked, I said to them. "That statement was made to me by Bishop Pigott in response to my request for an official ruling on this point."*
>
> *I raised this point with him because it was repeatedly cropping up in the questions asked at our lectures, and many people had taken exception to my statement that the Liberal Catholic Church was not a Christian church in the sense in which the word is ordinarily used, as being a church dedicated to that manifestation of the Christ-power which came through Our Lord Jesus the Christ, but might more properly be called a Maitreyan Church, being especially concerned with the work of the Coming World-Teacher. This conclusion I had arrived at as the result of the study of Bishop Leadbeater's books, in which this viewpoint is put forward without any equivocation whatever, and after conversations with several different priests and prominent members of the laity of that church. These conversations*

took place in the presence of witnesses who are prepared to come
forward and vouch for what was said on those different occasions.

For his part, Bishop Pigott gave his own side of the story in the
Bishop's Notes in the "The Liberal Catholic" magazine.

Some of our Churchpeople, in the country more than in London,
have been misled and somewhat disturbed by a statement, quoted
recently in a monthly journal, to the effect that I had said that
"the Liberal Catholic Church is not concerned with the Master
Jesus at all." The person from whose writing the journal quoted
this sentence, persists in declaring that I actually used those
words in conversation in spite of my denial and repudiation of
them, and further asserts that they were spoken as an official
declaration on this point.

As I very much dislike controversy I should leave this matter
alone were it not that it has been represented to me that some of
our people believe that I actually used these words and used
them officially. For their sake I will just say that I have never
believed anything of the sort and cannot believe that I ever used
the words attributed to me or any other words conveying the
same sense.

Furthermore, though I have no reason for concealing anything
that I may have said at the particular interview in question, I
was under the impression that the conversation was a quiet and
friendly chat over an afternoon cup of tea, and in no sense an
official interview.

I do not know how the mistake has arisen, but I hope it will
remove any difficulties that any of our churchpeople may have
felt if I state here, quite expressly and definitely, that in my
opinion, both now and so long as I have had an opinion at all
about the Liberal Catholic Church, that Church so far from being
unconcerned with the Master Jesus, has no other reason for
existing than to try to serve Him.

If by the Master Jesus is meant the Lord Christ, I cannot see
that a Church which had no concern with Him at all, could have
any right or reason to exist. But if by the Master Jesus is
understood the great Master Who, according to Theosophical
teaching, was closely associated with the Lord Christ in His last
earthly manifestation in Palestine, though not identical with Him,
I still affirm that the Liberal Catholic Church is very intimately,
and, I trust, very reverently concerned with Him.

Whatever words I may or may not have used in a friendly

conversation last November, the above is the opinion that I held then and hold now and have held since the day when the Liberal Catholic Church began its existence, and I can have no possible reason for disguising that belief. I hope therefore that no other people will be disturbed by what is really on the face of it an absurd statement to put into the mouth of a Bishop of a Christian Church.

One begins to see some of the problems that arise when theology is discussed without prior definition of terms. So much depends upon what is meant by "the Lord Christ" and also "the Master Jesus", the latter also somewhat obscured by the Theosophical practice of referring to Masters as well as the Divinity by capital letters.

Is the Lord Christ synonymous with the Hindu conception of the Lord Maitreya? Is Jesus not the Second Person of the Trinity, as taught in the trinitarian Creeds, but one of the like presumably of Krishnamurti?

Dion Fortune devoted a long article in the July issue of the "Transactions" to spelling out the origins of the dispute, and her reasons for pursuing it so doggedly.

Three years ago, just a year before the announcement of the Coming of the World Teacher, I received instructions from the Inner Planes to join the Theosophical Society, and as is usual when instructions are received in this way, I asked for a sign to be given in confirmation so that I might know that my imagination was not deluding me. The sign appointed was that the two signatories of my application should be Mrs. X., a well-known Theosophical worker, whom I had once known slightly, but had lost sight of some years previously, and Mr. Y., who was known to me only by name and reputation. I was also told the time at which the signing would take place. The sign appointed was thus a triple sign, difficult of fulfilment by coincidence. As is customary in such matters, I told no one except those who were assisting me in my esoteric work.

When the time arrived, I was reminded from the Inner Planes of the instruction, and told to hold myself in readiness. Within three days of receiving the second intimation the sign was fulfilled in no less than five particulars: 1 and 2, the sponsors named appeared spontaneously; 3, at the time appointed; 4, they appeared in the order in which they had been named; and

5, the exact words the Master had made use of were employed by Mr. Y. in writing to me. I therefore took it that the message of instruction had been properly signed and counter-signed and that I had received my credentials for the mission to which I had been appointed, and for the same reason I give the incident in these pages so that those whose support I seek for the carrying out of the work entrusted to me may know that the Master who gave the order was also able to give the "signs following".

To those who claimed she was using the Transactions of the Christian Mystic Lodge, not to expound Christian mysticism, but for her own purposes as a means to attack the Theosophical Society, she continued:

I feel that I can do not otherwise than stand up in the Name of the Master Jesus, relying upon Him for protection, and raise my voice in protest against conditions which "sin against the Light". I ask those who are in sympathy with what I am doing to remember that thought power is potent for protection and support, just as it is for attack, and to lend me their help on the Inner Planes. My task is not a light one. But as long as I am responsible for the conduct of this magazine I will follow the example of the Master, Who, while He had compassion for those who fainted by the way, had a scourge for the backs of those who made His Father's house a den of thieves.

The "den of thieves" she had in mind were officials who intercepted or destroyed letters of hers to the editor of "The Theosophical Review", and those who ran other Theosophical Society journals and refused to publish announcements of meetings of the Christian Mystic Lodge in their columns.

The whole situation seemed to be generating more heat than light. "The Occult Review" quoted her as regarding the present position of the Theosophical Society as "profoundly unsatisfactory", owing to (1) credulity, (2) personality worship, and (3) devious methods.

The upshot was that by October she had resigned as President of the Christian Mystic Lodge. A staunch critic of the latter day trends in the Theosophical Society, the plain speaking editor of the American magazine "The O.E.Library Critic" very much regretted this apparent capitulation. In the issue of February 1928 he wrote:

All this is natural enough. The treachery and shameless dishonesty of the officials of the T.S. in Great Britain on various occasions is a matter of record and fairly smells to heaven. The opening of letters by spies to whom they have not been addressed and the refusal of publicity to dissenting members is an old story. It is a deliberate attempt to force the vagaries of Mrs. Besant on the Society and to prevent by fair means or foul any attempt to oppose them. No one can be in good odour in the T.S. in Great Britain who does not stand for these. Those who will not endorse the absurdities of the Leadbeater cult are subjected to ostracism if not to actual persecution. I am no advocate of retiring under such conditions, but as the talented president of the Christian Mystic Lodge believed herself the recipient of orders to withdraw, and to carry on her mission independently, perhaps she was right, even at the cost of leaving the "thieves" in possession of the Father's House. Nevertheless, I regret it.

From now on Dion Fortune and her group no longer worked under the banner of the Christian Mystic Lodge of the Theosophical Society but declared themselves as the Community of the Inner Light.

Before the end of the year she embarked upon an intensive series of lectures, not only at her own headquarters but also on wider public platforms. The titles speak for themselves: "The Inner Light of the Higher Self"; "The Path of the Inner Light"; "The Work of the Inner Light in the World"; "Preparation for the Dawning of the Inner Light"; and "Dedication to the Service of the Inner Light." The Community, later Fraternity, of the Inner Light was on its way, having shaken the dust of the Christian Mystic Lodge from its feet.

Loveday expressed a wish to be able to take part in activities of the Christian Mystic Lodge of the Theosophical Society from time to time, even after the Community of the Light had been founded, but in practice was able to find little time to do so. A kind of task force was, however, left behind. Seven like minded volunteers were addressed by Erskine, who it seems was not entirely best pleased by the way that things had turned out, with the overt warfare of personality politics into which Dion Fortune and Loveday had become drawn.

He told the band of volunteers that it was necessary that a point of contact be kept within the group mind of that organisation so that those souls who belonged to the west might be touched and held.

The contact is maintained by the presence in that organisation of those who are under the contacts of the West standing in the Name of the Master of Masters, Jesus, Whom we all serve.

Those who undertake this task, undertake a serious responsibility. Little will be asked of them on the physical plane, but much on the inner planes, and I will not conceal from you the fact that it is a mission which has not only its difficulties but also its risks. You will have to stand in the midrush of a force and stem it. It will be for you seven, standing together, to keep open the contacts and stand against the rush of that force. You are offering yourselves as sacrifices for your brethren...

Do not fight personalities; uphold principles. Do not contradict them; act as if they did not exist. You have been side tracked once into personalities, do not make that mistake again. Remember you are dealing with those who are cunning. You are also dealing with a formidable occult force. Remain in your own territory. Uphold the standard of the Master Jesus. Invoke His Name, and summon to His standard those souls who belong to Him.

But let this be your test – it is Jesus the Christ for whom you stand. Jesus-Christ, the Son of God. God made manifest to man. Born of a virgin. Suffered under Pontius Pilate, was crucified, dead and buried. The third day he rose again from the dead, and is the Head of our Order, and His Power, transmitted by the Holy Order rests upon you, and in its Name you go to your task. If you are faithful over few things you shall be made ruler over many. You, who have sought the Brethren, now meet Them. Do you, with this knowledge before you, desire to undertake this task?

All answered in the affirmative.

You are then all clear and one minded in this matter? For if not so, now is your time to withdraw.

It is well, my children, you shall have not cause to regret it.

Your task then is to maintain the point of contact for the Masters; to uplift the standard of the Cross and see that it is kept before the eyes of the brethren; and to see that they are taught to invoke the Sacred Name of Jesus. That is all that is required of you on the outer plane. On the inner planes you will have to stand firm against pressure, but you will not be left unsupported.

As Socrates had predicted, all was largely a matter of waiting for the right tide and the inner forces would do their work. The Order of the Star in the East was brought to a sudden end in 1929 when Krishnamurti repudiated the role that had been cast for him.

As for the Christian Mystic Lodge, Ernest Butler, who used to lecture to it before and after this time, succinctly summed it up in conversation with Janine Chapman. In his eyes it was a body that consisted for the most part of "half a dozen people huddled round a gas fire" until Dion Fortune became its President, when it considerably livened up, only to revert to its original condition after she left.

The focus of Christian practice within the Community of the Inner Light became the Guild of the Master Jesus, after 1936 the Church of the Graal, which held regular Sunday services open to the public at Queensborough Terrace from 1928 until the outbreak of war in 1939. Much of its order of service has been published in "The Story of Dion Fortune" by Fielding and Collins (Thoth Publications).

21

Dr. Thomas Penry Evans
and the Master of Medicine

Before all the intensive campaigning commenced, there appeared in the May edition of the Transactions of the Christian Mystic Lodge a notice in the arch phraseology not untypical of the times.

NEWS OF THE PRESIDENT OF THE CHRISTIAN MYSTIC LODGE

By the time these pages are in the hands of our readers, I shall have taken the great initiation of the sacrament that is given and received in marriage.

The man who will share this sacrament with me is well known to those of you who are able to attend our lectures, being one of the inner group of workers who help me in my work, and a member of the Christian Mystic Lodge, Dr. T. Penry-Evans.

This great change in my life will not, however, withdraw me from my work for occultism in general and the Christian Mystic Lodge in particular, for Dr. Penry-Evans, for some time past, has been in close co-operation with me in both these lines of activity, and our marriage will render that co-operation more effectual.

Dion Fortune.

An accompanying notice is anodyne and amateurish enough as to look not out of place in a parish church magazine, despite the simmering tensions underneath, and gives a vignette of what the ambience of the organisation, soon to become the Community of the Inner Light, was like at that time.

We remind our friends again that this great expansion of work throws a considerable strain on our workers, and we should be very glad of offers of regular service. We are afraid that some of the offers of service which were made were not recorded, and we would ask all our friends who have time or talents to give us, whether they have already offered their services or not, to make their offer in writing to our secretary, stating what they can do and what time they can give; then their names will be put upon our register and they will be called upon as required.

Would anyone like to take charge of the lecture room?

Would anyone with a garden like to keep the lecture room and sanctuary supplied with flowers?

Are there any cake makers who would send us cakes regularly for lodge teas?

Is there anybody "at a loose end" who wants to serve? Let them all come. We are a painfully active lodge, and there is work for everybody.

The marriage of Dion Fortune and Thomas Penry Evans at Paddington Register Office on 6th April 1927 did however place some additional strains upon the group.

It is not certain how they met, one story is that he was interested in the psychological side of medicine and he attended one of her lectures and things started from there. Another, that the introduction came through Moriarty. He had been a tenant at the Queensborough Terrace house since 1925 as this is the address he gave when he took his first job after qualification, as House Surgeon and Registrar at Charing Cross Hospital in that year.

He had qualified in 1924 at the age of 31 having started his medical studies immediately after the war, and was of relatively humble origins, his father being a tin plate worker at Pontardulais, though later gaining some form of promotion to Llanelli in South Wales. At the outbreak of war he had been one of the first to enlist, in the Artists' Rifles, but transferred to the Machine Gun Corps when it was formed in 1917, ending the war with a commission and the rank of 2nd Lieutenant.

It was something of an achievement for someone of his working class background and financial status to have found a place in medical school in those days. His younger sister Hazel also came to London and lodged at Queensborough Terrace while studying to be a nurse. They must have had a certain interest in esoteric matters for she later married Edward Maltby, an early member of the Fraternity and its Director of Studies for a while.

With the coming of Tom Penry Evans, the centre of gravity of the group must have undergone a specific and radical shift. Not only had another male figure appeared, closer to their leader than "his Nibs", C.T.Loveday, but the new man was more of a natural pagan than a Christian mystic, and was soon nicknamed "Merlin" or "Merl".

Matters were explained to the rest of the group in esoteric terms, that he had brought an Elemental initiation, particularly for their leader, and this would enable her to raise the whole scope and power of the group. The goal was to be able to operate at Greater Mystery level.

Erskine was regarded as being at the centre of these events, and said he regretted the uncomfortable speed at which they had developed. In those days and in those social circles it would have been considered proper to have announced an engagement at least six months beforehand. However, the Masters wanted the group to be functioning at a higher level by the Autumnal Equinox of 1927 and so he had felt it necessary, or at any rate worth the risk, to precipitate matters. It was a period when very strong inner tides were flowing which could be taken on the flood.

The group were also warned that they must expect a certain change in Dion Fortune's demeanour, at any rate for the time being. They must expect to see more of her ordinary personality rather than the exemplary figure of a dedicated esoteric leader as in the past. In short, if they made allowances for this in the immediate future she would in the course of time revert to the teacher they had come to respect but would be the better for it.

You have, no doubt, been conscious of a withdrawal of the Higher Self of your leader. This has been away in the Elemental Kingdoms taking its initiations. This has left you with the Personality. In due course the Individuality will begin to recontact the Personality and will then speak with authority.

The terms in which this was expressed may seem somewhat precious and stilted, but we must remember that the words are passing through her own mediumship, and bear in mind the difficulties of obtaining accurate communication in any area where personal feelings are involved.

It was in any case probably the kind of language that went down best with a somewhat inexperienced group who had raised their leader rather high upon an esoteric pedestal and might have found it something of a let down to find her acting like a normal human being.

Anyhow, the underlying message to the group was loud and clear. They had to make the best of things and get their house in order, literally and metaphorically, by the time of the Autumnal Equinox, for then the work was to go ahead at a higher and more powerful level.

As a kind of foretaste of the kind of thing that might be expected they were vouchsafed the contact of a visitor from the elemental kingdoms, who came at the close of their Summer Solstice celebrations, a couple of months after the marriage.

I have come at the Master's request to give certain specific instruction in practical magic.

You are now contacting the Elemental forces. These are non-human, and can only be handled by human beings by means of ceremonial. You cannot handle coals of fire with bare hands, you must have tongs. Never try and handle the elemental forces save with ceremonial. Never attempt to contact them in meditation. Always use a formula. Elemental forces are dangerous to humanity if approached direct.

If you are about to do an invocation prepare for yourself the symbols by means of which the force shall be brought into manifestation. Surround yourself with those symbols. For Fire you would have a triangle of Fire – the pyramid of Fire – the Fiery planets – the Fiery triplicity and their symbols – the herbs, incenses and unguents of Fire – the chant of Fire composed around the keynote of Fire. You would arrange all this on a festival of Fire, in a place of Fire. You would have a dance of Fire – a movement of Fire in the ritual. Movement, sound, incense, colour and symbols – thus, concentrating on all these, you bring the power through into full consciousness and are aware of it.

> *If you have not this form aspect then you will make within yourselves the subconscious Element of Fire which is within your own natures. Any fool can wake the hidden Elements of his own nature below the threshold of human consciousness, but the Magus masters the Elementals of his own nature and brings the force through into consciousness. All the work of the Magus is conscious – willed – deliberate.*
>
> *I have given you this teaching, will you reply to it by accepting my people as pupils? It is the custom of the Adepts so to accept. I myself was so trained, and will be vouched for by him who trained me. I will vouch for those I send you, that they are worthy. It is the custom among us. For we are the creations of the created. We have no souls unless they are developed in us by contact with those who have souls.*

Immediately after this, Erskine made a somewhat surprising claim, indicating that he was by no means just the simulacrum of an 18th century lawyer.

> *Greeting my children. You have had some teaching from one competent to speak. He was my creature. I took him from the Fire, going on his belly like a snake of the dust, and trained him till he won his salvation and stood upright in human form. He is to be trusted. There is only one danger to be guarded against in dealing with the salamanders, and that is that they may accidentally set something on fire. It would not be wilful, but both you and they need to learn to handle these forces.*

They were, enjoined, however, that to handle forces such as these, they needed the qualities of the Christian initiate.

> *You have to learn, not only the evocation of the Elemental forces, but the control of them; and that is why you are trained first in the Christian dispensation, in order that the discipline of humility – purity – selflessness – compassion – and gentleness may have moulded your souls. These five points form the five-pointed star, which is the pentacle. The pentacle is the symbol of humanity and the controlling symbol which rules the Elemental forces. Interpreted, its symbol means that these five qualities are the characteristics of humanity, and distinguish the Man from the lower orders of creation. These qualities must be the controlling factors in the consciousness which would handle Elemental force as an Adept, and avoid being handled by them.*

The marriage of Merl to Dion Fortune was seen as a two-way initiation. He was bringing the initiation of the Elements to her and she bestowing the higher Spiritual contacts to him. It obviously brought a great deal to her, if we are to judge by a passage from one of the romantic thriller novels she later wrote – "Beloved of Ishmael":

And as he played and rejoiced and made love, she gradually changed from rather a startled and bewildered but adventurous maiden into the full flowering of womanhood and love; for these things are not done in a day, and though a girl may technically lose her virginity in one night, she takes longer than that to change from maiden into wife; and sometimes she never changes and the marriage goes wrong. And when she comes to marriage without her virginity, having played lightly at love and been passed from hand to hand, she never knows that wonderful flowering at the touch of one man, and its sacredness. And when a man has given a woman that flowering, no other woman can ever be to him what she is.

In terms of "The Esoteric Philosophy of Love and Marriage" it was at first looked upon, during the honeymoon period at any rate, as a union upon the 7th Plane. However, subsequent events suggest that although they did valuable work together and contributed much to each other in many ways it was not quite so elevated a partnership as had been hoped.

Within a few weeks Merl obviously began to find a conflict between his ambitions for a medical career and his close involvement in an esoteric group. By the August Bank Holiday Erskine was admonishing Merl that any difficulties he currently faced were of his own making, and that the way forward demanded a one pointed commitment.

Lord E: *Do you see your way clear, my son, in your present stage of the work?*
Merl: *I think I do, my Lord.*
Lord E: *Then you are prepared to go forward, confident that future stages will open up in the future as they have done now and in the past?*
Merl: *Yes, certainly.*
Lord E: *Because it is useless to go forward with a divided heart. It must be all or nothing in this work, and if you give your youth to this work, you may rest assured that your age will not be left unprovided for by the Masters.*

It would seem that, understandably, Dr. Evans had some doubts about committing himself wholeheartedly to what must have appeared a somewhat gimcrack exercise in the context of his recently commenced and hard won medical career.

In esoteric terms, he was being presented with what amounts to a demand for the Unreserved Dedication of the Greater Mysteries, after having been an initiate of the Lesser Mysteries for only a few months. However, those who marry so ambitiously in the esoteric scheme of things, even unintentionally, can hardly expect an easy ride. Added to which, we have to bear in mind that the contact with Lord Erskine was coming via his wife's subconscious.

Nonetheless, the marriage seemed happy enough at this stage, with the new Mrs. Evans affectionately being referred to as "the princess" as opposed to her more general nickname within the group as "Fluff" – apparently deriving from her pronouncing this word in mock denunciation when inspecting the standard of communal housework.

It may at this stage be opportune to clarify their name as a married couple. They are sometimes referred to as Dr. & Mrs. Penry-Evans but the Penry was simply his second Christian name. This floating use of a hyphen in names seems to have been quite common in those times and we have similar occasional discrepancies with regard to Curtis-Webb, Tranchell-Hayes and Campbell Thomson.

For Erskine the priority remained the formation of some kind of semi-enclosed community dedicated to working out certain archetypal ideas by means of ritual and meditation so as to uplift the spiritual life of the nation. Their task was to develop a system embodying the deeper issues of occultism, among which would be the training of initiates, the community life and esoteric therapeutics.

I therefore say to you – have now no more fear of the future than you have had need to of the past. For those who come in under instructions will not be left uncared for; but you can choose whether you can continue in the competitive way of existence or by the love and service of brethren in the happy family group.

Moreover, an esoteric development close to the heart of Dr Evans was about to take place. Early in August Carstairs came through with an announcement:

You are about to meet a teacher whom I believe has spoken to you once before, but who will come to you more frequently in the future.

Without further ado this other contact came in, announcing that he would address them on the occult side of physiology, pathology and the therapeutics of mind and body. It turned out to be a re-appearance of the Master of Medicine, who had first made desultory contact in the 1921 trance experiments with Maiya and possibly Dr. Curtis-Webb.

Wasting no time, on 9th August 1927 he began to dictate a book. Its title was "The Principles of Esoteric Medicine", and by the end of the month three chapters had been completed.

The dictated work was interspersed with sessions of question and answer between Dr. Evans and the communicator, about whose identity there was considerable speculation. The great Renaissance physician Paracelsus (1493-1541) was a popular supposition, but Carstairs intervened in his inimitable style, and advised caution on any public claims as to identity. He suggested using the title "the Master of Medicine" but being Carstairs, could not resist putting in a few supplementary hints of his own.

Hello. Seems to have settled down to his job quite happily. Decided to take you on. So you have been looking him up in "Who's Who?" He was a big Greek initiate, and he brought through what he knew, and the consequences you know. He came back again later on, and that is the incarnation you haven't traced; his last time. He has been back since the middle ages one, not so long ago either. That is his secret anyway. Hahnemann [1755-1843 - the founder of homeopathy] learned his ideas from him. But it doesn't matter who he is, the question is what he gives. If you are satisfied with that, all right. I should recommend that for all practical purposes you call him Master of Medicine. Avoid names, too many Shakespeares and Platos about. Never brag about your rich relations – only gets you disliked.

At the same time he made one or two important points about the problems and quality of mediumship in general:

When you claim to contact the great minds of antiquity it is like putting a two-inch pipe into a big lake, you are limited by the capacity of your medium. You are fortunate in that you have got a large bore pipe, and get quite a lot through it. But you will never get the whole through any medium, for if she were a lake she would not be a medium. If you had a pipe the same bore as the cistern, it wouldn't be a pipe.

He went on give one or two concealed hints as to the communicator's most recent incarnation:

No reason why you shouldn't trace it if you can. If you can catch him you have got him. I gave you hints - 'bugs'. He was the father of modern drugs but he was the father of more than that, and the mother of bacteriology, but he miscarried, or to be more strictly accurate his professional brethren aborted him.
I use the word 'bugs' in its drawing room sense!

A week or two later however, Carstairs referred to him directly by name - as "old Semmelweiss". This identification is very much in line with the series of concealed hints in the words we have quoted above, notably "mother," "miscarried" and "aborted", for Ignaz Semmelweis, (1818-65), one of the pioneers of bacteriology, made his name from success in maternity wards. He showed how puerperal or childbed fever, which killed a large percentage of hospitalised patients, could be virtually wiped out if doctors washed their hands in chlorine solution. This was in the days before Pasteur and Lister, and microscope technology, which eventually allowed the scientific investigation of microbes – or what Carstairs calls 'bugs'.

There seems a problem with Carstairs' assertion that Semmmelweis influenced Hahnemann, in that he only graduated the year after Hahnemann died. However, this is clarified later.

Despite this detailed information as to identity Carstairs again cautioned them about being too eager to pin down contacts to specific incarnations.

Don't be in a hurry to identify your contacts. They are apt to be rather shy birds till they get to know you better. But I will tell you whom the last one was if you like to know. He was the one you thought, [i.e. Paracelsus] but that was not his last incarnation. His last will give you a clue to his psychology. I don't know how he pronounces his name. It begins with an S – Semmelweiss. That is the nearest I can get to it. He was an Austrian. [Actually he was born Hungarian, but he qualified, and for the most part practised, and died, in Austria.] *He had a pretty tough time of it and it didn't do his temper any good. He does not suffer fools gladly, and that was one of his troubles.*

In response to some direct questions about his identity, the Master of Medicine declined to be specific, but afforded some statements which supported Carstairs' identification.

I do not see that you need very greatly concern yourselves who I was or what I was. It is sufficient for you that I am willing to teach, and know what I am talking about. However, since you have framed certain questions and seem perplexed I will endeavour to clear matters up.

With regard to the teaching used in some of my works, let me say that I wrote for my age, and I wrote in cipher, and the outward form of the cipher was in the language that the populace were accustomed to associate with learning. I wrote with my tongue in my cheek, but I got my results, and my pupils knew what I meant; but if you will translate terms of matter into terms of consciousness you also will get what I mean. You understand? If I had spoken of consciousness and the faculties of the soul, I should have been trespassing upon holy ground. It was enough that I should estrange my professional brethren, without transgressing the rules of Holy Church into the bargain. [This seems to support the Paracelsus identification, along with an interesting hint upon the way to approach Paracelsus' obscure, alchemically loaded, written texts.]

I have had certain work to do in medicine, I took my initiation in Greece, and it was an initiation of the way of healing; and before that I had been one of the Therapeutoi of Egypt. On my initiation in Greece I won my freedom, but I elected to return. I returned twice. I wanted to put through certain tasks in relation to medicine. In each case my success was partial; the reason being that my initiations were imperfect and incomplete. I have justly been called the Father of Modern Drug Systems.

There are two main systems, as you know. Of one I myself laid the foundations personally. The other was founded by my favourite pupil – reincarnating for the purpose; and I assisted him, as I am assisting you. [This would clear up our little time problem, mentioned above, if he inspired Hahnemann from the inner planes, before reincarnating himself.]

I never intended to reincarnate again, therefore I sought to work through my pupil; but I had to reincarnate again, because

I had the science of medicine in my care. It might be said that I was its patron saint, though I had but little claim to saintliness.

I reincarnated again in order to try and deal with surgical sepsis, and I failed, because I came too soon. I came before the high-powered microscope, and therefore I could not demonstrate my discoveries. It remained for another man [probably Lister 1827-1912] *to do that work, but it has been done, and that is all that matters.*

You will never see again what I have seen, when from one ward we were losing eighty percent of normal confinements. We had to close the wards, it was all we could do. I have seen hospitals pulled down because the mortality was such they dare not continue them. They were known as 'Pest-hausen' in my time. They were well named. [A double play on words – he refers to the Maternity Clinic at Pest, a town which is now part of Budapest.]

I have been the father of the modern system of drugs. I was the forerunner of modern asepsis. I desire to be for the third and last time a pioneer in medicine. After that, I shall take my freedom and go on.

The work I have in mind this time concerns the inter-relation of mind and body, the mental factor in disease, and the mental factor in therapeutics.

In confiding this high purpose he went on to give some heartfelt advice.

Now my friends, and brother of my profession, I have made mistakes before in my work, and I do not want to make them again. I made them in that chief incarnation, of which you know, by estranging my professional brethren through what was really my bad manners and unpardonable conduct. I despised them, and I let them see it, which is fatal; and in my last incarnation I made the mistake again of estranging my brethren by alleging what I could not prove. I was right, and they know it now, but I had not got what Lister had – Pasteur's work, and the high-powered magnification. I knew, but I could not prove. You will know, if you listen to me, a good many things which you will not be able to prove. Learn by my experience.

A still tongue, my friend, saves many a broken head and a broken heart. If you desire to give a strong tonic, you give it in measured doses; but I took my patient, the medical profession, by the nose, and forced the bottle between its teeth, and poured down the dose, and my patient had convulsions.

The measured dose for new teaching, my friend. Too much medicine can be poisonous, and so can too much truth.

Indeed the Master of Medicine developed a somewhat acerbic reputation, who did not suffer fools gladly, even idealistic and well-intentioned ones.

The following episode illustrates a problem that recruitment for the group met at that time. Many had been on the esoteric scene for some time, and had probably been influenced largely by eastern-based ideas that the work of the Theosophical Society over the previous forty years had done much to popularise. It is certainly doubtful if they had ever come up against contacts like Lord Erskine or the Master of Medicine before.

The former was lobbied to advocate vegetarianism for the group but declined to do so, giving his reasons as follows:

We are in and of the race, and that is why we deprecate vegetarianism. The forces we use for your initiations are designed for use on a vehicle in and of the race of men of the Western world. That vehicle is, from the spiritual standpoint, a very dense vehicle, and the forces we use are concentrated in order to penetrate it. You will therefore see why it is that it is not desirable that you should produce a sensitive condition of the physical vehicle by means of diet.

You may say that such an action is unpardonable from the humanitarian point of view. The solution of the problem of human suffering was not found when humanity abandoned cannibalism; and the solution of the problem of animal suffering will not be found when humanity abandons meat eating, for the genus homo sapiens is but one among many carnivores.

The reason vegetarianism is required of the candidates for an Eastern initiation is on account of its physiological effects. For the same reason we ourselves use it when specifically indicated. But the very races which employ vegetarianism as a religious discipline are diabolically cruel to their beasts...

If we believed that the problem of animal suffering could be affected by a change in diet, we would unhesitatingly demand it of you. But common sense shows that the roots of the problem do not lie there, and you are bailing out the Atlantic with a spoon, and you might be much better employed.

What many found more shocking was that the Master of Medicine declined to condemn as a matter of principle the existence of laboratory animals, even if he did hold out a crumb of comfort for them personally:

As a matter of fact, in the researches of esoteric medicine, animal experimentation will be of very little use to you, because in human beings the mental factor is a very large one and falsifies many of the results. But you must remember this, that all your esoteric medicine which concerns the boundary line of mind and body can have no other basis than a sound knowledge of anatomy and physiology. There is only one way to learn anatomy, and that is by dissecting a dead body; and there is only one way to learn physiology, and that is by the examination of the living body. If anyone can suggest a substitute we shall be very glad to hear of it. But hitherto, no one has suggested any other method. I do not suggest that as individuals it is incumbent upon you to take up this line of research work, but I would counsel you not to decry the work of those upon whose results you must base your own researches.

At this point the Greek Master interceded, doing his best to temper the wind of the Master of Medicine's plain speaking:

The Master of Medicine did not tell you that you were to be deliberately cruel. But he did tell you that you must face facts – and that is what we all tell you – you cannot evade facts, my children. We may just as well face them. You may say "these things are deplorable, is there anything that can be done?" But you cannot say they are not so, and that is why we train you; because the tendency of the spiritually minded is to be nice minded. Now we do not want you to be nice minded, we want you to be true minded. There is a distinction.

This confrontation ended with David Carstairs in private conversation with Merl reviewing the current state of the group.

Things are looking quite healthy. You seem to have succeeded in thumping a certain amount of sense into them. You will need to replace the ones that run in the baking. Ever seen a batch of pots come out of the kiln? Some of them sit down. That is what you will find with some of your initiates – they sit down and slip over to one side.

You get them licked into shape. Once your discipline is established you will have comparatively little trouble. You see, where you hit a lot of snags is that you are working over ground that has been cultivated before. If you made an altogether fresh start with people who never had this sort of thing before, they would listen. But when you take them half-hatched, they argue. That is when you get difficulties.

You get a lot of people with preconceived notions. They say "that is right and that is wrong". What they don't realise is – this thing is a lot broader gauge than they ever bargained for. The average man has got blinkers on, and he doesn't see the truth – like the owl who blinked at the sun. When you take initiation the blinkers are taken off, and a lot don't know what to make of it.

Now do you see what these chaps are driving at?

Merl: To establish a school on the basis of discipline?

And they don't want molly coddles. If you can't stand up to a hammering, go home, see. ... It is not a bit of use pretending it is a bed of roses; it isn't. There is a great deal of difference between half ideals and true ideals. That is what they are hammering into you.

But we are not out for those short cuts to comfort. We are out for something much bigger than that. ... That is why they are banging away at you. Take the rough with the smooth, it is no good being squeamish in this line of work.

However most of the contacts with the Master of Medicine were in direct dialogue with Dr. Penry Evans, and at times the scripts read like a chat between two old general practitioners. This confirms the earlier statement that those present at a trance address or conversational exchange contribute considerably to the quality of the communication. In later years when Dr. Evans was no longer available Dion Fortune had to seek out other qualified medical men to renew worthwhile communications with the Master of Medicine.

Meetings between the Master of Medicine and Dr. Evans continued throughout the next five years. The initial ambitious intentions included not only writing a book but also founding a school and indeed a clinic with special facilities to provide an approach to esoteric medicine on four levels – spiritual, mental, magical and physical.

That is to say it would be a centre manned by medically quali fied staff who were also trained in forms of esoteric diagnosis by intuitive and clairvoyant techniques. It would include a magical temple devoted to healing, and those with the necessary skills to perform exorcisms, the breaking of rapports, and the investigation of traumas in past lives. In short, it would be very much like the establishment fictionally described in "The Secrets of Dr. Taverner." No small ambition indeed.

In the beginning regular meetings were conducted at a place called "Heathlands" in Dorking, Surrey, whose location was not revealed to all.

It was generally referred to as "the House on the Hill". The third person making up the triangle for these meetings was invariably Edith Thrupp, familiarly known as "Thruppie" or occasionally "Fruppie", whether or not because she had a London accent, who knows? She was initiated into the group very shortly after Penry Evans and Arthur Firth. It may have been she who made the house available. It is referred to as a favoured location for advanced work with the advantage of being upon a height and resting on gravel based soil rather than London clay.

Their association with it did not last for long but it is an interesting coincidence that the house is currently still connected with healing, as a nursing home catering for elderly mentally and physically handicapped people, but would appear to have no esoteric affiliations.)

Although the meetings between the Master of Medicine and Dr. Evans continued for some time it is surprising how few and far between they came to be. Only six meetings occurred during the whole period from 1928 to 1932, resulting in just 24 pages of typescript, no more than had been received in the first burst of enthusiasm in August 1927. Nonetheless much of the material is of perennial interest and of wider application such as practical instruction for developing etheric vision and clairvoyance as a diagnostic technique.

One problem, apart from the early alarms and excursions with the Star in the East and Moina MacGregor Mathers, was undoubtedly the general expansion of the group's work in setting up a school of initiation along general occult lines. It meant that the more specialised medical line tended to be squeezed out. Also, for a good part of this time, as a practising professional medical man, Dr. Evans' time was not entirely his own either, to say nothing of the experiments in food production that he seems to have undertaken, a further development of interest in the soya bean.

Nonetheless over the course of time an interesting dossier was built up on techniques of alternative healing and diagnostics. Few people knew about this because of its specialist nature. As with "The Cosmic Doctrine" copies of relevant material were privately circulated mainly to senior students and trusted associates.

Some of the material, because of the passage of time or its technicality remains unsuitable for general publication, but that which remains relevant has now been prepared for publication under the title "Principles of Esoteric Healing". (Sun Chalice, 2000).

In the meantime Dr. Evans lent his weight to the work of founding the Fraternity and getting it over its growing pains.

22

A Time of Testing and Dedication

Erskine's counsel in the setting up of their new level of work at the Autumnal Equinox was to do so quietly, and with the minimum of fuss, so that no adverse forces would be provoked against them. After the alarms and excursions of 1927 it no doubt seemed wise to let things simmer down a bit before any serious new work was undertaken.

They also needed to make a greater distinction between their inner work and their outer work. It was one thing by public lectures and writings to let people know that there was a deeper teaching, but newcomers should not unceremoniously be thrown in at the deep end. A graded system of instruction and development had to be fashioned.

They would also need to learn to stand on their own feet as a group and not seek affiliation to other organisations. In the course of time they would attain recognition and respect from other organisations and groups, and to this end it would help if they produced a magazine and built up a library of their own.

They also had to learn not to try to swim beyond their strength, and to bear in mind that, because of her close involvement with inner plane tides, the strength and availability of their leader would of necessity be variable. It was a mistake to try to work continuously under pressure, regardless of the tides. Inner plane work is essentially tidal.

The secret of coping with this fact of nature was to build up a stock of material in hand to help keep up the momentum over slack periods.

The general forecast for the work ahead was that until the Autumnal Equinox they build up the mundane organisation, and set their house in order, literally and metaphorically. There would be a brief period of storm at about that time but they would not experience any internal difficulty.

Between the Autumnal Equinox and the Winter Solstice they should get their public meetings programme organised. This would provide an Outer Court to the Temple of the Mysteries they were building.

From Winter Solstice to Vernal Equinox would be a period of inner teaching, and after that a further period of withdrawal by their leader.

The work would be organised around three centres: the House on the Hill for inner plane work, the outer court work done at Queensborough Terrace, and a holy centre maintained at Glastonbury. Each centre should be regarded as of equal importance and they should not become rivals of one another. Once the training and outer court work had been established the therapeutic work could be opened up, at first experimentally on a small scale at the House on the Hill, and then, probably after three years, opening out on a larger basis.

The community system would always form the nucleus of the work, with the ideal in mind that the work at all three centres should be conducted entirely by members, with no need of hired outside help.

So much for the aims and ideals. By the time the Autumnal Equinox came round the mundane work had not advanced nearly as far as had been hoped. Nonetheless, general prospects remained promising, so they were given another year to consolidate their position and to attract and train the necessary personnel.

They were left in no doubt that as long as there was any insecurity, friction or disorganisation upon the physical plane, it would not be possible to open up the higher work. Those on the inner planes therefore had to wait upon the activity of those upon the outer plane.

The mundane organisation should consist of their leader, Dion Fortune, at the apex of an executive triangle of three men, each of equal standing and responsible for a particular department of activity, one to be in charge of teaching, another of members' discipline and the other of mundane functioning.

Up to now, the propaganda and teaching side of things had come up to standard. Indeed the first issue of "The Inner Light Magazine", published in October 1927, had a 500-copy print run that sold out in a fortnight, quite a remarkable achievement.

It was on the domestic side and in the quality of membership that things lagged behind.

Erskine, when asked by Merl to point out the areas in which they had failed said quite unequivocally, in terms that must jar a more feminist age:

> *Your trouble has always lain in your domestic sphere – in the sphere of your women – always a troublesome spot. The reason being that, in spite of the opportunities afforded, the women remain primarily less disciplined, less educated, less efficient; and your problem in your domestic sphere is the problem of ignorance and indiscipline.*

The male chauvinist edge to these remarks should be taken in the context of the times and of the circumstances. In 1928 it was through no fault of their own if women lagged behind men in education or opportunity, it was only in this year that they were trusted with the vote. The men of the group, Charles Loveday, Penry Evans, Edgar Homan and Arthur Firth, were all professional men. The ladies of the group would have been of a certain class and background, those who had the leisure to devote to philosophic and esoteric pursuits.

Indeed, most of the members were women. There were just five men to twenty-one women in the group at this time. The indications are that this was not felt to be entirely satisfactory, if only from heartfelt remarks made by Dion Fortune some years later that she wished never to have to preside over an all female lodge ever again.

Two of the women members of the group at this time remained members for many years, into the nineteen sixties. One of the original Accolades, Miss G.P.Lathbury, remained a redoubtable stalwart of the organisation for the rest of her life, filling many roles from Secretary to Magus. The daughter of a Field Marshall she went by the nickname of Dragon and stood shoulder to shoulder with Dion Fortune when they were bombed out of their headquarters during the war. I recall her interviewing me as a candidate for membership of the Society in 1954, a seemingly frail old lady yet with great black eyes you could drown in.

Another long serving member was Katherine Barlow who joined in January 1927, and although educated enough to be a brilliant translator of Russian technical texts she otherwise lived up to her nickname of "Doodah", for that was the state in which she commonly appeared to be. She was a deeply committed Christian mystic of unswerving loyalty to the cause for the rest of her life, despite being afflicted with severe health problems which may have contributed to her occasional disorientation.

Other grand old ladies from the earlier days figure in Janine Chapman's "Quest for Dion Fortune" whom I also recall being impressed on meeting in the evening of their days, Evelyn Heathfield, Katherine Clark and the like. They were the nucleus in what otherwise was likely to have been in a somewhat dilettante initial membership.

However, from the inner planes, plans were set in motion to forge a tightly disciplined community from what had previously been little more than a small circle of friends. Erskine spent a lot of time discussing with Dr. Evans the practical details for the formation of such a community. This included whether residents should be subject to a medical examination, the concern being that they could not take on board anyone whose ill health might become a financial and moral liability. There was also some concern as to whether anyone who might have a weak heart should be subjected to powerful ritual conditions.

The 1st Degree was to be one of character building, principally the development of the will through the discipline of keeping a daily meditation diary. On the mundane side they should be willing to perform the necessary humdrum tasks of any household community.

The work of the 2nd Degree should be concerned with training the mind. Principally in image building, this being a basic requirement of magical working, together with a verbal imagination to develop the elements of clairaudience and inner plane communication.

The 3rd Degree was thought of very much in terms of the Greater Mysteries in so far that it involved an Unreserved Dedication to the work of the Masters. Here there might be a relaxation of the disciplines of the lower degrees although it was recommended that all initiates should maintain some kind of handcraft.

Erskine had cause to admonish Merl over the burden of tasks that Dion Fortune had to contend with and at the same time act as an efficient medium for the contact of the Masters at the Vernal Equinox ceremony. Merl suggested that perhaps they could cancel her Monday lecture, to meet with the somewhat exasperated reply:

No, the lecture will not disturb her, that is part of the work. But why you should employ the cosmic medium in washing dishes is more than I can understand.

Erskine, despite his 18th century persona, was therefore not quite such a chauvinist as Dr. Evans, but one wonders if Merl speculated about a certain element of feeling from the subconscious mind of the medium in this response!

The Master, however, had his eye upon the essentials and went on to say:

You cannot have it both ways. Unless you are capable of undertaking the management of your household, it is not possible for the deeper occult work to be done. No man can serve two masters, and no person can concentrate on the inner and the outer planes simultaneously. You must arrange among yourselves that these mundane matters are taken over and attended to, or there will be no Vernal Equinox. This is foolishness, this business about many things when the great tides are running.

The type of new membership that Erskine desired was of a high standard, nor did he have any illusions about the general quality of the average occult seeker:

For it is only out of a body of men and women, highly disciplined and highly trained, that the great work can be brought through, and we must have the nucleus at the centre, however small the nucleus may be. All you need are seven. And if we try and discard seven hundred we will wait till we get what we want, and we shall get it.

Then again, in admitting, you would be wise to accept not the extremes, but to look for normality; and you will find in your work so much abnormality and unbalance attracted to this line of thought – so many souls who, through injudicious instruction, are rendered abnormal and unbalanced that you must choose wisely whom you admit. Restore the balance before admitting – not after.

*Avoid extremes, for your work lies in the soul of your race,
and therefore even extremes of good are unsuited, for yours must
be the middle path, and the saint and the ascetic and the hermit
and the unbalanced psychic are just as unsuited for your
community life as the worldling and the sinner. For it is designed
that you should be in the world, and of the world, in order to
leaven the world. It is for you to show how the life of the day can
be lived from the spiritual standpoint.*

The year was not without some strain and disappointment, and it
seems that of necessity the work of Master of Medicine had been
pushed somewhat to one side. On 26th May 1928 there is a somewhat
plaintive interchange between him and Merl:

*M. of M.: I shall be very glad indeed when this matter can go
forward. No doubt you will also. The delay is annoying to both of
us. Can you see your way at your end?*

M: Not quite clearly yet, sir.

*M. of M.: Then all we can do is to get on with the theory, and you
must work out the practice as best you can. It is not possible to
do our form of therapeutic work except in a place in which we
can make our mental atmosphere. Just as the surgeon must have
his conditions, so must the psychologist. On the plane of the life
forces it is the mental atmosphere which is your principal means
of therapy, and that you make with the trained mind of your group.*

A little light relief however was provided at the Summer Solstice
with an address to the Group by Carstairs.

*Hello. It always seems to be my fate to take these personally
conducted tours. How are you getting along these days?*

*I think they reckon they have taught you enough of the
preliminaries, and expect you to get on with your job. Next they
will let you have the forces to handle. I suppose you know the
way you are spread out on the Rays?*

*Lord E. does the Hermetic stuff. The Greek has the Christian.
Why, I don't know. He is B.C. – but he does. And I am in outer
darkness. Salvation went off me like water off a duck's back. I
am the basal line of the Triangle.*

*There is a very curious thing about Elementals. Have you
noticed it? They are Elemental... ...*

You cannot contact Elementals with your intellect, make up your mind to that. You contact them with your feelings; but there is one thing on the Elemental contacts, which is the same as salvation on the Christian contacts – you know what it is? It is the saving grace of the Elemental contacts – Beauty. That is your keynote. That is an important thing. It is beauty that keeps the Elemental contacts right side up. I am sadly lacking in it myself, and you must take my word for it, but it is a fact. As long as you hold to your sense of beauty you are alright in the Elemental kingdom. Think it out, there is a lot in it.

That is the big difference between the Norse gods and the Greek gods; and between the Greek gods at their prime and the Greek gods when things began to go to pieces. But you people of a Nordic race in a north country will find the Norse gods your surest contacts. They are native to the soil.

You must remember that as far as a practical demonstration of nature forces goes, it is not much good trying to do it in a city. The only time you will ever get it in a city is in a high wind. Because when you touch Elemental things in a city, the layer you strike first is the human passions. That is what you get in a city, and that you do not want. You do the things of the mind in a city. The things of the Spirit you can do anywhere, it is of a different plane. But the Elemental forces have each to be worshipped with their appropriate ritual. You have got to have the right conditions for that sort of job, and that is what we want.

These nature things are on a different plane to the Order. We generate the force, the Hermetic Mysteries make the machine, and the Spiritual aspect drives the car, and one without the other is no good. The only thing you can get with petrol is a flare up, yet the machine will not run without it, and with no one to steer, the car is of no use. The drive comes from the Elementals every time – believe me; and the machine is the carefully constructed technique of the Hermetic Order, and the Spiritual ideals do the steering.

Now what you want to aim at is men and women who can range freely – free-moving, right round the triangle, who don't jam anywhere. Maybe they will work the Hermetic forces, though the machine is not guided by Spiritual ideals; and maybe they will make the machine for the service and lack the Elemental driving power. It is only alright if you have got all three, and all working together, but if you have only two or perhaps only one, nothing happens. The man who has got the Elemental force and the Hermetic machinery, but no Spiritual ideals is a black magician, and if the man has got ideals and the Hermetic machine but no Elemental force, then again, nothing happens. He never gets going, and he is always scared of the Elemental forces.

Now, see what has been going on hitherto. Training has been preparing the Personality for the work. Your next job is to build the machine, and you will be on rituals for your next stretch. What you will want to do is, to construct the appropriate rituals for your different festivals, and work them; and the more they are worked the better they get. And another thing is this – the people who are taking part get first-hand experience, not second-hand experience. Trance work is only makeshift. You get your rituals going – that is your job.

Take the present festal occasion, what you want is a magical circle, and in the middle, the tripod. The tripod should be on a level with the eyes when standing up, and that ought to have the brazier, with fir cones burning in it. Then you have got a basis for manifestation. It is quite simple to manage. Have the thing made of wrought iron, that is all. With a fire basket, six to eight inches in diameter, and a good big tray on the floor to catch the ashes. And so you get a fire of pinecones burning, but don't light it with newspapers – light it with bits of the cone. If you are doing a magical act, everything is magical - unless you want to materialise the ghost of Alfred Harmsworth! [a newspaper magnate of the day]. *That is what you want, otherwise you have no basis for manifestation for a Fire force. It is a pretty sight when you get the fire going. That takes the place of your altar. It goes in the centre. Never mix your symbols. Remember that Fire and Air go together, and Earth and Water, and they are mutually destructive.*

Now don't think that because you have had no surprising manifestation that things have gone amiss – they have not. The Elemental forces have touched your souls all round, though they have not manifested on the physical plane. By this time next year I hope we shall have something more tangible to show you. A good many things will probably have happened by this time next year.

You have got your foundations in now. That is what all the preliminary work has been. The worst of your troubles are behind you, and the interesting parts are beginning. You are beginning to see the fruits of your labours. You have got to about the end of your first stage.

You will find that trance will take on a secondary position, and ritual is the thing. It means instead of one person doing a stunt, the whole lot will do a stunt. Don't you see what happens in ritual? The whole team shifts consciousness. That's the game.

Merl said to him before he closed, *"You know we have decided to go all out for the work next autumn?"*
To which David Carstairs replied:

And didn't you gather power when you made up your mind to go for it? Sacrifice is the secret of power. The sacrifice of mind gives you the key to the mysteries. You play ducks and drakes with your career, and then the Hermetic Mysteries get under way.
   You know what sacrifice really is? Sacrifice is the translation of power from one plane to another – it is transmutation – it disappears on one plane, and reappears on another.
   Well, I must be getting along.

Nonetheless, all was not quite plain sailing. An interview between Merl and Erskine on 9th October gives some indication of the strains currently being felt.

Merl informed Erskine that they were contemplating holding over the full community scheme in the house for the present, and they would like to let out part of the house to outsiders, who knew nothing of their work but who, they felt, would not disturb the group harmony.

Erskine agreed somewhat reluctantly to this as a matter of temporary expediency, pointing out that they had now been in the house four years and had only completed three years of the intended work. He gave them a piece of general advice on how to comport themselves in the immediate future.

You are not yet ready to cope with an expansion of your work, therefore we do not intend to give it you. Prepare your machinery, then will be the time to extend your operations. Aim above all things that your own lives would be the lives of initiates. For it is your own serenity and discipline and harmony which will produce that tone of serenity, discipline and harmony throughout your fraternity. As you yourselves are disturbed, and as you yourselves are serene and harmonised, so will you make others serene and harmonised.
   Aim at reducing your work to an impersonal system. But from

the solid nucleus of the inner group, waiting its time, making secure as it goes, there will come a sure and steady growth upon a firm foundation. For the first time you have a firm foundation under your feet. Your three years task is fulfilled.

Loveday asked if he could do anything further in the matter of religious services, to which Erskine replied that in due course this would meet with considerable response but it needed Dion Fortune to write the ritual for it. First she had to finish her current tasks with the magazine.

Penry Evans hoped that it would be possible to hold regular meetings of instruction with the Master of Medicine, while Loveday hoped for more instruction from the Greek master. Erskine's reply to all these aspirations was that they would get what they invoked for.

Finally, at the Winter Solstice of 1928 they started the ritual side of things again from scratch. The Lesser Mysteries of the Fraternity of the Inner Light were inaugurated, with Dion Fortune, Thomas Penry Evans and Charles T. Loveday functioning as principal officers.

The Fraternity of the Inner Light was ritually established.

23
THE WRITTEN AND SPOKEN WORD

1927, by no means an uneventful year, also saw not only the publication of the last book under her maiden name, "The Problem of Purity" but the publication of the first of Dion Fortune's occult novels "The Demon Lover". This was very much in the tone of the "Dr. Taverner" stories of 1922, which had been published in book format by Noel Douglas the year before..

Then in 1928 came the first of her major textbooks "The Esoteric Orders and their Work" closely followed by its companion volume "The Training and Work of an Initiate" and in 1930 by the ever popular "Psychic Self-Defence" and a collected edition of her "Sane Occultism" articles.

This flurry of activity was helped by the services of a young literary agent, Christine Campbell Thomson, who would later become a member of the Fraternity of the Inner Light. She had at this time no overt interest in occultism but some years earlier, when working for the large literary agency, Curtis Brown, had handled the last novel of J.W.Brodie-Innes, close friend of MacGregor Mathers, and head of the Alpha et Omega Temple. At that time he observed that she might have the aptitude for study "along certain occult lines," although she had not followed the matter up, possibly assuming it to be a well-tried opening gambit of elderly occultists to attractive young ladies. In the meantime she had directed her energies more to the outer world and founded her own literary agency.

It was some years before Dion Fortune returned to writing her classic series of occult novels but this first one shows the lineaments of her typical heroine, a downtrodden female who in spite of all wins through and saves her man from the worst side of himself. The heroine of her last two novels, it should be said, was very far from being downtrodden, but of this, more later.

In this early work, Veronica, just out of commercial college, is lured into the clutches of Justin Lucas, the secretary of a mysterious magical fraternity. He exploits her natural psychism under hypnotism, in his plot to discover the occult secrets of his superior brethren, to which he is not entitled. When the punitive ray is evoked upon him his efforts to escape it take him beyond the grave, where in his efforts to maintain an etheric body by vampiring off the vital spirits of others we have an elaboration of the first of the Dr. Taverner stories, "Blood Lust", which was, of course, based upon the circumstances of her early meeting with Moriarty, an event that obviously made a great impression upon her.

A great deal of practical knowledge is expounded within the book, particularly of trance conditions and of post mortem pathologies. However, the denouement, a magical action which summons up a storm and a flood to enable them to snatch Justin's body from the cemetery, and his rejuvenation, minus the eyes, which have been removed in the autopsy, is somewhat more melodramatic and grisly than is the usual lot of members of esoteric fraternities in real life. Veronica however, in saintly fashion, agrees to marry and care for him despite his affliction – which in the circumstances he could probably count himself lucky was not a lot worse. They had of course been closely connected in a previous incarnation, in which was contained much of the causation for this one.

One interesting aspect of the publication of "The Demon Lover" was that its dustjacket was designed by Mary Bligh Bond, the daughter of Frederick Bligh Bond. She was a friend of Dion Fortune and had very strong Elemental contacts that are apparent in her art work, and not least in the cover of the "The Demon Lover", not so much in their subject matter, but in their raw power – a very far cry from the rather fey approach to the Elemental Kingdoms. She was also herself the author of an occult novel of disturbing power, "Avernus", that harked back to Atlantis, and its effects in the lives of certain people in contemporary life, a theme that was to be found in the background to a great deal of Dion Fortune's work and thought.

In "The Esoteric Orders and their Work" and its companion "The Training and Work of an Initiate" she provided a theoretical structure for anyone who sought initiation in the Western Esoteric

Tradition, whether through her own organisation or another. After a general traditional history she went on to describe the function of different types of school, the use and power of ritual, seeking a Master and the path of initiation through right choice of an occult school. It was a book, accessible to the general public, which was aimed foursquare at the serious seeker for esoteric wisdom according to the western way, and such books were very rare in those days. "The Training and Work of an Initiate" covered much the same ground from the point of view of the experience of the individual and the ethical, theoretical and practical considerations of following the Path.

The writing of books was far from being her only literary activity, for the "Inner Light Magazine", launched in October 1927 had to be filled with articles, and the burden of filling its twenty pages every month fell largely upon her.

Some of these early articles were later made up into published books. The first of these, "Mystical Meditations upon the Collects", published in 1930, was a series of short meditations upon the selection from holy scripture chosen each week for the liturgy of the Anglican church. This emphasised the Christian commitment that the Fraternity showed throughout the whole of the pre-war period, not only from its origins as the Christian Mystic Lodge of the Theosophical Society but as pursued in its Sunday services of the Guild of the Master Jesus, later known as the Church of the Graal.

A second series of articles comprised evocations of her impressions of Glastonbury which, as we have already mentioned, were later issued in volume form as a kind of popular esoteric guidebook, as "Avalon of the Heart" in 1934.

In addition to these articles and books there was also the matter of public lectures, junior and senior study groups and correspondence courses, to say nothing of writing the liturgy for the Guild religious services, and of course her continuous call of duty as a trance medium.

We have no record of the lecturing activity taken on before November 1928, but certainly from that time, and presumably well before it, she was engaged in two lectures per week, on a Monday evening and a Wednesday afternoon, not repeating herself once, until the end of 1929. The afternoon lectures were then dropped but she continued with Monday evening lectures throughout the whole of 1930, apart from four occasions taken on by C.T.Loveday.

— Part Four —

THE FRATERNITY AT WORK:
1928-1939

24
THE LODGE OF THE LESSER MYSTERIES

The aim under the new dispensation was to establish an even balance of men and women members, the one sex not to outnumber the other by a ratio of more than two to one.

> In 1929, there were nine initiations, two men and seven women.
> In 1930 ten initiations, five men and five women.
> In 1931 eight initiations, three men and five women.
> In 1932 five initiations, two men and three women.
> In 1933 nine initiations, four men and five women.
> In 1934 ten initiations, six men and four women.
> In 1935 eight initiations, four men and four women.
> In 1936 four initiations, one man and three women.

So by and large they kept within the desired proportions and there seems to have been no need for any positive discrimination of individuals on grounds of gender. The role call of the Fraternity must have been, in the mid 1930's, allowing for perhaps two resignations per year, somewhere around the fifty to sixty mark.

The initial ritual team consisted of Dion Fortune, Dr Penry Evans and Charles Loveday as the three principal officers, with the four minor offices, (one of which was temporarily doubled up) filled by Miss Lathbury and Edgar Homan, (who was also the Secretary) and his wife.

Ritual seems to have been something of a low key affair in the early stages for we find Loveday being instructed that it really was not appropriate for the minutes of the last meeting to be read out at the commencement of the next. This suggests that there was a residual element of formalistic "old boy" masonry as opposed to working the offices with magical power at this time.

In the beginning members were known in lodge by their surname, prefixed by the term Brother, irrespective of sex. In the case of married couples the initial letter of the first name of one of them would be used to distinguished between them, as for instance Brother Homan and Brother B. Homan for the secretary and his wife. An exception was Dion Fortune who was known as Brother Dion Fortune whilst her husband was Brother Evans.

Within a year this convention gave place to a system whereby members chose an aspirational name for themselves. To quote from the Lodge Records of 1st October 1929:

The name taken to be that of one of the Saints or Sages with whom the Member feels an affinity and whose name the Member would choose to be known in Lodge; the form of address to be "Serving Brother of ... ."

The title Serving Brother was very soon abbreviated to Server, and names chosen included Servers of Thoth, Orpheus, Socrates, Merlin, Harmonica, Maimonides, Ra, Hermes, Harpocrates, Pan, Arnolf, Athena, Richard Coeur de Lion, Plotinus, and Dionysus. Christian saints were also popular, including Saints Raphael, Michael, Mary the Virgin, Anselm, Francis, John, Paul, Christopher, Patrick, Luke, Ambrose, Theresa, Joseph of Arimathea, Alban, and of course the Master Jesus himself. Should more than one elect to have the same name they were called the 1st, 2nd, 3rd Server of whoever it was. Thus there were three Servers of St Paul, and also of Hermes and of St John, whilst eventually they reached no less than a Fifteenth Server of the Master Jesus even though the First Server had long since resigned.

When new members had passed through the Outer Court course and examination they were proposed and then, if not blackballed, ritually initiated into the Lesser Mysteries. They were then allowed to meet the Masters, that is to say a personal introduction to Lord

Erskine through the entranced Dion Fortune. This was no mere formality and pertinent advice might well be given, and at some length.

One of these occasions was recorded after the initiation ceremony of the first two initiates in January 1929, another man and wife team.

The husband, who had chosen to be known as Server of Thoth, had some experience of teaching other students in the Outer Court and asked for advice on this. Erskine's remarks are worth quoting for their continuing relevance to any officer in ritual lodge or public speaker on occult subjects:

> *When you come to meet your pupils, visualise myself. Thereby I shall be enabled to pick up contact with you. Then, putting aside all voluntary endeavour, allow the teaching to flow through you.*
>
> *Let come what will come. You will find it a mistake to over prepare your lessons; and I will give you this advice – do not refer to it on the day on which you give it. Then, when you come to meet your class, learn to listen mentally to the atmosphere of that class. You will soon learn to sense it and, like the conductor of an orchestra, you will soon be able to pick out the sounds of the individual instruments of the orchestra.*
>
> *The great secret of success in occult work is to learn to work off the subconscious mind, and to do that you must allow impulse and intuition to function, and speak without thinking the first thing that comes into your mind. If the lesson be thoroughly prepared in the course of the week it will sink from consciousness to subconsciousness. Then leave it alone on the day in which the lesson is given. You will have the general outline only in your head, and you will fall back on the subconscious mind, and then your class will begin to draw from you what they need, and it will flow out to them, and through you they will be drawing on the Masters.*
>
> *Always remember this, that when you stand up to speak on esoteric matters, you are standing up in the name of the Masters, and if you allow it, the Masters will come and speak through you, and you will find yourself giving utterance to things you have never known. Learn to trust to the impulse, and do not be afraid to give utterance spontaneously to things that are coming through you.*

This is advice that requires a certain amount of talent and advancement on the part of the one doing the teaching. If followed by one who is not ready for it the results can be dire, as much modern "channelling" can bear witness. However, it is the means whereby any real progress is made in the magical arts and the theoretical structure behind them.

The next to be introduced, the wife of the former neophyte, elected to be known as Server of the Master Jesus. She was particularly keen to offer what she considered a special gift of healing to the Masters, and to this end her interview was extended to include a meeting with the Master of Medicine. She was, however, given a certain degree of forewarning about this contact from Lord Erskine:

> *You must remember, in dealing with him, that he is a man who, in his last incarnation, which of course is the personality in which he manifests, was accustomed to deal with medical students a hundred years ago... A man of noble soul, and vast intellect; and you must strive to see the compassionate heart behind the rough tongue. It is because he was a man of extreme sensitiveness of nature that he covered himself with a thorny covering.*

The interview, thorns and all, proceeded as follows:

M. of M.:   *Well, my daughter, now what about this special gift of healing? What makes you think you have got a special gift of healing?*

S. of M.J.:   *Because I have used it. I have been told I have it.*

M. of M.:   *And you have used it and got results? How long have you been using it?*

S. of M.J.:   *For a year.*

M. of M.:   *How many cases have you had?*

S. of M.J.:   *Only three, but one continued for eight months.*

M. of M.:   *It isn't the length of time, it is the results you have got. It is no especial virtue to have a case a long time, rather the other way about. Now of your three, in how many cases was the original diagnosis confirmed? In how many were they discharged cured? In how many were they improved? In how many was there no change? And how many were killed? It is no good coming to me and saying I have got this case cured. What you want is the necessary statistics. That is the test.*

S. of M.J.:   *I have not given the treatment.*

M. of M.:   *That is rather peculiar – yet you have had three cases.*
                How many have you cured?

S. of M.J.:   *Two, and the third was a faith cure.*

M. of M.:   *It does not matter what, if you cured the case. Perhaps it*
                was due to lack of faith. But it does not matter what you
                call it – if you cure by faith or jalop, I don't mind, if you
                have a cure. Two out of three – that is a presentable
                proportion.

S. of M.J.:   *The one I had for eight months was a different thing.*

M. of M.:   *There is as much skill in managing the patient as in*
                treating the human body. You cannot put a patient in a
                strait waistcoat. One does not treat the disease and forget
                the patient; and that is where experience comes in, and
                the art of handling human nature, which is as much
                part of the art of medicine as the technical aspects. A
                man may know his science side, but unless he can
                handle human nature he is not going to succeed in
                practice. Well now, what do you want to do?

S. of M.J.:   *Can I be trained?*

M. of M.:   *You can be trained, certainly. I cannot make anything*
                of you till you are trained, that is quite certain. And I
                will give you a word of warning – healing is not a
                simple thing. So my advice to you is this – learn the
                technique of the thing you want to do. And remember
                this – never start your treatment till you are sure of
                your diagnosis, otherwise you are no better off than
                the vendor of patent medicines. Now what do you
                understand by spiritual healing?
                Come along. Don't crib.

S. of M.J.:   *I was told...*

M. of M.:   *Don't tell me what you were told. What do you mean*
                by spiritual healing?

S. of M.J.:   *Laying on of hands.*

M. of M.:   *I call that massage. What have the hands to do with*
                it? Think it out.

S. of M.J.:   *Being a channel to flow through.*

M. of M.:   *What is the spiritual force?*

S. of M.J.:   *The Christ force.*

M. of M.:   *Of what kind is that?*

S. of M.J.:   *The gift of healing.*

M. of M.:   *Now we are back where we started.*

S. of M.J.:   *I want to learn.*

M. of M.:   *Clarity of ideas is the beginning of wisdom. So unless you begin to think more clearly, I cannot teach you. Now what do you mean when you say spiritual healing? You have got a label, but you don't know what it is tied to. What do you mean by healing?*

S. of M.J.:   *Take a case of hernia – by laying on of hands I have reduced the hernia.*

M. of M.:   *How do you know it was a hernia?*

S. of M.J.:   *It was diagnosed.*

M. of M.:   *How do you know you reduced it?*

S. of M.J.:   *By examination.*

M. of M.:   *And how did you heal it?*

S. of M.J.:   *By putting my hands on it.*

M. of M.:   *You see, my daughter, if you want to function with spiritual healing, and don't know what spirit is, and what healing is, you are not a safe guide. What happens when you do this? Shall I tell you? You are going into a medical hospital, into the dispensary in the dark, and you are taking down the first bottle you lay your hands on, and you are pouring some into a glass and handing it to the patient. Now there is a glyph for you to meditate on. One of these days you will be giving the wrong bottle.*

S. of M.J.:   *But I am not doing it.*

M. of M.:   *That is a relief to my mind. Now spiritual healing is a very important thing. I will tell you what it is, since you can't tell me. "Healing" means making the abnormal normal; bringing that which has got out of line into line. And "Spirit" is the parent essence of life – life before it takes on form. Spiritual healing means straightening things out, beginning at the top, and that force has to be translated down the planes; and on each plane it functions according to the nature of that plane. In spiritual things it functions spiritually. In mental things it functions mentally. In astral things it functions astrally. And in physical things it functions materially. And what you need to learn is, to know at what point in the planes lesion has occurred, and pick it up there. And if the lesion is on the spiritual plane, nothing but spiritual healing will touch it, and no surgeon or physician can do anything for it. If on the mental plane, you must express your healing in terms of psychology. If on the astral, you will express it* in terms of magic; and if on the physical plane, you will express it in terms of surgery and medicine. And what you need to know is, how to place your case; otherwise, my daughter, you are going to burn your fingers. So that is what you need to know if you do spiritual healing.

S. of M.J.:   I have no intention of treating anyone unless I am trained.

M. of M.:   That is sound policy. Mind you stick to it. You probably won't. That is why we say spiritual healing is not nearly so simple as it looks, and the trouble comes when you get hold of the wrong type of case. And that is where the technical knowledge comes in – in sorting out the cases. But I will say this – there is no case in the world that would not be the better for spiritual healing. But there are only a small percentage of cases where spiritual healing is going to cure by itself. It is part of a much larger whole. You are playing one instrument in a quartet, and you will make some very funny noises if you play by yourself. And the true therapy contains all the elements I have mentioned – spiritual, psychological, magical and physical; and in every case they are present in different proportions, for everything that happens on one plane reflects down the planes always. And therefore, my daughter, the spiritual healer plays a part in the orchestra – not a solo. And what you need to understand is the technique of what you are doing. See what you are doing. Why you do it. How you do it. When to do it, and still more important, when not to do it. Of the non-physical healings there are several types. Spiritual healing is only one. There is also psychological healing; and magical work; and etheric healing. So there are four distinct types. Now, my daughter, I have told you something of what it means; and I have tried to make you think. If I have succeeded in making you see that it is not as simple as it looks, I have done you considerable service. Now is there anything else, or have you had enough?

S. of M.J.:   I thank you for all you have said. I will think it over, because I wish to serve the Masters, and that is all I think I have got to offer. Perhaps I can serve in some other way.

M. of M.:   That is more sensible. It is more to the point to do what is wanted, than what you want to do.

It is perhaps not surprising that this particular initiate subsequently resigned "on instruction from an authority higher than any on Earth," and her husband followed suit upon "instructions received in another place."

It was obvious that a new rigour was moving through cosy esoteric circles with the advent of the Fraternity of the Inner Light, and also one that was more outgoing than the secretive inward-looking enclaves that many of the old Golden Dawn Temples had become.

The "Inner Light Magazine" attracted a wide readership, with subscribers in the United States, Canada, South America, South Africa, West Africa, East Africa, India, China, Australia and continental Europe.

A note by Dion Fortune to her readers sums up their general sense of mission:

> At the present time "the fields are white to the harvest". A spiritual message gains a ready hearing nowadays. The terrible years of the Great War have awakened mankind; the old forms have been broken up, and men and women are crying aloud for spiritual food. The churches are not empty because people are less religious, but because they are more religious, because they are no longer content to be put off with empty words but demand spiritual realities. They have realised that religion is a real and potent thing, and not a matter of compliance with set forms.
>
> Whether the viewpoint of the "Inner Light" is acceptable or not, at least it represents actual spiritual experience. Here is no repetition of stereotyped phrases, but an endeavour to describe that which has been known and felt, and which can be felt and known again, given the right conditions.
>
> Scientists test the accuracy of an experiment by repeating it independently. The same test should be applicable in the life of the Spirit, if true, and we recommend it to our readers.

Strange as it may seem in a modern consumerist age when retailing has allegedly been brought to a fine art, in the years before the war, despite being typed up and run off on a duplicator, the "Inner Light Magazine" could be ordered through any branch of W.H.Smith, the leading bookselling chain.

In the pages of the magazine, as well as the descriptive articles on Glastonbury and the Mystical Meditations on the Collects, she had started a series under the title of "Spiritualism in the Light of Occult Science" in which she strove to define the distinction between mediumship as she knew it, and as it was practised within spiritualist circles and churches.

The community ideal had not yet come to pass at the Queensborough Terrace headquarters and they were advertising guest rooms to let for most of the year. It would seem that there was not a great rush to have a bed sitting room at the headquarters of an occult fraternity, or perhaps they had quite rigorous standards for vetting any applicants.

The doors were open for lectures on Monday evenings and Wednesday afternoons and a run down of the list of talks Dion Fortune gave week in week out gives an idea of the extent of her range.

January
 14th The Initiate's Philosophy of Life
 16th What is Initiation?
 21st Merlin and the British Mysteries
 23rd Stages on the Path
 28th The Master Jesus and the Cosmic Christ
 30th The Esoteric Explanation of the Sacraments
February
 4th The Power of the Mind and its Use
 6th Esoteric Concept of the Universe
 11th The Esoteric Concept of Death and Birth
 13th Esoteric Concept of Evolution
 18th Lent and the Tides of Purgation
 20th Esoteric Concept of Man
 25th The Psychic Influence of Places and Things
 27th The Dedicated Life
March
 4th The Esoteric Significance of Avalon
 6th The Elemental and Nature Contacts of the Green Ray
 11th The Initiate – his Training and Work
 13th Glastonbury – "the holyest erthe in England"
 18th The Esoteric Interpretation of the Crucifixion
 20th The Power Tides of the Christian Year
April
 8th Esoteric Science: whence comes it?
 10th Esoteric Methods of Character Building
 15th Esoteric Science: what is it?
 17th What Initiation really is
 22nd Initiation by the Way of the Cross
 24th The Western Esoteric Tradition

29th Our Atlantean Heritage
May
    1st Occultism and Spiritualism
    6th The Living Christ
    8th The Use of Symbolism in Mystical Thought
    13th The Inner Light
    15th Esoteric Teaching concerning the Forgiveness of Sins
    27th The Hidden Powers of the Mind
    29th The Mystic as Citizen
June
    3rd The Celtic Esoteric Tradition
    5th The Use and Power of Prayer
    10th Mystical Christianity
    12th Mind Training
    17th The Green Ray of the Nature Contacts
September
    30th The Esoteric Interpretation of Life
October 1929
    2nd The Sacramental Concept of Life
    7th The Tree of Life and the Jewish Qabalah
    9th Through the Gates of Death
    14th The Way of Initiation; its Method and Discipline
    16th The Rationale of Divination
    21st The Psychology of Psychism
    23rd The Mystic Way
    28th The Esoteric Aspect of Christianity
    30th The Occult Path
November
    4th The Evocation of Spirits
    6th The Esoteric Concept of Love
    11th The Hidden Side of Nature
    13th Meditation and Mind-training
    18th The Tarot Cards of the Bohemians
    20th The Regime and Discipline of the Way of Initiation
    25th The Etheric Body and its Projection
    27th The Astral Plane
December
    2nd Some Practical Applications of the Doctrine of Reincarnation
    4th The Sources of Occult Energy
    9th The Rationale and Psychology of Ceremonial

The summer months were taken up with Chalice Orchard, which was now open from Whitsuntide to the end of September as a guest house and social centre "for all those interested in Esotericism, Mysticism, Spiritualism, New Thought, and similar subjects," with vegetarian or ordinary diet provided.

Here, lectures were provided also, and a library, as well as "motoring expeditions arranged at moderate cost." The hostel was described as being situated "high up on the shoulder of the Tor, and the sheltered garden and large verandas are ideal for an open air life."

A booklet on the Aims and Ideals of the Fraternity had also been produced (price three pence, post free three pence halfpenny) which no doubt had also fallen to the lot of Dion Fortune to produce, along with a Correspondence Course which was now available for students living at a distance, and something of an innovation in its day.

This first year of the inauguration of the Lesser Mysteries also saw publication by Riders of "Sane Occultism", a collection of articles that Dion Fortune had written over previous years for "The Occult Review", an influential monthly magazine run by this company, which was the main occult publishing house of the time.

These articles had brought a fair amount of wrath upon her head, when they first appeared, including from Moina MacGregor Mathers. In making general comments about what she felt to be abuses on the occult scene, she had apparently struck painfully close to some of the practices and peccadilloes of leading occultists. Her sallies included essays on Credulity in Occult Research, the Use and Abuse of Astrology, Records of Past Lives, Secrecy in Occult Fraternities, the Left-hand Path, Psychic Pathologies, and Eastern Methods and Western Bodies.

Most of the articles read as freshly today as when they were written, and it is interesting to speculate who might have been offended by what.

25

CONSOLIDATION OF THE WORK

Some of those joining in this first seven-year period made their mark in the annals of the society and indeed of occultism in general. W.E.Butler was initiated into the Fraternity in July 1930, having been demobilised from the British army the year before, but had first made contact with Dion Fortune at Glastonbury in 1925. She turned out to be "the lady with the rose" to whom he had been directed by Annie Besant from whom he had sought esoteric instruction when he was serving as a soldier in India. His fascinating story is told in Janine Chapman's "The Quest for Dion Fortune". In later years he wrote a number of books on magic and occultism and became a co-founder and Director of Studies of the Servants of the Light organisation.

The Lesser Mysteries system of the Fraternity of the Inner Light was complete in little more than a year after its commencement. A 2nd Degree had been opened on 9th April 1929, and a 3rd Degree on 28th January 1930. Progress through the degrees could be surprisingly rapid, subject it seems only to a rule that a student's stay in any one degree should not be less than three months. Some initiates, such as Miss Barlow or Miss Lathbury, were of course old hands who had seen service in the earlier group.

The general guidelines laid down from the inner planes were that the full curriculum should last three years. There should be one year in the Outer Court, one year in the three grades of the Lesser Mysteries, and one year in the Portal that prepared for the Greater Mysteries. Beyond that, said Erskine, "open up many lines of study and adventure".

Despite the possible speed of passage there was a rigid barrier between the degrees. In the beginning, 2nd degree meetings took place immediately after 1ˢᵗ degree meetings, and on those occasions initiates of the 1ˢᵗ degree had to leave the lodge. The same procedure occurred with early 3ʳᵈ degree meetings, but this meant that the whole evening's events had to be started earlier on account of this piggy back system.

Only senior initiates were permitted to be present at Equinox and Solstice celebrations, in complete opposition to later practice when such events were all but compulsory for all members.

Senior members became known by the initials of a chosen motto once they had passed through the graded system. Dion Fortune retained her Golden Dawn designation of Deo Non Fortuna, C.T. Loveday's deep mystical Christian commitment was reflected in his motto Amor Vincit Omnia, while Dr. Evans characteristically chose a Celtic motto, Bid Ben Bid Bont, which are Bran the Blessed's words from "The Mabinogion" and translate as "He who would be chief, let him be a bridge" as he lay himself over a wide river to let his men pass over him. These names were usually rendered by their initials, D.N.F., A.V.O. and B.B.B.B.

A new phase in the work was announced at the Vernal Equinox of 1930. The three degrees of the Lesser Mysteries now being established, Dion Fortune could withdraw to work more upon the inner levels, the result of which was expected to be the opening of a Threshold Degree, probably by the Autumn, when the celebration of the Greater Mysteries could then follow.

She intended to make only occasional appearances in 1ˢᵗ Degree lodges from now on, perhaps to give an address, and her function as Magus of the Lodge was taken over by Dr. Penry Evans.

This was not his only function for Erskine was also pressing him to extend the boundaries of the Fraternity, to make the teaching more accessible, and do something about getting "The Cosmic Doctrine" published, which they seemed to regard as a confidential document for senior students only. Erskine did not see it quite in that way.

Your aim should be to spread your boundaries as wide as possible, merely guarding sedulously the highest degree working – the quick of the Fraternity.

So also in the matter of your Script. That is intended for mankind. It is not a secret teaching. I would have you publish it,

*would have you circulate it, lend it freely, sell it. It is for
circulation. It is only your Lodge which is secret.*

Merl replied that they would publish as soon as they had enough
money, however Erskine maintained a far more radical and pragmatic
attitude.

*But meanwhile, my son, let it go forth. Do not conceal your
light under a bushel. It is for the instruction of mankind, and,
my children, if someone were to steal one of those MSS and
publish it, it would be saving you much expense. It were better
for mankind to get the teaching than for you to get the profits
for the sale of such a book, for there would not be much! By
guarding it sedulously you merely ensure for yourselves that
you have the sole right of paying expenses. It is not a thing
anyone will steal because it is of no value on the physical plane.
No man will make a fortune from it. Let it go forth, it is for the
enlightenment of mankind and the more that can be enlightened,
the better.*

If he had been speaking in modern times he would no doubt have
suggested that the text be displayed upon the internet.

At the same time, Erskine encouraged them by saying that
changes were on the way and financial tension would be less acute.
He also told Loveday that he would be approaching a time of
personal growth and might expect to take on responsibility for the
Outer Court.

The expansion of Dion Fortune's inner work took the form of
a number of out of the body experiences. They were related to a
major literary work upon which she was about to embark, although
she did not yet quite realise it at the time. This was "The Mystical
Qabalah", upon which she worked consistently from 1931 to 1935.

The opening up of these powerful visions impelled her to seek to
go into some kind of retreat, preferably at Glastonbury. However, it
seems that there were some intractable domestic problems there.
Whoever was currently running Chalice Orchard seemed not best
pleased to accommodate any such new arrangement.

As a result, Merl found himself in the somewhat uncomfortable
position of having to seek a compromise. In a meeting of 23rd July
at Glastonbury he was however able to tell Erskine that agreement
had been reached that the place would return to Dion Fortune's

disposal by the following Easter, and that with this assurance she has been content.

Lord Erskine dryly remarked:

That simplifies your problem. You have only one warring woman to deal with instead of two. And you yourself, are you feeling happier about matters?

Merl replied that it relieved the situation considerably. Erskine went on to say how they were beginning to realise just what Chalice Orchard could do for them, and that at a later date certain rituals could be performed there. It was too important a spot lightly to be abandoned.

He considered it unwise for Dion Fortune to try to return there immediately because of the violence of the reaction it would cause, but it would be no bad idea if Penry Evans himself undertook the task. He should enter the place and possess it, to be held for the group mind of the work.

The exact root of the problem is unclear, but it would appear that someone, perhaps only half associated with the group, probably some kind of housekeeper, had possession, and would not lightly give it up. There is mention of there having been some similar kind of problem the year before in relation to this person and another member of the group. Erskine was convinced that if Merl stepped into the breach the problem would be sorted out, and the person concerned would either be absorbed into the group or take herself off.

He also gave Merl some very practical advice on how to go about it.

Make your conditions what you wish them to be – taking them for granted. Do not approach people as if you were trying to put a halter on a horse running free; take it for granted that they accept conditions as a matter of course. In this way you have the halter on them before they have seen it.

The next day, Merl was able to report that he had taken possession and the first results were already apparent. Erskine was much impressed.

You see how potent is thought and how necessary it is to guard it. You see how readily you can reach out into the Unseen. It has

*been no doubt a surprise to you, the facility with which this can
be done. You would not have believed it possible had you not
seen the results for yourself – but this is only possible to the
trained mind. The untrained mind, constantly fluctuating, cannot
fix the fleeting image.*

*And do you not feel a peculiar intimacy growing up between
you and this place? You will become increasingly conscious of
its personality, and it will become increasingly conscious of yours.
It is this relationship between the soul and the place which gives
the consciousness of home or the consciousness of holiness as
the case may be. Your aura cannot expand except in the
atmosphere which is home to you.*

Merl replied that he had resorted to flying the Celtic flag from the
veranda – with good effect. To which Erskine replied:

*That is a good device, for the symbol of the scarlet dragon is
eloquent of the old gods. It is the colour of war and the symbol of
sin. You have chosen well! Now you will see why your aura can
expand in this atmosphere. And as you say, it is beginning to feel
homelike. In other words, it is the symbol of the elemental forces
in their most primitive form and the man who can ride the red
dragon can ride anything!*

He went on to remark that it was not for nothing that Penry Evans
had been called after Merlin, the "mid wife" to King Arthur, and no
doubt he recognised many aspects within his nature that gave him a
peculiar title to bear that name.

Merl said that he had indeed felt a strong pull towards Merlin
but could neither understand nor explain it, to which Erskine replied
that Merlin would be his initiator. Merl demurred, saying that if it
were in his power to choose, he would feel honoured enough to
received initiation at the hands of Erskine. Only to receive the reply:

*I am one of the lesser Masters, I am not Lord of a Ray, and
Merlin is Logos of the Green Ray in these islands. I myself am on
the Hermetic Ray and the Lord of my allegiance is Thoth, the
Wise Ibis.*

However, all did not run completely smoothly. By the end of
September Dr. Evans withdrew as Magus of the Lodge. This was
apparently in response to a call of his medical career that he felt he
could not refuse. Consequently, Dion Fortune had to take over again.

In a eulogy given in lodge she spoke of the valuable work he had rendered the Fraternity and how most were probably unaware of the great sacrifices he had made. He had given up an important post and income to devote his whole energy to putting the work of the group on a firm foundation. This had now been achieved and a strong group mind had been built up.

Certain qualities were necessary for this work that he possessed – strength, rulership, capacity for hard work, willingness to bear blame and enforce discipline. He had brought stability to the Fraternity and done a more valuable piece of work than any of the brethren realised.

Others, including C.T. Loveday, added their personal gratitude, not only for Dr. Evans' medical skill and kindness, but for the mental and moral leadership he had given.

To take some of the burden from Dion Fortune the Wednesday afternoon lectures were dropped from the beginning of 1930 and Loveday stood in to give a talk from time to time. He had a deep interest in cosmology and esoteric philosophy and gave talks on "The Cosmic Doctrine", as well as writing a series of magazine articles on aspects of Blavatsky's "The Secret Doctrine".

He was also closely committed to the Guild of the Master Jesus, in support of which Dion Fortune wrote a long series of articles called "The Guild of the Master Jesus" that ran from January 1930 through to April 1932.

The aim of the Guild was to provide a response to those who wanted to follow the mystic way and study the esoteric Christian tradition. Of the Fraternity's members about half had chosen Christian saints as their aspirational names.

Services were held at eleven o'clock every Sunday morning. Its ministrants made no claim to ordination or apostolic succession, with both men and women eligible for office. Apostolic succession had been offered to them at one point but their instruction from Erskine was politely to refuse affiliation to any other organisation and rely on making their own contacts.

On the Hermetic side of things a most important entry appears as a laconic note in the Lodge Records at the end of 1930, that had more significance than its brevity might suggest:

December 14ᵗʰ, the London Centre of the Hermes Temple is consecrated.

This refers to the Bristol temple of the Stella Matutina that Dr. Felkin had established before his departure for New Zealand. It was currently run by a good friend of Dion Fortune named Hope Hughes.

Dion Fortune referred to her connection with the Hermes Temple and Hope Hughes in a letter to Israel Regardie a couple of years later:

I have known her for some years and am very fond of her. As a matter of fact, it was she who turned up at Glastonbury seven years to the day from the starting of our work, as I told you, and brought me the contacts I needed after they seemed to have been broken forever.

This raises some interesting speculation about dates, including which date Dion Fortune considered to represent the starting of her work. If it was immediately after her meeting with Loveday and the contact with the Company of Avalon on 5ᵗʰ August 1922, as Loveday himself has suggested, then it would appear that Hope Hughes made contact with her in 1929, a year or so after Moina Mathers was safely out of the way, and officially restored the Golden Dawn contact at the end of 1930.

Much of Dion Fortune's writing time over 1929/30 was spent on "Psychic Self-Defence" which was published at the end of the year. In commercial terms it has probably been Dion Fortune's most popular book, somewhat to the chagrin of the more serious and philosophically minded of her students. It has a somewhat sensational and credulous tone in some respects, hence its general popularity. It is largely autobiographical and full of personal experiences and speculations, and so might be termed the more human side of "The Esoteric Orders and their Work" and its companion volume "The Training and Work of an Initiate". It is, in effect, a candid account of some of the vicissitudes of finding her way on the Path in the first forty years of her life.

Its main drawback was that it could act as a magnet for a range of life's victims with real or imagined problems. One can thus sympathise with those manning the front desk of the Society in later years if they felt that "Psychic Self-Defence" would have been better left unpublished. An occult Fraternity is not a psychic hospital or first aid post and seeks students of potential quality, not those who come seeking help for problems. Ministering to the afflicted is highly skilled work, demanding specialist knowledge and resources, not least psychiatric and medical. If, however, the hopes and plans of Dr. Penry Evans and the Master of Medicine had come to fruition, and a school of esoteric therapeutics been established, then it might be a different story. "Psychic Self-Defence" was written at a time when hopes ran high for the establishment of such a clinical centre, but for various reasons, this was not to be.

For the more serious student the major publication of this year was "The Training and Work of an Initiate", a companion volume to "The Esoteric Orders and their Work" and which may also have been spun from the early efforts of the Fraternity to provide instruction for potential members, not least with a Correspondence Course for those who lived further afield. 31st May 1932 was seen as a red-letter day in that it saw the initiation of the first candidate who had done all her preparatory work by correspondence.

With the correspondence course in operation, supported by these two books Dion Fortune had laid down in clear unequivocal terms the existence of the Path of initiation for modern western students.

26

SPIRITUALISM
IN THE LIGHT OF OCCULT SCIENCE

Throughout the whole of 1929, the "Inner Light Magazine" had carried a series of articles by Dion Fortune entitled "Spiritualism in the Light of Occult Science" and in the Spring of 1931 this was made available to a wider audience in book form by the occult publishing house of Riders. It had been followed up during 1930 by a series of articles aimed at a more general readership, particularly the bereaved, under the title of "Through the Gates of Death".

The publication of "Spiritualism in the Light of Occult Science" caused considerable controversy and it is possible that because of this "Through the Gates of Death" may have been rejected by Riders. At any rate it became one of the first titles to be published by the Fraternity itself, in July 1932, under the imprint of The Inner Light Publishing Company. It was aimed not at occultists or spiritualists as such, but at the bereaved, who might be contemplating spiritualist assistance.

Dion Fortune had taught herself to be a trance medium and had functioned as such since at least 1921 and maintained this ability until she died. She drew a distinction however between the normal Spiritualist medium and what she called a cosmic medium, that is to say, one who makes contact with higher intelligences such as the Masters, or higher Guides, rather than the more domestic ambience of the average spiritualist control.

There is of course a broad spectrum of ability and function in this whole field and in some cases it is not easy to draw a hard and fast dividing line, in cases such as "Imperator" a teaching guide of the early spiritualist Stainton Moses or latter day teachers such as "White Eagle".

Dion Fortune was quite categorical in her belief that mediumship provided the power for invigorating her Fraternity, although there had always been a certain ambivalence, verging at times upon duplicity, as to how far occult teaching relied upon techniques shared with spiritualism. That is to say, how far did the founding fathers of the Golden Dawn rely upon their wives' or their own psychic abilities for communicating with "masters" or "secret chiefs". There was controversy about this in the schismatic troubles at the turn of the century, with Dr. Felkin of the Stella Matutina openly advocating astral contact with a being known as Ara ben Shemesh, while others would have nothing of such goings on. The dispute rumbles on to the present day and was also the cause of a major eruption in the case of Israel Regardie and his trenchant views of the Stella Matutina Hermes Temple into which he had been initiated.

Maiya Tranchell-Hayes (formerly Curtis-Webb) later opined to Bernard Bromage that she thought Dion Fortune had wasted her gifts by indulging in mediumistic practices which anyone with a fraction of her talent could have as effectively done. Nonetheless this did not prevent Maiya from aiding and abetting Dion Fortune in these practices both at the beginning and towards the end of her occult career.

There is also evidence that during the nineteen thirties, when once the Fraternity was established as a ritual group, the amount of direct mediumistic work conducted by Dion Fortune decreased, and certainly surviving records of any such work dry up radically between 1931 and 1940. This is much the same time that she began to have the Qabalistic visions and at the same time saw her greater commitment to the written word, not only in "The Mystical Qabalah" but in the series of novels. The first became the principal textbook for at least a couple of generations of esoteric students and the latter marked a high point in the somewhat recherché genre of occult fiction.

A change of emphasis from mediumship to ritual had indeed been forecast in the early stages of the launching of the Fraternity. This now seems to have come about. At the same time Dion Fortune has remarked that when writing articles or books it is not easy to draw a firm dividing line between what was coming from her own mind, conscious or subconscious, and what may have been put there by higher inner plane contacts. This is an impression that a number of writers of esoteric works may well confirm, and it is in effect not very far from the techniques of "channelling" or "mediation" in full consciousness rather than the unconscious mediumship of complete trance.

During this same period it seems that an attempt was made to share out some of the mediumship. The Lodge Records for April 25th 1933 record an address "received from a Master upon the Inner Planes" through one of the officers although it is no more than a short sermon of generalities, and a far cry from the specific detail and sense of presence that came through any such address via Dion Fortune. The same might be said for some of the "Words of the Masters" that were published from time to time in the "Inner Light Magazine".

In this context another interesting development in May and June 1933 were some trance communications through E.F.Maltby, who had been initiated early in 1931, with the recently initiated Colonel Seymour acting as scribe. At the end of one of these sessions Carstairs turned up with a typical greeting, and a reference to Loveday who was going to be present later in the week:

Hello, you have not met me before. No? Well, old Nibs will tell you all about me on Friday. A new telephone. I am not used to it. Well, I just thought I would look in, I would not keep him under too long at first.

In a formal statement made by the Fraternity in 1942 it was claimed that Dion Fortune's mediumship had hitherto been kept a strict secret from the outside world, although it has to be said that a number of articles in the pre-war "Inner Light Magazine" had either revealed or implied the fact.

In "Spiritualism in the Light of Occult Science" the intimate detail of her descriptions of the psychological experience of trance mediumship suggest that they could only have come from close personal experience. Whilst in an article on "The Masters and the Fraternity" in April 1938 she stated quite baldly the use of mediumship and her own involvement with it.

Those who have some acquaintance with the inner workings of the Fraternity of the Inner Light know that it possesses a quantity of teachings that have been received psychically and that are referred to generically as "The Words of the Masters". These have been published in part in the pages of the "Inner Light", are read aloud at some of the meetings, and are used as the basis of certain of the inner group teaching. Persons who have had access to these MSS say that they have a very marked effect upon the consciousness of those who read them – an effect out of all proportion to their intrinsic content.

These communications were received by means of trance mediumship, myself acting as medium and various Masters who are behind the Order which is behind this Fraternity acting as controls.

She also set great store by the power that could come through such mediumship, leading her to assert that only an esoteric group that had this type of combined communication and power source at its centre was likely to be anything more than a discussion group.

In "Spiritualism in the Light of Occult Science" however, she made plain certain reservations she had about the uses and abuses of Spiritualism. She had already done much the same with regard to occultism in "Sane Occultism". This was Dion Fortune the plain speaking reformer, the same who had fallen foul of Lillias Hamilton for speaking out of turn at college, who had stood up for the agricultural workers on the farm, and who was now running true to form with regard first to the occult and then to the spiritualist worlds.

There is of course a difference of attitude, motive and purpose between the two movements. The spiritualist seeks to provide evidence for the survival of personality after death, and the principal direction of service is to those who have been recently bereaved, and more generally to any member of the general public seeking some kind of personal evidence of life beyond death. The occultist, on the other hand, is seeking to probe more deeply into metaphysical realms, and follows a quest for personal spiritual development often in the comparative study of various ancient traditions.

There is of course no hard and fast dividing line between the two. Some spiritualist guides provide teaching of a philosophical and self-developmental nature and occultists share some of the theories and techniques particularly of clairvoyant and clairaudient mediums.

The watershed between them is perhaps best illustrated by comparing Dion Fortune's "Spiritualism in the Light of Occult

Science" with her "Through the Gates of Death". The first seeks to throw light on spiritualism from the technical point of view of an occult practitioner, while the latter seeks to give good advice to the recently bereaved.

Her general advice to the latter is what one might expect from one who always took a commonsense middle of the road approach to most questions. That is to say, that there is a perfectly good and normal intuitional form of communication between the living and the dead without having recourse to mediums. From this it follows that if we should feel compelled to try to communicate with our recently deceased loved ones through a medium we should consider our motives carefully, and the possible effect we are likely to inflict upon those who are called back to make an appearance in the séance room.

There are unhealthy emotional dependencies in life in the world that certainly should not be extended beyond the grave. There is more than one kind of love, and one of the less salubrious forms takes the form of a hunger for affection, care and attention, rather than concern for the interests and well being of the alleged beloved. This indeed can be a form of emotional vampirism, and it is possible to envisage an ironical reversal of the traditional roles of vampire and victim, when the emotional vampire is of the living and the victim one who is being persistently called back to continue to provide the support given during physical life.

At a slightly higher level there are those who seek to relieve an inner emotional tension by pouring demonstrative affection and service upon the loved one irrespective of the latter's needs in the matter. It is thus equally reprehensible to try to continue this kind of possessiveness beyond the grave.

In short, Dion Fortune did not so much decry all attempts at communication with the departed but said that it should only be done for very good reason, and exceptionally, as a response when there was good reason to believe that the departed had in the first instance attempted, via a clairvoyant or medium, to contact us. It followed that members of the Fraternity were not encouraged to attend spiritualist meetings, which led to some heart searching amongst members who had a sympathetic rapport with the spiritualist movement.

In the midst of all this she was still trying to divest herself of her more general duties in the lodge that had been thrust back upon her by the departure of Penry Evans from office the previous autumn.

At the Vernal Equinox of 1931 Dion Fortune announced once more her need to withdraw from general lodge work, and Nibs Loveday was appointed Magus of the Lodge. He continued in office for the next three years, although Dion Fortune stood in from time to time, attended as a visitor or sometimes gave an address.

By June of this year other competent members of the Fraternity had also begun to take up the burden of public lecturing – Edward Maltby, (who had married Dr. Evans' sister Hazel), Francis Davey M.A., Victor York and W.E.Butler. Between the Vernal Equinox of 1931 and that of 1932, out of a programme of thirty lectures, Loveday gave ten, Ernest Butler and Francis Davey gave four each, and Edward Maltby two, including manning the cinematograph on one occasion, and Victor York one. This relieved Dion Fortune of two thirds of her lecturing workload.

27

ISRAEL REGARDIE
AND THE HERMES TEMPLE

Dion Fortune split the lecturing about half and half with her colleagues in the following year, from Vernal Equinox 1932 to 1933, and was now the better able to concentrate upon the literary work for which she has justly remained famous, "The Mystical Qabalah".

This was also the year when Israel Regardie arrived upon the scene in England, which brought about some reverberating consequences, not only in respect to the Golden Dawn tradition in general but to Dion Fortune's relations with it in particular.

Regardie had just written two books "The Tree of Life" and "The Garden of Pomegranates", upon magic and the Qabalah respectively. Although both books were based upon the Golden Dawn system of correspondences, Regardie had not, at this time, ever been a member of this organisation. He had picked up most of the material when acting in the somewhat flexible position of secretary to Aleister Crowley between 1928 and 1931.

He was British by birth, having been born to Jewish parents in the East End of London, who emigrated to America when he was very young. The family ended up in Washington D.C. which was fortunate for him, as he could study locally in the extremely well stocked national Library of Congress. He developed an interest in esoteric subjects in his teens and applied for admission to the Washington Temple of the *Societas Rosicruciana in America*, which used rituals largely derived from Golden Dawn sources, advancing to the grade of Zelator. Coming upon the books of Aleister Crowley at the tender age of 21 he was so impressed that he wrote to the author out of the blue, made his way to Paris, where the Master Therion was currently resident, and was somewhat surprisingly taken on in an irregularly paid and ill defined job.

By 1932 he had parted company with Crowley, and although he retained considerable affection and respect for him, did not care to be associated with his particular brand of magic. From what he had learned he wrote a book upon the Tree of Life called "The Garden of Pomegranates" which was accepted and published by Riders. When he arrived in England in August 1932 he had recently completed the manuscript of "The Tree of Life", a book on magic, which he duly sent to Maiya Tranchell-Hayes with a request for her comments upon it.

He also wrote to Dion Fortune who replied at the beginning of November.

Nov. 1ˢᵗ 1932

Dear Mr Regardie,

I am so sorry not to have answered your letter before. At the time it came I was away doing some occult work, and then, of course, everything got left; and since I have been home, there have been arrears to catch up with.

Riders have just sent me both your books with the request that I will do an article on them, and this I am now at work on. I think very highly of both the books, and especially of "The Tree of Life". It is quite the best book on magic, in my opinion, not excepting either Crowley or Levi. I think it is an exceedingly fine piece of work.

I am sorry there is no chance of meeting you in the near future; I think a talk would have been very interesting. Ceremonial magic is a matter that especially interests me, and we are well equipped both here and at our Glastonbury centre for doing it. Glastonbury is particularly interesting for workings, as our place is on the side of the Tor, the "Hill of Vision". Perhaps some time you will be able to visit us there.

I judge from the correspondences given in "The Garden of Pomegranates" that you are using the old "Golden Dawn System", which is the one I use myself. I think it is far and away the best. Crowley gives it away in 777, but I have also got the Mathers MSS to check it by.

I myself am doing some work on the Tree of Life, and it is coming out serially in my little magazine. I should much value your opinion on it, and will send it to you as far as it has gone if you would care to see it, and would do me the kindness to comment

*on it. It is a subject that requires very careful counterchecking, it
is so easy to make a slip in the correspondences.*
With every good wish for the success of your book,

Yours sincerely,
Dion Fortune

A couple of weeks later she wrote again, having had time to consider
the possible consequences of the very open revelations in Regardie's
book, which were quite revolutionary at the time. There had also
apparently been some problems with the delivery of her first letter.

Nov. 14ᵗʰ 1932

Dear Mr Regardie,
*I enclose the letter and its envelope I sent to you so that you may
see its travels and perhaps be able to prevent other of your letters
from meeting with the same fate.*
*I am at work now on the review of your two books, and am
extending the scope of it to cover the sources of the system and
the repercussions your Books of Revelations are likely to have in
the occult movement.*
If only Mr. Strutton [editor of the "Occult Review"] *does not
"cut" me too much, there ought to be interesting developments.
I suppose you know you have given away the old "Golden Dawn"
system, lock, stock and barrel? It is guarded by oaths with the
most appalling penalties. I trust you have not been slain by
invisible forces! There will be some very angry folk in certain
quarters. However, what you have said, badly wanted saying; I
have done a certain amount myself in that direction, but not as
much as you have. You have made my discrete contributions look
like the day after the fair!*
*I hope the opportunity for us to meet will occur in the not too
remote future.*

Yours sincerely,
Dion Fortune

This suggests an interesting situation. Regardie of course had not
been initiated into the Golden Dawn and therefore could hardly be
held guilty of betraying oaths he had never taken. In any case all
this was to be as nothing compared to later events, when he *had*

taken such an oath, and had gone ahead and revealed the complete system, with a good degree of gratuitous vituperation into the bargain.

At any event, his current revelations obviously struck a sympathetic chord with Dion Fortune and resulted in their meeting, which in turn brought an immediate response from her:

Nov. 16th 1932

Dear Mr Regardie,

I am so glad you liked us, because we liked you! I hope your visit will be the first of many, for there are some interesting things we could discuss together. I do so much laying down of the law to those who simply sit at my feet and open their mouths that it is a great pleasure to meet someone to whom I can talk "on the level". It would be very interesting if we could do some practical work together; the equipment and conditions are here for the undertaking. We must meet again in the near future and discuss possibilities.

Very many thanks for your kind words about my Qabalah article. You are perfectly right about the spelling, and I must see what can be done in the future, but it is very difficult to alter a sound with which one has become magically familiar. The Qabalah article was written before I read your book.

Your point about Eheih [sic] being in the future tense is very interesting; it certainly suggests the dynamic idea of becoming rather than the staticism of pure being, which properly belongs behind the Veils of Negative Existence.

I appreciate your offer of help in Qabalistic matters, and shall take you at your word if ever we are in difficulties in that respect. I should like you to read the typescript of my "Mystical Qabalah" when it is finished.

No, I had no thought whatever of spying in connection with you, and hope that you had none in connection with my interest in A.C., for whom I have a sneaking regard. I wish one could do something for him without burning one's fingers over him. Something ought to be done for the kidney condition you describe. It is absolutely an occupational disease of magicians. No ordinary doctor can treat it.

With kindest regards, in which my husband joins me,

Yours very sincerely,
Dion Fortune

One consequence of this meeting was an impression of Dion Fortune and Penry Evans as a married couple as seen by an independent witness. Regardie's view was not entirely flattering, although he did qualify it by saying that he was very young at the time, (about 25). His impressions were thus possibly afflicted with the somewhat intolerant expectations that go with youth, and particularly Israel Regardie's youth. He felt a little uncomfortable at the time because he felt Dion Fortune put down, even hen pecked, her husband in the course of their meeting. He thus recalls Dr. Evans as being a little man physically as compared to his wife, which certainly does not appear to be the case in a photograph of the two of them standing together some five years before, at any rate as regards height. It is possible though that she had put on more weight in the interim.

Not long after this meeting they received news of Regardie's impending initiation into the Hermes Temple of the Stella Matutina at Bristol, which they enthusiastically welcomed.

Dec. 13th 1932

Dear Mr. Regardie,

I have just heard from my friend, Miss Hughes of Bristol, that she will be seeing you on Wednesday afternoon. I was so interested to hear that you were in touch with her. You may remember I told you that I was working with a branch of the old G.D. that had survived all cataclysms, and had found it satisfactory. I think Miss Hughes may tell you something about it.

I have known her for some years and am very fond of her. As a matter of fact, it was she who turned up at Glastonbury seven years to the day from the starting of our work, as I told you, and brought me the contacts I needed after they seemed to have been broken forever. It is curious that you also should be linking up with her.

I saw Strutton the other day, and suggested he might run a symposium in the pages of the O.R. on occult secrecy, and that Waite and Garstin should be asked to write in favour of secrecy, and you and I against it. It ought to be a lovely dogfight! My article is coming out whole! I had hardly dared to hope for that. I asked him to delete the part you thought risky.

I hope we shall meet you again soon. The interview with Miss Hughes ought to be interesting, for she is a very interesting woman, and a very fine one.

Would you be kind enough to tell her from me that we are looking forward to seeing her. I ought to have written to her, and am ashamed to say I have not done so, and she may not get my letter at Bristol before she starts if I write now.

I hope the books are going well; my article and the symposium ought to stir things up for them.

My husband joins me in all good wishes,

Yours sincerely,
Dion Fortune

Immediately after Christmas Dr. Penry Evans wrote to Regardie saying that they had received dates for his "vaccination" from Miss Hughes and inviting him to stay with them at Glastonbury for a long weekend, during which they would take him across to Bristol for the ceremony and return with him to London a couple of days later.

Things did not work out too well apparently, as he was physically indisposed for much of the time, but he was particularly appreciative that they should have taken the trouble to be present at his initiation.

Moreover, in the January 1933 issue of "The Occult Review" Dion Fortune's article duly appeared, supporting a relaxation of the cult of secrecy in an article entitled "Ceremonial Magic Unveiled". In the course of this she stated:

... the veil of the Temple of the Mysteries is being drawn back at the present moment... So far as I can see, ceremonial magic is coming out into the open... For any organisation to try and close the sluice gates against it by oaths of secrecy, is to keep back the Atlantic with a broom.

This did not enamour her with the traditionalists, and it all had a very bitter sting in the tail.

Israel Regardie rapidly went through the grades of the Stella Matutina but resigned from the Hermes Temple within two years, in December 1934, with considerable acrimony.

His reasons were much the same that had caused Dion Fortune to criticise the Order some years before, as being run by "widows and bearded ancients" who were more interested in grandiose titles than real magic, but Regardie was not one to go quietly. He had his own agenda and understanding as to what the Order should be all about.

He would have no truck with the idea of Secret Chiefs or Masters, and insisted that the aim of the teaching should be the development of the initiates' own inner genius, not attempts to contact astral entities. He made his views very plainly known in a polemical book of 1936 called "My Rosicrucian Adventure" and pilloried Hope Hughes and her temple in no uncertain terms:

> ... *immediately after my initiation into the grade of Adeptus Minor, or rather the day following, the Chief ushered me into the Vault, and there alone we two were visited by the so-called Invisible or Secret Chiefs of the Order. It would be useless repeating any of the chaotic communications received at any of these meetings...*

So much for poor Hope Hughes, who was plainly of the same mind as Dion Fortune when it came to contacts with Masters behind the Order, whether or not her facility at contacting them was on a par with that of Dion Fortune.

Nor did Dion Fortune escape criticism from Regardie in all of this, despite her favourable review of his books in "The Occult Review" and support of his stand against stifling secrecy. Indeed, he based his criticism of her upon this very article, in which he also accused her of playing the secrecy game for her own ends:

> *Though her purpose was ostensibly to review a book purporting to outline the general fundamentals of Magic, the whole orientation of that article was in an utterly false direction. The book mentioned contained no single reference to Masters, stressing from the first page to the last that the principal object of the Great Work consisted in the acquisition of a nobler and wider consciousness, which there was termed the Holy Guardian Angel. Significantly enough, however, Dion Fortune ignored this repeated definition. The concluding paragraphs of her article give utterance to the baseless view that Magic and the Golden Dawn system were devoted to "picking up contacts" of the Masters, to use the horrible clichés of a neo-occult movement. Yet neither "The Tree of Life" nor the Golden Dawn system itself were concerned in any way with Masters or their "contacts".*

There we have it. There is obviously a fundamental difference between Israel Regardie's view and experience of occultism and that of Dion Fortune and the Stella Matutina branch of the Golden Dawn.

He continued to campaign vitriolically and in August 1935 we find a letter from Dion Fortune to him declining to publish an article of his in "The Inner Light Magazine". Her reasons are much the same as the editor of "The Occult Review", who had also refused to publish it.

I cannot, however, print your caustic remarks about the G.D. any more than Strutton could. The law of libel is very heavily weighted against the press, and any one who knows the ropes can twist one's tail properly. It is not worth the risk. I should be wary, if I were you. They could make things frightfully hot for you if they had a mind to, and if you twist their tails, it is quite likely they may have. I happen to be rather well up in the law of libel at the moment, having just been twisting the tail of an editor myself for a scurrilous review. He did not say the half of me that you have said of the G.D. but my lawyer chased him from Dan to Beer-sheba and back again, and he had to print a withdrawal and apology, and pay my lawyer, and presumably his own. I do not suppose he was out of it at a penny under fifty pounds. There are so many ways of nipping a man who is technically on the wrong side of the law without actually taking him to court. I should not risk it, if I were you. The game is really not worth the candle.

   With all good wishes,

Yours sincerely,
Dion Fortune

But that was Israel Regardie, and part of the whole man. When I was briefly his publisher some thirty years later I can recall having to render him much the same advice, which brought about some even more vitriolic comments about what he thought of the laws of libel in the United Kingdom. He was, let me say, in spite of all this, a very likeable and sincere man, although he had probably mellowed somewhat since his salad days.

Between 1937 and 1940 Regardie followed through by publishing all the secret rituals and teachings in the four volumes of "The

Golden Dawn", by Aries Press, Chicago, on the grounds that if he had not done so then the whole corpus of valuable material might have been lost to the world. He believed that as those whom he called the "inepti", (as opposed to "adepti"), would attract no new recruits of talent, and destroy their papers before they died.

In this he might well have been right. To those Golden Dawn Temples that were not already moribund Regardie's revelations proved a deathblow. Their initiates felt that with the publication of the secret rites their efficacy had been destroyed, and even Maiya Tranchell-Hayes, in despair, buried her regalia at the bottom of her garden. This being on a cliff top, by a quirk of fate and coastal soil erosion, it fell to the beach below many years later to cause a ten day wonder in the local press.

As for Hope Hughes, she evidently felt that Dion Fortune, in supporting Regardie, had gone beyond the pale and thrown in her lot with dark forces. Thus ended their friendship, and for the second time, Dion Fortune's affiliation to a Golden Dawn temple.

It was no doubt Hope Hughes that Dion Fortune had in mind when, in a brief note to Regardie in June 1938, she summed up matters by saying:

So far as I am aware, I have no occasion to complain of your behaviour to me personally, though I think you have treated some of my friends very badly.

Indeed, as a consequence, they were her friends no longer.

28
COLONEL SEYMOUR -
"THE FORGOTTEN MAGE"

If the Masters had been looking for the kind of initiate responsive to military discipline, with wide experience of the world, and a well-stocked mind, they must have been very pleased when Colonel C.R.F. Seymour became a member of the Fraternity.

He had been born in the west of Ireland on April 9th 1880, and so was now in his mid-fifties and active with it. In his youth he had studied Russian at Trinity College, Dublin before joining the Hampshire Regiment of the British army. He saw active service in the Boer War and was drafted to the Indian army in 1902. There he served with the 13th Rajputs, the Rangoon Volunteer Rifles, the Burma Rifles, and at the Staff College at Quetta. During the 1st World War he was wounded fighting in what was then German East Africa. His skill as an interpreter was called upon in a diplomatic mission to Moscow in 1917, and after the war he was mentioned in despatches for police work in Iraq in 1920/21. He retired with the rank of Lieutenant Colonel and went back to university to gain an M.A. degree in 1929.

He was initiated as Server of St. Patrick in January 1933 and soon made his mark within the Fraternity. He worked his way through to the 3rd Degree within ten months and by February 1934 was taking senior office in lodge, as Philosophus, second only to the Magus in the ritual scheme of things. At the subsequent Vernal Equinox he was appointed to the newly made post of Executive Officer of the Fraternity, responsible for running the Outer Court, (the training and testing of all students), thus lifting a considerable burden from the Secretary.

Shortly after, in June 1934, Dion Fortune announced a new regime for the Outer Court. It would be reconstructed to lay emphasis on three lines of development – Hermetic, Mystic and Orphic – or what was in those days sometimes called the Blue Ray, the Purple Ray and the Green Ray. This was a portent of what became a reorganisation of the whole Fraternity at the Vernal Equinox of 1936 , when what was called "the New Epoch" was put into force. Colonel Seymour also became active as a lecturer and contributor to the "Inner Light Magazine", in which most of his articles were signed with the initials of his senior lodge name: F.P.D. His first lecture in the Fraternity's programme had been given when he was still a student on the Study Course, on 28th November 1932, but he got well into his stride in 1934 when he gave nine lectures in the regular programme, with titles including, "Mithras, God of the Sunrise", "Temples of the Mystery Religions" and "Life in the Mystery Temples" – illustrated by magic lantern, precursor of the modern slide projector. He also laid on a special course of lectures on Thursday evenings on behalf of the Guild of the Master Jesus on "The History of the Esoteric Aspect of Religion."

In the magazine he became responsible for long series of articles between 1934 and 1939 that were in effect short books. They included "Ritual and Religious Experience", "Magic in the Ancient Mystery Religions", "The Esoteric Aspect of Religion", "The Old Gods", "Meditation for Temple Novices" and "The Old Religion", The bulk of his writings have subsequently been published as "The Forgotten Mage", edited by Dolores Ashcroft-Nowicki.

From 1933 onwards Dion Fortune, Dr. Penry Evans and Colonel Seymour gradually took the lion's share of the lecturing with occasional slots filled by C.T.Loveday and Victor York, another Green Ray enthusiast. Merl's lectures were advertised with his full title and honorifics – Dr. T. Penry Evans M.R.C.S., L.R.C.P. – and were on topics such as "Where Mind and Matter Meet", "The Whole Man", "Mind in Medicine", "The Healing Gods", "Christ Within" and "Pan Within".

Previous lecturing stalwarts such as Edward Maltby and Ernest Butler seem to have dropped out of circulation. Edward Maltby went his own way some time after Seymour's arrival, perhaps unhappy with the changes in organisation that affected his role in Outer Court responsibilities. Ernest Butler may have been disaffected by Dion Fortune's line with regard to Spiritualism, although he did obtain permission from her to open a subsidiary lodge at Guildford some time in 1938. When I first met him, in 1962, he was no longer a member but rejoined in 1965, although was never entirely happy with the new regime that had come into force in 1961.

The 1st Degree Lodge of 27th February 1934, in which Colonel Seymour first took principal office, was also the occasion of two significant initiations. One was of W.K.Creasy, who subsequently became Vice-Warden of the Fraternity, and the other Christine Campbell Thomson, Dion Fortune's literary agent.

Dion Fortune had made contact with her back in 1927 to help place some of her books, a task which she continued to do effectively. Despite Brodie-Innes having remarked that he thought she had potential for occult training she had not followed it up. She had subsequently launched her own agency and embarked upon what proved to be a somewhat disastrous marriage.

In the summer of 1932 Dion Fortune invited her to come to some lectures she was giving on magic, and this seems to have struck a spark. She enrolled upon the Fraternity's Study Course and within eighteen months was initiated as Server of Arnulf.

Just turned 35, she was one of the more physically attractive of female initiates of the time. This reputedly drew the remark from Penry Evans, who was Magus at her initiation, "At last, we've got a priestess of Isis in the house!" Her husband, Oscar Cook, had also embarked upon the Study Course but unfortunately could not make the grade, despite the generous assistance of alcohol.

Thus she was not having an easy life at this time, and with a young child, was gradually drifting into the state of single parenthood, sustained as best she could by her literary agency. Dion Fortune proved a great source of strength and support, acting as a general protector on the occasions when Oscar telephoned or turned up at the house in an abusive frame of mind. Eventually, with the help of an inner plane consultation, she advised the young initiate to separate from her husband.

In return Christine was of considerable help to Dion Fortune beyond the usual call of duty of a literary agent. They spent long lunches knocking novels into shape and deciding on a suitable pseudonym for the non-occult ones. Christine favoured Violet

Orchard but Dion Fortune preferred the more machismo V.M.Steele.

She advanced creditably through the degrees, entered the 3rd Degree in June 1936 and on January 26th 1937 took the senior ritual office of Philosophus at a 2nd Degree meeting. From the middle of this year she began working specifically with Colonel Seymour, although it was a magical collaboration that did not particularly attract her at first. Nonetheless it developed momentum and carried on for a number of years, eventually independently of the Fraternity.

As such their further progress would not form part of our story but for a certain light that it throws upon esoteric custom and practice within the Fraternity at this time. Despite holding an important executive position in the Fraternity, and working closely with Dion Fortune in her Rites of Isis of 1937/8, it seems that Colonel Seymour was never told the identity of the Masters with whom she worked.

Despite her public enthusiasm for pulling down barriers of secrecy, and her open declaration of the importance of her contacts with the Masters, the closest that Colonel Seymour got to the identity of her principle contact was that he was referred to as "Lord E." and had once been Lord Chancellor.

On the face of it, it looks as if he badly wanted to make this personal contact himself, and looking up the history books, assumed "Lord E." to be Lord Eldon instead of Lord Erskine, and thus picked out the wrong Lord Chancellor. The confusion is quite understandable for Erskine was Chancellor only for a year, in Fox's ill-fated Whig administration of 1806. Lord Eldon, on the other hand, was by far the more successful Chancellor and had famously filled that office before and after Thomas Erskine's temporary occupation of it.

The evidence is only circumstantial, and one may be doing Seymour a grave injustice in assuming that he had simply jumped to a wrong conclusion, for he was capable of making a range of contacts which owed nothing to Dion Fortune. These included the ancient Egyptian Setne Kha'm-uast, Priest of Ptah, and the Spartan King Cleomenes III, which according to his later associates, seemed to work well for him. Oddly enough, one of Dion Fortune's more important contacts, Socrates, appeared to turn up at a later meeting conducted by Seymour and, not being liked the look of, was promptly banished!

Theoretical conjecture is unlikely to bring much clarification to any of this. Indeed it is a situation that can provide cheap ammunition for sceptics, including possibly Israel Regardie, who claim that the whole business of contacts is deluded imagination anyway. Nonetheless a sizeable proportion of practical occultists do work with such contacts, not least Dion Fortune, whose experiences with them from 1921 to 1945 dominated her life.

It is not so much their existence as their identity which proves something of a problem. A pragmatic if somewhat cynical line was expressed in a statement made by W.G.Gray to Alan Richardson. He said he did not know the names of his contacts, and what is more would not believe them if they told him!

This is typical of the man, and from personal acquaintance with this redoubtable old occultist, I can say that I take this remark with a pinch of salt. He knew very well who one or two might be, but his attitude is a salutary exercise of deflation against too much credulity and at the same time a self-defence against sceptics.

There is no doubt that it does help to have some kind of personal identification to make and maintain a contact. Yet because of the risk of misunderstanding it may be no bad thing to keep that identity to oneself. Hence, probably Dion Fortune's refusal to reveal her principal contact by anything more than an initial. In later years her principal contact refused to give any personal identification other than "the Magus Innominatus" – the unnamed Master.

The identification of Thomas Erskine with Thomas More, it should be said, which has been widely assumed to be the belief of Dion Fortune, did not occur until as late as 1958, through the mediumship of Margaret Lumley Brown.

It seems odd, however, that Dion Fortune did not take Colonel Seymour more closely into her confidence. For whatever reason it appears that a certain lack of sympathy began to appear between them, the roots of which may have stemmed from the New Epoch of 1936. On this occasion, Dr. Penry Evans was appointed head of the Green Ray work, despite having been more concerned with other interests for some time. Seymour, who had worked unstintingly in many ways for the Fraternity in this direction might well be considered to have had a powerful claim to be appointed to this position.

In the records of his work with Christine Campbell Thomson there are signs of this increasing disaffection. An entry of March 15th 1938 notes that he has a feeling of no longer being wanted at Queensborough Terrace. Ten days later another note says that he is "very fed up" with Dion Fortune's Isis Rite.

This seems odd, coming at such a time, for he was, during February and March, in the thick of giving lantern lectures in tandem with Dion Fortune on the Worship of Isis and the Worship of Pan, illustrated by her chanting. And by July Penry Evans was no longer around, having gone off to Barcelona to advise the Republican Government on child nutrition during the Spanish Civil War.

It has to be said, with regard to the lectures, that according to at least one independent witness, not every member of the general public was enraptured with Dion Fortune's chanting, and Colonel Seymour may have been aware of this reaction, or possibly even shared it.

Things seemed to hit rock bottom on February 13th 1939 however, when he saw himself in a vision, in ancient times, being sacrificed at Avebury by a wolfish evil looking figure whom he identified as Dion Fortune!

At the outbreak of war Seymour was drafted to Liverpool for a time and when he returned to London. He drifted away from the Fraternity, taking Christine Campbell Thomson with him.

He died unexpectedly on 24th June 1943. Christine Campbell Thomson went her own way, despite an olive branch extended by Dion Fortune. She later married one of her authors, and under her married name of Christine Hartley wrote a couple of books herself, "The Western Mystery Tradition" and "A Case for Reincarnation".

29
THE MYSTICAL QABALAH

In following the vicissitudes of Israel Regardie and Colonel Seymour we have somewhat over-reached ourselves in time. In May 1931 a new series of articles began to appear in the "Inner Light Magazine", that carried on for four years. This was "The Mystical Qabalah".

It remains one of the milestones in Dion Fortune's occult and literary career and a fitting memorial to her and is still used for training Qabalistic students to this day. It was even welcomed by Israel Regardie in fulsome terms when published as a book by Williams and Norgate in 1935:

An extraordinarily lucid and learned exposition of certain ideas fundamental to the Order philosophy. In future years this book must undoubtedly be considered a masterpiece in its own sphere.

Strange as it may now seem, Dion Fortune felt she was taking a great risk in publishing "The Mystical Qabalah", such was the ambience of occult secrecy that had been inherited from the immediate past of the Golden Dawn tradition.

Although it is a theoretical book, albeit a very accessible one for the middlebrow student, it is rooted in practical experience, which began with several visions and portents, in a series of Qabalistic visionary experiences during 1930 and 1931 before ever she set pen to paper.

She published two of these in "The Inner Light Magazine", which indicate a type of experience altogether different from mediumistic trance and the expression of verbal communications.

She had learned the basic principles of the Tree of Life and the Golden Dawn system of correspondences on her initiation into the Alpha et Omega temple in 1919. She later said that she was not at that time of sufficient grade or experience to make the most of it before being pitch forked, after three short years, into the seven-year task of founding the Fraternity of the Inner Light.

Over the years a certain unconscious development had been going on, however, that when the time was ripe, caused her to abandon her more usual methods of working and to work more specifically with the Tree of Life.

She began by revising her knowledge of the Tree and its intricate system of symbols, reciting to herself each morning the primary correspondences of the Ten Holy Sephiroth. That is to say, the Names of God, the archangels, choirs of angels and planetary spheres.

Then she began to work upon each Sephirah, one at a time, rehearsing all its relevant correspondences. As she began to work with the Sephiroth in this way she began to find a change coming over the spirit of her meditations, difficult to describe.

I would be sitting in my accustomed chair, conscious of the sounds of the house, the touch of my clothes on my limbs, and all that makes up the sum total of impressions that keep us in touch with the external world when the eyes are closed. Then I would commence my mental rehearsal of the sacred names, and would suddenly find that I was aware of mental pictures only, to the entire exclusion of physical sense impressions. Nevertheless I retained full co-ordination of consciousness, for I knew that I was conscious of the pictures, and that the physical impressions would return unless I maintained my concentration on the images arising in consciousness, and did not allow it to wander.

She realised, when she thought this over later, that her consciousness had been transferred from her dense body to a subtle body, and without realising it, she had passed within the Veil, from the objective to the subjective sphere.

Thus she systematically went down the Tree, reviewing it Sephirah by Sephirah, conscious of power and a kaleidoscope of mind pictures, deep in meditation, oblivious of her physical body and its sensations.

Eventually she came to the ninth Sephirah, Yesod, and as she rehearsed the Divine Names, a picture suddenly formed in consciousness, at first as if seen through a window, and then as if she stood in the midst of it.

The scene was a sandy desert by moonlight; at my feet a lake or inland sea rippled against the sand; a few scattered palm trees were on my left, a little behind me, and on my right, in the middle distance, a string of camels moved slowly away.

For quite a while she surveyed this scene and it continued to grow in reality the longer she gazed. She could absolutely hear the wash of the calm water as it lapped the sand and see the flash of moonlight reflected from the ripples. In the far distance, across the water, she could dimly see the white walls of a city, round white domes dominating it, still and asleep in the moonlight.

Then as I stood and listened, a change occurred. Out of the sky over the water a vast angelic figure began to form, and I saw what I felt to be an archangel bent above me in a vast curve, crescent shaped. The colouring was all in moonlight greys and misty mauves and blues, in keeping with the dim yet luminous scene. The face was calm and still, not so much sad as absolutely unsmiling, and very intent. This vast being leant towards me and showed me a symbol which he held in his hand. I had some difficulty in making out what it was, but he persisted, and finally I saw it to be a slender cone of white plaster, point upwards, which in some way I associated with the round white domes of the distant city. It seemed to be made of the same material.

Thus the vision persisted until the time came to draw the meditation to a close but as she started to do so by visualising herself entering the purple disc of Yesod upon the diagram physically before her she felt a strange sensation, and seemed to vibrate backwards and forwards between the objective and subjective like a shuttle. The purple disc appeared to come off the chart, to expand in size and to pass within her own aura, and she was not quite sure what she was meant to do with it.

Then, for some unknown reason, the sphere itself took charge, and seemed to slide right inside the physical body till it took up its position resting upon the floor of the pelvis, just in front of the spine, and reaching upwards to the level of the lowest ribs. I was exceedingly conscious of this disk of quivering purple light in this position, and also of the appearance of my own skeleton, and the sense of the objective reality of this disk still remains with me, in marked distinction from the rest of the Sephiroth which have not been thus magically formulated.

The following day she looked up all the minor associations of the symbolism of Yesod and was amazed at how closely they correlated with what she had seen in her vision. As she remarked, it took her much longer to look up the symbolism and verify it than it did for the vision to formulate itself spontaneously before her inner eye.

This vision followed upon a similar one experienced some time before in connection with the Path that leads between Malkuth and Yesod, the 32nd Path, attributed to Saturn, whereon she also experienced the curious sense of objective reality. There she had seen a vision of the Great One of the Night of Time with reaping hook and hourglass, ever after which she had felt a peculiar sense of familiarity and security upon that Path which is usually considered difficult and dark.

In another vision she had a more comprehensive vision and experience of the Tree of Life as a whole. She found herself in her astral body, in white robe and striped headdress swooping and soaring like a bird before taking her seat in a temple on a stone block facing the east. Then she rose up, with the whole block, through the roof into bright sunlight and up through clouds. The sky began to darken into indigo with a very bright crescent moon and she realised she was symbolically ascending the Tree of Life. From the Moon Sphere of Yesod she rose to the Sun of Tiphareth in a deep golden sky, and continued to rise with breathless rapidity. She entered a great sphere of blinding white light in which she no longer had her astral form and was just a point of consciousness. She looked down the Tree of Life as if backed into it, and found she had taken on a form of enormous size, a towering cosmic figure, with feet planted on the bluish globe of the Earth seen through clouds.

She did not know quite what to do as she had never experienced anything like it before. There was a feeling of terrific force pouring like water from the palms of her hands, her solar plexus and forehead which rained upon the altar in diamond sparkles of light.

These were the type of experiences that led her to seek a place of retreat at Glastonbury in order to concentrate upon them away from the demands of the outer work at the London headquarters. As we have seen, this at first caused some organisational difficulties which required the personal intervention of Penry Evans to sort out.

This led in turn to the idea of creating a permanent Sanctuary at Chalice Orchard. This was mooted at the end of 1931 and an appeal launched for its implementation.

> We want to establish at Chalice Orchard a sanctuary for meditation and practical occult work, and we ask all those who are interested in our Centre there if they will contribute to the fund we have opened for that purpose.
>
> Glastonbury is essentially a place of pilgrimage. No one who visits it can fail to realise its strong spiritual atmosphere. We feel that it would be of very great value to have there a quiet place set apart for prayer and meditation, where those who desire to do so may enter into the silence.
>
> We are therefore asking all those who realise the significance of Glastonbury and who have felt the inspiration of its influence, and especially those who know and love the little hostel in its sheltered garden, to contribute to this fund in order that we may make a sanctuary and keep a perpetual light upon its altar.
>
> We make this appeal despite the financial difficulties through which the world is passing, because we feel that in such times as these, there is especial need for a place set apart for the renewal of spiritual resources.

This was of course hardly the time to think about expanding organisations or taking on new building projects. It was the time of the great depression, and as Dion Fortune remarked in an annual report to members at the end of 1931, it had been the most critical twelve months since the Great War on both the inner and outer planes. Occult movements everywhere were restricting their activities or coming to an end altogether.

Nonetheless they went ahead and raised the money and built the Sanctuary at Chalice Orchard. She continued to rally her troops with a positive message. Midsummer Day marked the end of a seven-year stage in their work, (she was obviously counting from the reconstruction of Moriarty's ritual work in 1924) and so changes could be expected upon the horizon.

Not least of these changes already in process was, she felt, a change within her own temperament:

> ... a change which discerning readers may have observed in my writings as they appeared in the "Inner Light", for they have

*begun to re-open for me those deeper aspects of occult work
which were perforce closed to me while the strenuous work of
building up our organisation was going on.*

*Simultaneously with this change in myself the time arrived
when the students who had been training in our study groups
began to graduate out of them and become ready to take on
responsibilities in connection with our work.*

The work at the Queensborough Terrace headquarters had indeed
gone forward steadily, with a gratifying improvement in attendance
at public lectures. The most marked sphere of growth had, however,
been the Correspondence Course. The Library also made great
progress and was very well patronised. Consequently large numbers
of books could be bought and added to the shelves, attracting yet
more subscribers. This era was a time of great popularity for private
"circulating libraries" which were to be found as an appendage to
W.H.Smith, the main chain bookstore, and even Boots the Chemists,
and in many small privately owned shops. Dion Fortune felt that
the Fraternity's library might claim to be the most up to date occult
library in the United Kingdom, and in addition, the "inner library"
of rare books was also made available to serious students.

In the sphere of her personal occult experiences she was also
aware of the relevance of the psychology of Jung, particularly with
regard to the racial subconscious. This was also noticeable in Israel
Regardie's books at the time. The Jungian psychology was beginning
to make an impact in esoteric circles, with its sympathy to mythology
and even alchemy bringing, it was to be hoped, also a certain
respectability and credibility to the occult field. It was not long
before Dion Fortune was in touch with Olga Fróbe-Kapteyn, founder
of the famous Eranos Institute in Switzerland, with whom she
exchanged information over a number of years.

This interest in Jungian psychology continued for the rest of her
life. On the assumption that an initiate should have as well balanced
a personality as possible she flirted with the idea that some kind of
psychoanalysis would be a desideratum for members of the
Fraternity. However, if occult secrecy was to be considered important
this raised the problem of secrets being given away to a non-initiate
analyst. This implied the need to have a resident analytical
psychologist within the group. But no ready-made Jungian

psychologist ever joined the Fraternity in her time, and any plans to have a member specially trained proved unrealistic.

Dion Fortune was always aware however that psychology was no substitute for occultism, because it went nowhere deep enough. She said as much in an earlier chapter of "The Mystical Qabalah".

Dr Jung has a great deal to say concerning the myth-making faculty of the human mind, and the occultist knows it to be true. He knows also, however, that its implications are much farther reaching than psychology has yet suspected. The mind of poet or mystic, dwelling upon the great natural forces and factors of the manifested universe, has, by the creative use of the imagination, penetrated far more deeply into their secret causes and springs than has the scientist.

During the four years of her writing her Qabalistic textbook, the Fraternity continued on its way, with the usual minor ups and downs of any human organisation, but the general trend was one of growth.

Given that about half the brethren had named themselves after Christian saints it was perhaps slightly surprising to find in June 1933 Charles Loveday expressing regret that more did not attend the Services of the Guild of the Master Jesus. For an experimental period from October 1932 to October 1933 the time of services had been changed from Sunday morning to Sunday evening but apparently without very much improvement. He addressed this matter to an entranced Edward Maltby, who had been attempting to stand in, in this way, for Dion Fortune for some months. The reply Loveday received may seem slightly on the lukewarm side, considering their roots in the Company of Avalon and the call to arms in the Christian Mystic Lodge some few years before:

Yes, my son, if you can draw more into the Christian side it would be to the good I think, for it keeps the group mind healthy, but though you can lead a horse to water, you cannot make him drink. It is difficult to see how this side can be developed. Perhaps you can do a little in your discussion talks. I will keep the matter in mind.

Anyway, it seems that everybody rallied round and that there was a concerted attempt to keep this side of the Fraternity's activities going. From notes of a Guild Meeting earlier that year by Katherine Barlow it is evident that the Qabalah was introduced to help things along. Her report concludes:

> *Nowadays, when there is much talk in various quarters about the reunion of Christendom, this can probably only be brought about by a return to the ancient truths of the Mysteries, which are once more being made manifest to humanity, and in which the Qabalah has an important place.*

As we have earlier seen, Colonel Seymour also did his bit with a special lecture series under the aegis of the Guild entitled "The History of the Esoteric Aspect of Religion" through the autumn and spring of 1933/34 and also began a new series in the "Inner Light Magazine": "Ritual and Religious Experience" although his pagan affiliations were always pretty close to the surface.

In addition to her articles on the Qabalah Dion Fortune began to run another magazine series through most of 1933/44 called "Practical Occultism in Daily Life" that attempted to reach out to the more general reader and enquirer. This was published in book form along with "The Mystical Qabalah" in 1935. It dealt with such popular topics as reading past lives, karmic factors, divination, controlling the environment, and the old favourite of sexual expression, or lack of it, in a repressive society. She obviously still felt the constraints of traditional occult secrecy for it is hardly a teach-yourself manual of the magical arts. Nonetheless it expressed her usual commonsense approach to the frequently glamorised field of popular occultism.

Another book addressed to the general public at this time was the collection of her early essays about Glastonbury, published as "Avalon of the Heart" in 1934 by Robert Mueller, a general interest publisher. It made up into an attractive little tourist guide with an esoteric slant, whose evocative style made up for some of its factual deficiencies. More significantly, it contained the seeds of some of the more advanced Arthurian work upon which she would later embark.

30

THE OCCULT NOVELIST

Dion Fortune once said that if she had not been an occultist she would have been a novelist. There is no doubt that she enjoyed writing fiction because as well as her occult novels she wrote three romantic thrillers under the pseudonym of V.M.Steele written for the circulating-library market of the day. However, her occult novels were in a class of their own, because of her specialist knowledge

The complete list of Dion Fortune's fiction is:

The Secrets of Dr. Taverner	1922 (published in volume form by Noel Douglas 1926)
The Demon Lover	1927 (Noel Douglas)
The Winged Bull	1935 (Williams and Norgate)
The Goat-foot God	1936 (Williams and Norgate)
The Sea Priestess	1938 (Inner Light Publishing Company)
Moon Magic	1957 (Aquarian Press)

Together with the three non-occult novels under the pen name of V.M.Steele:

The Scarred Wrists	1935 (Stanley Paul)
Hunters of Humans	1935 (Stanley Paul)
Beloved of Ishmael	1936 (Stanley Paul)

Unfortunately occult novels, at any rate of the better kind, do not make attractive commercial propositions despite a flurry of interest from publishers in the nineteen thirties. Thus Charles Williams' fine series of novels, was taken on and then dropped by Gollancz, and the final two titles only saw the light of day because T.S.Eliot, on the board of Faber and Faber recognised their quality. Whilst Mary Bligh Bond's "Avernus", which Dion Fortune considered the most powerful novel ever written on Atlantean memories, and even Aleister Crowley's amusing *roman á clef*, *"Moonchild"* remained nineteen twenties curiosities. Even a master of Elemental atmosphere like Algernon Blackwood was beginning to be considered old fashioned.

Thus Williams and Norgate, who had taken on "The Winged Bull" and "The Goat-foot God" in the wake of "The Mystical Qabalah" declined to publish a third novel, even if they did purport to form practical illustrations to the theoretical text. Nonetheless Dion Fortune believed sufficiently in the worth of "The Sea Priestess" to publish it herself via the Fraternity.

Her work on "Moon Magic" may have been blighted by this experience. It suffered several false starts and remained unfinished by her hand at the time of her death, although it marked a new and promising line in her fictional endeavours – moving into the first person mode of story telling so that one learned of occult motivation and experience more from the inside.

Her early work, "The Secrets of Dr Taverner" was, as we have seen, originally written as short stories for general consumption in a popular magazine, and her first full-length novel "The Demon Lover", was what she and Carstairs regarded as the blood and thunder kind. Their main purpose was simply to make the general public aware of the extent of the unseen worlds about them.

She confirmed this in an article on the purpose of her novels towards the end of 1936:

> *"The Secrets of Dr. Taverner" had a purpose that lay very near the surface – it was written to point out the possibilities that lay in the application of psychotherapy of the knowledge to be found in occult science, and said so frankly in the foreword.*

> *"The Demon Lover" set out to be a thriller pure and simple, but developed a purpose spontaneously in the course of its writing – and ended up as a kind of saga of the purification of the soul through initiation; pointing out that once that process is set going, it will work itself out whether the neophyte likes it or not.*

These two books, she said, stand apart as early work, because when they were written she was than still engaged on interpreting occultism in the light of psychology. In the later novels however, she had begun to interpret psychology in the light of occultism.

The three novels that follow are therefore of a different calibre and were a deliberate attempt to supplement the theoretical teaching of "The Mystical Qabalah" by practical example. They are thus specifically teaching works as much as works of entertainment.

All her novels share an underlying theme, which applies to the non-occult romantic thrillers too. It is that of a heroine who, against all odds and often from a deprived or restricted background, saves the hero from the worst side of himself. The Dion Fortune heroine is always an initiatrix, a priestess of the feminine, even in the non-magical novels.

There is also an evolution in the status of the heroine in the series of occult novels. In the very early "The Demon Lover" Veronica Mainwaring, a very vulnerable unconscious psychic straight out of commercial college is imprisoned, forcibly hypnotised and driven into projective trance by an unscrupulous occultist, whom in the end she stands by when he meets with his just deserts. The anti-hero in this work is very much a villain, Justin Lucas, who abuses his position of trust in an august esoteric order to try to gain secrets and power beyond his grade.

In "The Winged Bull" Ursula Brangwyn has been badly mangled by involvement in a less than savoury occult group but wins through to magical courtship and marriage with the equally damaged hero, Ted Murchison. His problems have arisen from being a red blooded young man unable to fit into a sanctimonious and hypocritical post-war society amongst his shabby genteel relations.

Mona Freeman in "The Goat-foot God" is a struggling and not very successful artist who by her intuitive magical skills succeeds in reconstructing Hugh Paston, a poor little rich boy who has been ruthlessly exploited by all and sundry and who comes her way when he is on the verge of a nervous breakdown.

With "The Sea Priestess" however, we are met by a formidable heroine Vivien LeFay Morgan, who is more than a match for any man, knows exactly where she is going, and selects a local estate agent Wilfred Maxwell to become her partner and general factotum in some magical work she is doing. He has been driven into asthmatic attacks by his hectoring mother and sister but in the end, through

Vivien's guidance, has developed sufficient independence to marry a local girl of his choice.

The same heroine appears in "Moon Magic", this time selecting the highly dynamic Dr. Rupert Malcolm, who is a very successful surgeon but hopeless at human relationships, which is not helped by marriage to a career hypochondriac who leeches off him financially and emotionally. He is instructed how to help her in her magical work and in return becomes a more rounded and equilibrated human being.

As might be expected, there is more in Dion Fortune's occult novels than meets the eye, and she took the step of explaining something of this in "The Inner Light Magazine" in an article on "The Novels of Dion Fortune" in November 1936 and a long analysis of "The Winged Bull" , subtitled "A Study in Esoteric Psychology" over three issues from August to October 1937. The first article, which came out just before publication of "The Goat-foot God" was accompanied by a statement that the new novel formed an integral part of the training of the initiate.

Although there were those who asked her why she "wasted her time" writing "occult thrillers" she stated quite unequivocally that the occult novels formed an important part of the work that was being done by the Fraternity of the Inner Light. She went on to explain:

> ... there are a surprising large number of people in the world today who, though they have never seen the inside of a lodge, are of an advanced grade of enlightenment; and owing to the deservedly ill repute into which occultism has fallen owing to the knavery of some and the foolery of others, will have nothing to do with it. To these, and especially to those in whom the realisation is subconscious rather than conscious, as is often the case, a book such as my "Winged Bull" can have all the effect of an initiation because it speaks directly to the subconscious by the method of imagery, which is the only language the subconscious understands. "The Winged Bull", in fact, together with its two companions, ["The Goat-foot God" and "The Sea Priestess"] is an initiation drama.
> Now let us make another digression and consider the psychology of the initiation drama. In the dramatic type of initiation the initiate is made to identify himself with the suffering, death and

*resurrection of some semi-divine person or avatar of a god. By
this means he is given a profound emotional experience, effectual
in proportion to his powers of imagination and his sympathy with
the divine character portrayed.*

She went on to analyse the two types of readers of fiction: those
who read for intellectual pleasure and those who read to escape
from reality into a world of wish fulfilment. What is more, very few
readers read a book objectively, but tend, in varying degrees, to live
in it imaginatively, and if the type is congenial, to identify themselves
with the hero or heroine so that the book becomes a glorified day-
dream.

*Knowing this as a novelist, and also knowing as a psychologist
the part played by the day-dream, I decided to put the two together
and produce novels that should come as near an initiation
ceremony as possible; that is to say, that should produce in
receptive persons something of the same results as are produced
by the experience of going through a ritual initiation.*

In writing her novels, she said she used exactly the same method
that is used in the composition of a ritual. Furthermore, that those
who knew "The Mystical Qabalah" would see that her novels also
were Qabalistic works.

In each case she had taken a basic idea, attributed it to its
appropriate sphere on the Tree of Life and then proceeded to work
it out on that basis, not in the language of theoretical occultism but
in the dream symbolism of psychoanalysis. Consequently, anyone
who knows the Qabalah could "place them on the Tree".

She never specifically says to which Sephirah each novel relates
but we give away no great secrets in saying that "The Winged Bull"
has its roots in Tiphareth, "The Goat-foot God" in Malkuth, and
"The Sea Priestess" in Yesod. She went on to give the theoretical
justification for this.

*Now the peculiar function of the famous Tree of Life of the
Qabalists is to link the microcosm with the macrocosm. In other
words, to reveal the relationship between the different factors in
the soul of man and the corresponding factors in the cosmic life
from which they derive, causing a tremendous inflow of energy
and inspiration into the aspect of the soul thus linked with its*

cosmic prototype. These prototypes are invariably dramatised as angels, archangels, gods, elemental kings and "hoc genus omne". Actually these Great Ones are the projections and dramatisations of the factors that go to the make-up of the human soul. But equally they are something much more than that, according to occult tradition, reinforced by modern experience. They are the channels of the corresponding spiritual forces owing to the faculty of the mind for being energised by an idea.

Now supposing we get a novel that is at the same time an interpretation and a day-dream, have we not got something very potent; especially if that interpretation be a mystical and cosmic one? This is precisely what I have tried to do with my novels. I have tried to make use of the dramatic form of the thriller-romance, as a vehicle for a mystical and cosmic interpretation. Read by a person who has it in him to respond, these stories will put him in touch with the corresponding factor through his daydream identification of himself with the hero who is put in touch with cosmic factors in the course of the story. In fact each story is the story of an initiation, and if the reader identifies himself with the hero, or herself with the heroine, they will be taken through that initiation as surely as a young sporting dog is trained by being coupled to an obedient and gun-wise beast who knows the words of command.

It might be assumed that this might be loading rather a lot onto some poor unsuspecting reader who had been seeking nothing more than a good read. However, she felt that if a reader had no capacity for response at this level, then they would probably classify the stories as ordinary romantic fiction. Although she conceded the risk of treading upon someone's subconscious complexes, and cited with some gusto the story of the lady who had returned a copy of "The Winged Bull" on the grounds that she was so horrified by it that not only would she not keep it in the house, but would not place it in the dustbin lest it corrupt the scavengers.

In Dion Fortune's view, each book was a form of psychotherapy. An initiation to a particular Sephirah or a psychoanalysis according to the capacity for response of the reader.

She jokingly wondered if she might find a reviewer who had a similar violent response to the lady who returned the book, as in that case with the resultant publicity her fortune might be made. One wonders if the coincidence of her heroine's name in "The Winged

Bull" with that of D.H.Lawrence's heroine in "The Plumed Serpent" might have been a subconscious wish for a similar critical notoriety!

Since writing the novels, she had come across Friedrich Nietszche's "The Birth of Tragedy", which she had found as much a revelation as she had hoped her stories would be to other readers. She found in those rather difficult pages, analysed in terms of aesthetics and metaphysics, exactly what she felt she had been trying to do with her fiction.

In more accessible terms, and with scant regard for occult secrecy, she declared:

> *My novels are dramatised daydreams. They are not written; they are lived and recorded. Everything is seen and heard exactly as if I were watching a play at the theatre.*
>
> *Those who are acquainted with the theory and practice of magic, especially as outlined in "The Mystical Qabalah" ... will know that vividly visualised thought-forms become astral images, ensouled by cosmic forces – provided they are built upon cosmic lines – nothing, for instance, could vivify a hippogriff. Now my characters are human beings; even the reviewers who like them least have always granted me that. Consequently my books, so far as I can judge of my own work, appear to me to "come alive" in a peculiar way. They are, in fact, magical acts.*

This became more so in the subsequent novel "Moon Magic" where, after several false starts, she began to write in the first person, and almost to identify with the magical heroine of the novel, finding much knowledge coming to her that previously she felt she had not possessed.

In the meantime, after "The Winged Bull" had been out for two years, and "The Goat-foot God" for a year, and Williams and Norgate had turned down "The Sea Priestess" she made an assessment of how well her experiment in occult fiction had fared. She was quite frank in admitting that it had not resulted in all she had hoped.

> *The result of this experiment has been interesting. The novels have quite definitely spoken to the subconsciousness of their readers, exercising over some a curious and profound fascination, and throwing others into something not far removed from panic as they felt the stirring of the depths. They have failed in a large*

measure, however, to accomplish their main object, which was
the linking up of consciousness and subconsciousness, bringing
both to bear simultaneously upon certain things, and also bringing
them to bear on each other.

Accordingly, she proposed to take "The Winged Bull" apart to show the readers of "The Inner Light Magazine" what she had been trying to do. The key concept of the book, she said, had been frankly stated in the blurb.

"the relationship between a man and a woman in the light of the
forgotten knowledge of the ancients", and "the knowledge of
certain aspects of the sex relationship which are the carefully
guarded secrets of the initiates." That they are carefully guarded
is proven by the fact that Mrs. MacGregor Mathers nearly turned
me out of the famous "Fraternity of the Golden Dawn", in which
I received a part of my training, for touching on the mere fringe
of them in an earlier book of mine, "Esoteric Philosophy of Love
and Marriage."

She had tried to present a three-fold thesis in "The Winged Bull", which she described as:

Firstly, the radical unsoundness of the Christian attitude towards
sex;
Secondly, the remedial possibilities of a combination of
psychology and occultism;
Thirdly, the dangers of the black magic side of sexual magic.

With her method of writing off the subconscious, she found a similar effect as later on when she identified with the heroine of "Moon Magic". The amount of information in the book amazed her when she came to read it.

For speaking to the subconscious as it does, it likewise speaks
from the subconscious; and my subconscious, as all
subconsciousnesses must, contains a great deal more than I
realised was there till it rose to the surface in the course of the
writing.

There was an element of personal experience in her depiction of Brangwyn, the adept, who has obviously made some errors in letting his sister fall into the hands of the less than salubrious sex magicians.

Many of her readers felt that because he was an adept he should also be a plaster saint, which, she says, shows just how much they know about adepts!

The adept may have great knowledge, but is not perfect in wisdom.

Is this true to the psychology of an adept? I only know that it is true to my psychology; and the psychology of Mme. Blavatsky and Mrs. Besant, though whether any or all of us are adepts is a matter of taste. The explanation is simple. An adept is, ipso facto, a psychic, and therefore sensitive. Being sensitive, he is highly suggestible. As long as he maintains the guru-chela attitude, with the chela sitting safely at his feet, he is all right, for the chela is negative and receptive towards him, and this makes him positive towards the chela; but the moment he meets the children of this world on a level he is at their mercy. It is for this reason that I never deal directly with any save my senior students, but always through the intermediary of persons more worldly-wise and less sensitive than myself.

It might be argued that this cutting off from the outside world was not the best way to deal with such a problem, and in her later years she made some effort to expand her circle of acquaintances considerably. Others might challenge the idea that an adept must necessarily be psychic, arguing that a superior intuition is the more important and reliable criterion. However, much the same factors apply, whatever the level of inner perception. The true adept, in other words, should be able to maintain a balanced polar relationship with the outside world whatever the conditions. Or perhaps this is hankering after plaster-saintship.

In this respect she recalls the down side of the man whom she regarded as "an adept if ever there was one", Theodore Moriarty, in relation to one of the more unsavoury characters in her book, Hugo Astley:

My first teacher was a decidedly Isabella-coloured individual, and he had just such a hugger-mugger household as Astleys. It is a curious fact that if anything goes wrong on the inner planes, people seem incapable of keeping their mundane affairs in any sort of order; debts and dirt accumulate at a pace unknown among ordinary mortals.

However, in "The Secrets of Dr. Taverner", based upon the same character, the prototype had been the best side of her original teacher. The treatment of adepti in her books is an interesting study in itself. There is a triangular pattern of relationship in most of the novels. Apart from the main pair of protagonists, the heroine and the anti-hero, there is usually an overseer, who in relation to the others is some kind of adept.

In "The Demon Lover" this role was taken by one known as the Senior of Seven who holds high rank in the occult fraternity which Lucas has tried to betray. He bears a certain resemblance to various descriptions of the Master Rakoczi, and albeit in flesh and blood appears something like a *deus ex machina* to sort things out when they seem to have become absolutely impossible of resolution.

In "The Winged Bull" it is the heroine's elder brother and guardian, who is also a magical adept. A colonel of the regiment in the late war he is also a great epicurean, with most fastidious tastes, who lives in a custom designed maisonette that on the outside looks like a run down London slum. It is handily situated over an Italian restaurant with an obliging proprietor who provides unswerving loyalty and cordon bleu culinary services at a moment's notice as part of his tenancy agreement.

In "The Goat-foot God" the role is filled by Jelkes, although he is not really an adept except in a theoretical way. He is a second hand bookseller with a kind heart who once had aspirations to the priesthood and whose magical knowledge of occultism derives largely from the stock within his shop.

In "The Sea Priestess" the triangle is completed by an inner plane being of hierarchical status, simply called the Priest of the Moon. However, she herself has considerable claims to adepthood, and again, as with Colonel Brangwyn, has fastidious tastes, having the best of food and drink specially delivered from various parts of the world, and, in the London home described in "Moon Magic" also has a penchant for living in a dwelling whose scruffy outside belies its magnificent interior.

These accoutrements are also found, as it happens, with a couple of protagonists in the non-occult novels. The hero of "The Scarred Wrists", for example, lives in a converted warehouse overlooking the Thames that would have been the envy of Lilith Le Fay. He too, has a talent for attracting loyal servants and retainers, colourful paragons such as never walked this earth.

In much of this Dion Fortune is simply enjoying herself with a bit of wish fulfilment on how she would like to live, but she also takes the opportunity to settle a few scores:

> *The representation of the hero of the story as a fighting man, and his contrasting with the pacifist and vegetarian Fouldes, the second villain, together with the epicureanism of Brangwyn, is, I am afraid, a trailing of the tail of my coat before the idealists who form a large proportion of the ranks of the students of the occult, and of whom I have had a hearty sickener. So much mystical riff-raff has accumulated in the occult movement that in some of its aspects it is little more than a mutual admiration society of phenomenal foolishness, attracting what Kipling so aptly calls "The brittle intellectuals who snap beneath a strain." Every variety of lop-sided mind makes of it a happy hunting ground. I am far from saying that there is no truth and no virtue in any or all of the various ideals and "isms" I have seen exploited, but it is characteristic of a lop-sided mind that in reacting to an admitted evil, it tries to stabilise the pendulum at the extreme of the opposite swing, and the remedy is worse than the disease. I have spent the better part of my life among cranks and idealists and reformers of one sort or another, and am pretty thoroughly disillusioned concerning all their ways and works; consequently my hero stands for normality and simplicity and common decency as against the high-falutingness of Fouldes which ends in a mess.*

However, the main thesis of the book, insofar as it had a general message to mankind, was the contemporary unhealthy attitude towards sexual mores, which indeed may be considered to be shared by the other books as well. In "The Winged Bull", the flawed hero Murchison is a typical victim of this, his background being a suburban vicarage, where his brother with whom he boards, is portrayed with little sympathy.

> *The Rev. James Murchison is represented as sincere, narrow minded, and doing infinite harm by his mishandling of life through ignorance and false values. He reduces his brother, a fundamentally decent man, to complete rebellion against all he stands for in life and religion. Murchison waxes blasphemous. He bids his brother's God go to His own Hell and stop there.*

Dion Fortune was somewhat surprised that no correspondent or reviewer had taken exception to these blasphemies of Murchison and felt it spoke volumes for the state of public opinion at the time. There is thus no reason to think that Dion Fortune stood alone in the opinions she expressed in the novels. It is difficult to appreciate the climate of sexual repression at that time, when even a King of England was forced to abdicate because he wished to marry a divorcée. However, things were stirring. Charles Morgan, the dramatic critic of "The Times" and successful novelist had a play produced in London the following year, "The Flashing Stream" which met with great success and was also rushed out as a book with an introductory essay by the author. Dion Fortune felt this to be one of the great plays of all time. It was hardly this, but it gained by striking a nerve in public consciousness on the thesis that: "The face of the whole world would be changed if the experience of sex were considered to be innocent unless its circumstances made it guilty." This idea would be regarded as commonplace today, but in 1938 it was a daring thesis, and Dion Fortune hailed it as "a notable exposition of the principles underlying sexual ethics."

Apart from the general thesis of her novels, though, she also did her best to get around some of the inhibitions about secrecy that still dogged the esoteric scene, and which was not easily shrugged off by anyone of her generation. Thus throughout the novels were little snippets of information on practical details, even in the sphere of magnetic interchange.

It was not for nothing that the inner library of the Fraternity contained the classic works on "Shakti and Shakta" and "The Serpent Power" by Sir John Woodroffe or strange little books with inbuilt locks such as "Private Instructions in the Science and Art of Organic Magnetism" by Miss Chandos Leigh Hunt (1884) "Giving minute Practical Instructions How to Magnetise, Mesmerise, Electro-Biologise, Psychologise, Hypnotise, Statuvolise, Comatise, Fascinate, Entrance, &c., &c."

There is a fair amount of chaff that needed to be sifted from the wheat in all of this, and was not until February 1939 running through to August 1940, that she finally got round to dealing with the "principle of polarity" and what she called "the lost secrets of western occultism" in non-fictional form, in a series of articles called "The Circuit of Force" in "The Inner Light Magazine".

Ever the pioneer, there was always an element of breaking new ground in Dion Fortune's literary work, and this includes the three romantic thrillers published by Stanley Paul, not that they hold much interest for esoteric students. She was, however, always trying to extend the limitations of the genre, which did not entirely endear her to her publishers.

In all of them we are in a world of adventure and flirtation with low life together with a theme of romance, where the heroine succeeds in rescuing the anti-hero from the worst sides of himself. The redeeming heroine is a feature of the occult novels as well, of course, but in the V.M.Steele books she achieves her aims without recourse to the inner planes.

In "The Scarred Wrists" however the fallen male might well be classed as a paranoid schizophrenic. He has served seven years for manslaughter and the scarred wrists of the title are the result of the handcuffs used to restrain him. Nonetheless he is brought back to sanity by little Pat Stone, an unwanted illegitimate poor relation in a straight-laced household, who finds her first secretarial job with him. The book ends with him being restored to his rightful patrimony and so Pat Stone finds herself a viscountess. Despite the formulaic ending the dark side of the novel was not lost on the publishers who announced: *"A new kind of thriller with a new kind of hero – a man just out of prison with nerves and health shattered, who is trying to run straight."*

The next novel "Hunters of Humans" is much lighter and easier to read, with a possible unconscious resonance to the painful experience of the horticultural college, for the serial poisoner and villain of the book is named Studley. His daughter Ann is caught up in a conflict of loyalties when he is tried at the Old Bailey, complicated by her romantic attachment to one of the investigating detectives whom her father has also tried to poison, and been beaten up in custody for his pains. Hence the title, for criminal and detective are in a grim game of hunting each other. Once again, the author slightly bucks the genre conventions and the publishers are led to state: *"This is not a detective novel – a jigsaw puzzle of imaginary crime and arbitrary clues, but a story about detectives. Crime and detection form the background but it is the love, the hate and fear of hunters and hunted, that form the motive of the plot."*

The final novel "Beloved of Ishmael" is a colourful and eventful story and the greatest challenge yet to any reforming heroine. Lewis Cassalis is a renegade white man on the west coast of Africa who has organised an underworld of graft, gun running and slave trading. The heroine Nina Barnett finds herself married to him and by her attitude and example brings about his reform. The plot becomes ever more picaresque leading the publishers to describe it as *"a love story quite as much as a tale of adventure and intrigue in the tropics... V.M.Steele has again written a thriller that is out of the ordinary run of thrillers. "*

It was also to be her last.

The three non-occult novels bear witness to the fact that she must really have loved writing for writing's sake. With the amount of words she was already writing of an esoteric nature, in terms of lectures, rituals, articles, textbooks and novels, to turn to writing yet more novels seems a strange kind of relaxation.

Yet it may have been the only way she could break free from the constant occult ambience with which she was surrounded. She had earlier sought some kind of retreat at Chalice Orchard, and very soon after she abandoned novel writing we find her setting up in the Belfry and finally living in a separate maisonette down the street from her headquarters in Queensborough Terrace.

She was not the first or the last occult teacher to find that she was expected never to be off duty.

31

THE NEW EPOCH

This Vernal Equinox meeting of 1936 was an important one beyond all other. A New Epoch was proclaimed in the running of the Fraternity. In the new regime there was going to be a formal recognition of the three rays of expression, with an officer in charge of each.

Dion Fortune was Magus of the Lodge and therefore at the head of the Hermetic Ray. Dr. Penry Evans was from henceforth to be known as Priest of the Green Ray, whilst C.T. Loveday was designated Priest of the Church, the Guild of the Master Jesus being renamed the Church of the Graal.

This marked the end of the first seven years of the Fraternity's foundation of the Lesser Mysteries as a ritual group, and its period of finding its feet.

Whether Colonel Seymour felt in any way slighted by not being appointed Priest of the Green Ray we do not know. It would be understandable if he did in view of the great amount of work he had put in along these lines since he joined. Dr. Penry Evans had not held ritual office since the Autumn of 1930 except to appear as Magus of the Lodge for three meetings between February and April of 1934, after which he dropped out of sight again until this Vernal Equinox of 1936, although he had continued to give a few lectures each year between 1933 and 1935.

During 1936 and 1937 Dion Fortune once more became sole lecturer in the Fraternity's programme but with a less frantic schedule. She gave just one Monday evening lecture each month for nine months of the year.

The formal Lodge Reports which had been carefully kept, at first in copperplate handwriting, ceased for all three Degrees at the beginning of 1937. Whether this also signifies a cessation of the actual Lesser Mystery ritual work is possible, although would seem unlikely. The years 1936 to 1939 might be called the years of achievement. The Fraternity had survived its founding years and established itself as an important presence upon the contemporary esoteric scene.

Dion Fortune went on to develop the Hermetic side beyond the rigid Masonic type structures of the Lesser Mystery degrees inherited from Moriarty. She began to write and perform a series of rituals such as the Rite of Isis and the Rite of Pan, parts of which were published in her novels.

She also took up residence in another building, the Belfry, in West Halkin Street. This was a converted Presbyterian church of the 1840's era, some features of which are described in "Moon Magic" as the town house and temple complex of Lilith Le Fay. In physical reality it was not quite so striking as its fictional counterpart, but was large enough to house an audience for lectures or demonstrations of ritual work, and included a species of stage lift for producing dramatic effects.

The finance to lease such a place probably came from Lady Catherine Perry, who had been initiated in 1936 and was a notable supporter in this respect. She was later always remembered for her donation to the library of a magnificent first edition of Manley P. Hall's "An Encyclopaedic Outline of Masonic, Hermetic, Qabbalistic and Rosicrucian Symbolical Philosophy", a vast tome, too big for any of the shelves, that was ever after referred to as "Lady Perry's Pamphlet".

Performing rituals to a public audience, by Dion Fortune's own account, seems hardly the most effective mode of ceremonial magic. However, in this respect she was by no means the trailblazer, for a Rite of Isis had been performed by S.L. and Moina MacGregor Mathers in Paris when Dion Fortune was still in her cradle.

One member of the public who witnessed the rites at the Belfry was Bernard Bromage, a writer and academic of some distinction. He first met Dion Fortune and her husband at the start of a series of university extension lectures he had been asked to give in 1936. He had been rather surprised to be asked by the authorities to lecture upon the unusual subject of "The Literature of the Occult", and was quite intrigued to discover what kind of audience the subject might attract.

On the first evening, his attention was drawn to two figures seated at the back, who took no notes *"but who carried around them that curious and practically unanalysable aura which goes with practice and expertise in the occult and 'magical' field."*

It was the custom at lecture series of this kind to invite students to write essays in answer to certain questions if they so wished. At the end of his second lecture the lady handed him an essay entitled "The Beginnings of Occult Literature". It was signed Violet Firth, but she revealed that she was also known as Dion Fortune. The name was familiar to him as he had read with much interest both "The Mystical Qabalah" and her novel "The Goat-foot God."

He found her a striking figure who bore a marked resemblance to a well-known advertisement for Sandeman's port that featured a figure in long cloak and broad brimmed hat.

> *Her rather plump figure was swathed in a crimson gown of hieratic cut: on her head she wore a black flapping hat. There was an odd atmosphere about her of the sibyl, the prophetess, and the diver into deep occult seas.*

One might sense here a certain resemblance to the heroine of "The Sea Priestess" which she must have started to write at about this time.

She continued to submit essays during the course of his lectures and Bromage, not surprisingly, found them well written, with obvious enthusiasm and penetration. Indeed, he considered her his "star student".Eventually Bromage was invited to Queensborough Terrace for tea, and as a result of their mutual respect for each other's work they arranged to give a series of Saturday night lectures at her Bayswater headquarters in the Autumn of 1937. It would feature both of them as speakers and lead into a general discussion which would be chaired by a distinguished guest from the literary field.

Bernard Bromage mustered an impressive panel of visitors to take the chair. They included the novelists Marjorie Bowen and Berta Ruck, Claude Houghton, Christina Foyle of the famous book emporium, Elliot O'Donnell, an expert on haunted houses, and these literary figures were supplemented by Dr. Penry Evans, Colonel

Seymour and Christine Campbell Thomson. Despite being priced at double the usual rate, including season tickets, the events attracted a large and intelligent audience.

As Bernard Bromage put it later, they threshed out many of the problems which had preoccupied distinguished minds in the field of occult speculation. They made people think, and they came back for more!

In this respect the Fraternity of the Inner Light may be said to have "arrived" as a force upon the modern social and esoteric scene, and 1937/38 was, so far, its most successful year.

The programme of lectures for the Spring Term of 1938 shows a fascinating bill of fare.

Jan 17: Spiritual Healing: its Power and Limitations. By Dr. T. Penry Evans.
Jan 24: The Esoteric Tradition. By Dion Fortune.
Jan 31: Methods of Occult Training. By Dion Fortune & C.R.F.Seymour M.A. with practical demonstration.
Feb 7:   Ceremonial Magic. By Dion Fortune.
Feb 14: A Reconstruction of Isis Worship. Part 1. A Lantern Lecture by C.R.F.Seymour M.A. with Chanting by Dion Fortune.
Feb 21: The Esoteric Doctrine of Sex and Polarity. By Dion Fortune.
Feb 28: A Reconstruction of Isis Worship. Part 2. A Lantern Lecture by C.R.F.Seymour M.A. with Chanting by Dion Fortune.
Mar 7:   The Doctrine of Magical Images. By Dion Fortune.
Mar 14: A Reconstruction of the Worship of Pan. A Lantern Lecture by C.R.F.Seymour M.A. with Chanting by Dion Fortune.
Mar 21: The Mental Factor in Health. By Dr. T. Penry Evans.

The Fraternity's activities excited interest in the whole London esoteric world of this time. Even Aleister Crowley with a couple of his acolytes appeared on one occasion, although he was somewhat coolly received by Dion Fortune. He held her abilities in high regard however, and on publication of "The Book of Thoth" his book on the Tarot, he sent her a signed copy No. 9, in which he inscribed:

To Dion Fortune, this small tribute to her achievement and attainment in the Science of Wisdom and to her eminence as an Artist in Words. Aleister Crowley.

No. 9 to Dion Fortune, as to the High Priestess of Our Lady Selene.

"The number 9 is sacred, and attains the summit of philosophy" Zoroaster.

Bromage was engaged at this time in translating some Hindu tantrik texts, and this excited the interest of Dion Fortune. She said that she had come to the same conclusions as the Tantrists with regard to the interpenetration of the powers of mind and body. As Bromage later wrote:

I recall many discussions with her on these and kindred topics: on the nature of the love technique and how it is the woman, the positive dynamism, who awakens the energy in the male and so makes him positive; of the part played by the ancestral subconscious in the formation of character and personality; of the tremendous and sometimes terrifying power of suggestion and its use in propaganda; of the nature of the child and the perception of animals.

At this time I read all she had written and admired the courage and the insight with which she probed depths and stressed parallels which had not been sensed previously. A very active, ceaselessly speculative mind, with touches of genius.

He put at her disposal much of the material he had collected on Eastern religions and she began to write up some of her ideas on this in a series of articles called "The Circuit of Force" that appeared from 1939 to 1940 in "The Inner Light Magazine". Her view was that they constituted, in part, the "lost secrets" of Western occultism. In return, she invited Bromage to the Belfry for a performance of the Rite of Isis.

He found himself ushered very secretly into the converted church and conducted up several flights of stairs to the topmost floor, where all was in darkness, and he was given a seat in a small hand picked audience. At one end of the room was a platform behind a curtain which was illuminated when the Rite of Isis began.

The costumes were more Egyptian than Greek and Dion Fortune admitted afterwards to Bromage that it was the ancient Egyptian overtones to the Greek symbolism which had always attracted her.

In spite of what Dion Fortune has said elsewhere about the risk of disappointment for anyone insufficiently trained to be present at a magical working, Bernard Bromage seems to have been sufficiently well attuned to appreciate it, and he emerged impressed with his Saturday evening's entertainment. It remained in his memory as *"one of the best attempts I have ever witnessed to stimulate the subconscious by means of 'pantomime' drawn from the more ancient records of the hierophant's art."*

Of particular interest in Bernard Bromage's memoir of Dion Fortune is his mention of some severe cases of collapse or serious obsession that she, working in collaboration with her husband, had handled and cured. This suggests that the work with the Master of Medicine had not been confined to theoretical principles only, even if a full time clinic never came into operation.

Indeed, Bromage thought that Dion Fortune had all that was needed to be a successful healer in her own right, not least because of a superb and unflagging self-confidence. Watching her in contact with other people, particularly with those who needed some kind of support, he was continually struck by her power to quieten agitation and to still fears by her very presence. She had a kind of maternal strength of receptiveness which led the most timid to confide in her, to put themselves at her disposal and execute her behests.

He found in her a powerful natural intelligence and an apparently vigorous and resilient physical constitution, to which she had added a self-imposed system of training whereby she managed her body with a maximum of economy and the avoidance of unnecessary movement. She was one of the most unflustered people he had ever met. Nothing seemed to put her out. On the lecture platform he had rarely heard a speaker less nervous. She kept a firm grip on the reins of her audience, fully in control of the situation.

Dr. Evans also spoke of his work in manufacturing food products from soya. This was another practical extension of Dion Fortune's concerns, that went back to her 1917 experiments on soya milk and her 1925 book on the soya bean as an alternative food source.

Dr. Evans was one of the participants in the Rite of Isis that Bromage saw, however, he was soon to leave the fold and not return to it. In the middle of 1938 he was invited by the Spanish Republican Government to go to Spain to advise on the nutrition problems of children at the time of the Civil War. He accepted the invitation and set up his equipment in Barcelona only to be forced, after only eight weeks, to fly for his life on the victorious advance of General Franco's fascist forces. He left behind him £2500 worth of equipment, a very considerable sum in those days, when the average workingman's earnings were little above £200 a year. Nonetheless as he later said, although it was a failure he was more pleased with that failure than with anything else he had ever done.

On his return to England he found a post as Assistant Tuberculosis Officer at Southwark, the borough at the southern end of London Bridge, and there he met Ann Mower White, another Assistant Medical Officer for Health, whom he later married, after applying for a divorce from his wife which was granted, uncontested, on 30th July 1945. He became Medical Officer for Health for Beaconsfield, in Buckinghamshire, in 1941 where he remained, a popular figure in the district, with a keen interest in rugby football and music, until his death at the age of 66 in August 1959.

Dion Fortune soldiered on with the Fraternity still in reasonable shape despite her husband's departure and Colonel Seymour's gradual disaffection. However, internationally times were at a crisis, with gas masks being issued to the civilian population and rumours of imminent war. It was at this time she took a step back from herself and her work to review just where she stood. It was a revealing document she shared with the readers of her magazine, although she never completed it.

> I have spent so much of my life in explaining the work of the Fraternity of the Inner Light to other people that there are times when I feel a great need to understand it myself. There has, alas, never been anybody to explain it to me, and I have had to find it out and piece it together as best I could.
>
> This statement is neither paradoxical nor cynical, but the simple truth. I have never, until quite recently, had any complete vision of the work of our Fraternity. I have seen it as a growing thing gradually unfolding, and have not so much created it as watched it grow. I have, in fact, not been the leader of the Fraternity, but the ploughshare on the snowplough, which is a very different matter; as anyone will know who has ever seen a snowplough at work.

A leader goes on ahead; he has the plan of things in his mind; he knows the landmarks. The cutting blade of the snowplough, on the contrary, is propelled forcibly from behind, clearing the way for that which comes after. If the plough-share were conscious one could imagine its surprised interest as the road opened up before it; its indignant perplexity at the obstacles that opposed its progress, and its gradual realisation that its mission in life was to go shearing through them. Imagine, too, the surprise of the other parts of the machine when they realised that a ploughshare is a cutting instrument!

It was said to me once, and it gave me understanding of a good deal which had hitherto puzzled me, that I am the medium of my own work. This explained to me the nature of the curious "driven from behind" feeling which I have always had, and why my work is much larger than myself. Why people meeting Dion Fortune digging in the garden at Glastonbury have said: "What — that?!" and why it was therefore better that people should not meet Dion Fortune digging in the garden at Glastonbury. Not that I object to them, but that they are very apt to object to me, uplift not being my strong suit when I am off duty.

Our work, being an evolving and not a static thing, must be seen in perspective if it is to be understood, for what it is at one time is quite different to what it is at another. We have lost some members because they could not grow with the work. We have lost other members because they could not see that provision must be made for different types of people at different stages of development.

The power of a Fraternity to develop its members depends upon the presence in its midst of persons of a higher evolution than the average. If all the advanced people felt themselves at liberty to withdraw, then all the less advanced people would be well advised to withdraw also, for there would be nothing there for them. To serve, however, is part of the price of training, and the trouble is not with the really advanced people, for they realise this, but with the people of intermediate development, who have got too big for their boots before they have grown big enough for their wings.

I have, in consequence, not got a compact body of troops to manoeuvre, but a long line of battle deployed over broken country, which is not nearly so simple a matter, and which must be taken into account when judging the work of the Fraternity.

In the very early days of our work we had to put up a kind of scaffolding before we could start the actual building. This scaffolding consisted of a framework of the traditional Mystery method. But as the Mysteries fell into decay during the alleged Age of Reason, this scaffolding had to be constructed out of some pretty rotten timber. In other words, I had to teach a great many things which I could not verify, but which I could not afford to scrap because I should have brought the whole structure down if I had pulled them out.

I was, moreover, entangled in the traditional oaths of secrecy, and so were other people, and for all I knew to the contrary, the missing proofs might exist, but not be available for me at my then grade. There was, moreover, always the saving grace of intuition which sensed the presence of light and power behind the tumbledown structure of conventional tradition. This faith was ultimately justified, for I eventually discovered that historical fables were psychological truths, and merely required to be restated in terms of modern thought to be accurate working models of things ineffable. Trouble comes, however, when the fables and the framework are taken at their face value, for then they are very misleading and hampering.

It was on the strength of this realisation that I wrote "The Mystical Qabalah", which restates in terms of psychology the traditional material. Anyone who has had access to that material knows the kind of dead bones I had to work over. Yet, at the same time, the tradition was too valuable to discard. It was, in fact, all we had to work on, and we had to make the best of it. I am of the opinion, however, that no one who had not got the psychic half from the inner planes that we had, could have made anything of it. For it was by purely psychic means that we recovered the lost keys that turned the locks, and these are still in process of recovery, though the main doors now stand open. To know the Mystery system is one thing. To know how to make it work is another.

The keys have been cut by studying what is known as the records of the Mystery religions and applying to them the methods of modern psychology. This revealed some extraordinarily interesting knowledge concerning the nature of the mind, the practical results of which are very far reaching. Such knowledge, however, like classical music, is only available to the persons who have developed the capacity to appreciate it. Its practical application, however, is behind all the work of the Fraternity of the Inner Light.

Because of the difficulties attending the expression of it, there is much more of it to be found in my novels than in my other books. For in the novels it can be presented in pictorial form, which has always been the method of the Mysteries, for the excellent reason that it is the only possible one, as will be appreciated by those who have used the keys to turn the locks and have seen for themselves what is behind the closed doors.

— Part Five —

THE YEARS OF TRANSFORMATION: 1939 - 1946

32
The War Letters
and the Outer Court

The outbreak of war on September 3rd 1939 put a stop to all previous activities that had been in full swing. Many members were drafted and relocated onto various types of war work, and those who were not would have problems attending meetings, with the restrictions on travel. "Is Your Journey Really Necessary" was the headline of a major government poster campaign. It was thus perhaps not unnatural that in an occult society thoughts should turn to less physical forms of travel or meeting.

Dion Fortune met this problem head on within a month of the war commencing. In the October of 1939 she sent out to everyone on her mailing list an invitation to participate in a weekly meditation at the same hour.

MEDITATION INSTRUCTION

The members of the Fraternity of the Inner Light have been carefully trained in the theory and practice of meditation. Every Sunday morning from 12.15 to 12.30 certain members will hold a meditation circle in the Sanctuary at 3 Queensborough Terrace. Other members, scattered all over the country, will also sit in meditation at the same time. Thus a nucleus of trained minds will be formed.

All who care to join in this work are invited to participate. They should proceed as follows:

The weekly letters will be sent every Wednesday in order to ensure the punctual arrival in time for the following Sunday. On that day, but not before, study the contents of the letter in preparation for the united meditation at 12.15. It is inadvisable to study the papers sooner than this, lest the concentration on the previous week's work be disturbed. Success can only be achieved by single-pointed concentration.

The meditation work consists of certain well-defined stages, each of which must be carefully performed before passing on to the next. These stages are the steps of a stair on which the mind rises to a higher level of consciousness, performs certain work there, and then returns to normal. For convenience sake they are numbered in sequence.

Stage 1

Having studied the letter, take your seat if possible in a quiet, dimly lit room, secure from disturbance; face towards London; sit in such an attitude that your feet are together and your hands clasped, thus making a closed circuit of yourself. Your hands should rest on the weekly letter lying on your lap, for these letters will be consecrated before they are sent out in order that they may form a link. Breathe as slowly as you can without strain, making a slight pause at the beginning and ending of each breath, thus: breath in, pause; breathe out, pause. The attitude should be poised and free from all strain, either sitting or lying. If sitting, have some support for the back. The position should be symmetrical so that both sides of the body are the same. It should be taken up a few minutes before the meditation is due to start, so that you have time to settle down into a posture of balanced relaxation and stabilise your breathing. Once the meditation has begun, think no more about your breathing.

Stage 2

Commence your meditation by thinking about the subject allotted for the work of the week. Try and realise its spiritual implications but do not attempt to consider its practical ones, for this will distract you and cause mind wandering. Realise that ethical principles are involved. If you have any knowledge of the Qabalistic method, place your meditation on the Tree.

Stage 3

Having thoroughly filled your mind with the ideas set for the meditation work, picture in your imagination a symbolic image, figure or scene that shall symbolise it. Keeping this before your mind's eye, slow down your thought processes till you begin to "feel" rather than reason. Try, as it were, to "listen" mentally. Do not try to hold this mental stillness for more than a few moments, even if you feel that you are getting results, because it is a very potent method of mind-working and it is not good to do it for long at a time. However fascinating you may find it, discipline yourself to pass on firmly to the next stage, for it is here that the real work is done.

Stage 4

Mentally dedicate yourself in the Name of the All-Good to the service of the One Life without distinction of friend or foe; let the good that you are about to invoke come through for all, relying upon the Cosmic Law to adapt it to their needs or their healing.

Stage 5

Think of yourself as part of the Group-soul of your race; your life a part of its life, and its life the basis of yours. Then, invoking the Name of God, open your mind as a channel for the work of the Masters of Wisdom.

Stage 6

Meditate again on the subject set for the work of the week.

Stage 7

At the conclusion, say aloud: "It is finished". Imagine a pair of black velvet curtains being drawn across the scene you have built up in your imagination, as if it were on a stage. Let the curtains approach from either side till they meet in the middle, thus blotting out the scene. Rise from your seat and stamp your foot firmly on the ground to affirm your return to normal consciousness.

You must be careful to always "close down" after meditation, otherwise you may find yourself becoming over-sensitive. If this should occur, discontinue the meditation work for a week. If it persists, let us know. Meditation by this method is potent and has to be done carefully. It is not foolproof.

Every day, at any hour convenient to yourself, but always at the same hour and if possible in the same place, repeat this meditation. Keep strictly to the method and exclusively to the subject set for the week. It is only by single-pointed teamwork that results are obtained. A diffused benevolence never gets anywhere. Never attempt to deal with specific problems or to direct the course of affairs on the physical plane. Bring through spiritual force and leave it to that force to work its own way.

We shall be glad to hear from you once a month if you care to communicate with us. Please mark your enveloped "Meditation report".

The first of these weekly meditations was scheduled for October 8th 1939. Although giving such practical instruction for meditation may seem commonplace nowadays it was little short of revolutionary then and justifiable, in the minds of occultists of the old school, only by the dire national emergency – and somewhat doubtful even if then! As she later wrote:

Those who were with us in those days will remember how we opened our doors and welcomed all who would sit in meditation with us and taught them the esoteric methods of mind working that had never been revealed before outside the Veil of the Mysteries.

The weekly letters represent a case book of working occultism over a three year period and continued until October 1942, when the Fraternity began to reorganise itself in preparation for the post-war period.

What comes through clearly in the letters is Dion Fortune's faith in her task and her destiny and the cause she served, and the combination of firm vision and practical leadership that inspired those who gathered round her.

Dion Fortune was much impressed by a series of synchronicities at the commencement of this work. The decision to embark upon the work had been taken in mid-August, in the crisis just prior to the actual outbreak of war, and the first Sunday in October had been chosen for the first meeting "for psychic reasons as being the one on which the forces with which we proposed to co-operate would commence to flow." It was subsequently announced by the religious denominations of the country that this same day would be selected as a national day of prayer and intercession.

Those available assembled at Queensborough Terrace on this particular day, the 1st October, where, presumably through the mediumship of Dion Fortune, they were told that they were there assembled as a means of getting in touch with the group mind of the nation and that the ideas being used for the group meditations would inoculate that group mind and be re-expressed in influential quarters so as to ensure them a hearing. They were much gratified therefore, and probably surprised as well, to discover that at 8 o'clock on the Monday evening, some thirty six hours later, a broadcast on the radio by the Archbishop of York repeated almost verbatim the text of their own address and meditation. Was this coincidence, she asked, or further confirmation of the existence of spiritual influences at work on the inner planes? She drew attention to these things, she said, not because she wished to boast but because of the confirmation they give of the occult teaching concerning the invisible governance of the world.

By the fourth letter it was evident that the symbols they were using had begun to "come alive". This, as Dion Fortune decreed, indicated that they were being "contacted" on the inner planes. It was thus no longer necessary to use the imagination quite so strenuously in building the symbols. They had now taken on definite astral forms that appeared and maintained themselves of their own accord.

One of the early departures from traditional secrecy was the formulation of the rose upon the cross, the symbol that, since the seventeenth century, has represented the heart of the Western Esoteric Tradition. It was a symbol that came through more publicly as well. Government posters displayed in the London Underground air raid shelters as a means of maintaining morale during the time of the blitz featured the rose and cross in the form of a star. In the Fraternity of the Inner Light meditation group it became linked with an underground cavern beneath Glastonbury Tor, in which, over the course of a few weeks, seven figures in the colours of the rainbow, representing Lords of the Rays, were seen to be present.

Again, by the end of October they felt that the ideas and ideals they were trying to express had been voiced in a broadcast speech by the Minister for War, and a week later a speech by the Pope gave expression to the same ideals. Of these matters Dion Fortune wrote:

> *Far be it from us to suggest anything so foolish as that we are responsible for the Pope's speech, but we do claim that the incidents we have recorded from week to week are strong evidence in support of our contention that there is an active centre of spiritual influence on the inner planes that is "broadcasting" telepathically certain spiritual ideals.*

And so the work of the united Fraternity and its active sympathisers and associates continued on a daily basis, formulating and re-formulating the mental link between these spiritual influences and the group mind of the nation.

At the beginning of February 1940 they began to visualise angelic forces some of which patrolled the coasts of the British Isles. Soon after this a new symbol complex began to develop. At first it took the form of a triangle that linked three coloured spheres, red, blue and purple.

In the red sphere a mailed rider was seen grasping a sword, who was later identified as King Arthur. In the blue one a seated figure held a rod of power, and was later identified as Merlin, holding a diamond sceptre. In the purple sphere was a figure of the Christ holding the cup of the Holy Graal.

This triangle then transformed into a three dimensional pyramid at the end of April, with the figure of the Virgin holding the cup in the purple sphere, whilst the Christ rose to the apex of the pyramid. This was philosophically aligned with a three-dimensional representation of four of the spheres of the Tree of Life, the blue of Chesed, the red of Geburah, the purple of Yesod, and the gold of Tiphareth.

By June 1940 the meditation work had extended to become what was virtually a visionary journey, that in original Golden Dawn terms would have been called "scrying in the spirit vision", or in latter day Qabalistic workshop terms a form of "path working". It was an evocation of the old Glastonbury contacts, building a Rose Cross cavern beneath the Tor, which led up inside the sacred hill to various states of consciousness, represented to astral vision as a library, a chapel and a watch-tower. These were imaginable representations of spheres upon the middle pillar of the Tree of Life, although the connection was not overtly made at that time.

Some readers in recent times have found this emphasis upon national ideals as somewhat odd or even distasteful, but this may be because they have the good fortune not to have experienced being a citizen of a nation under attack and intense aerial bombardment. It was therefore not jingoism or mock-heroics that led Dion Fortune to write in her 41st weekly letter, for September 8th 1940:

> There is only one way to keep quiet and serene under bombardment – to be prepared to lay down your life for your country if necessary. Once that eventuality is accepted, one abrogates one's civilian mentality, and the passivity and helplessness that go with it. Regard the warning wail of the siren as an "alert" not as a "retreat", unless specifically ordered to get out of the way. Carry on as near normal as you can without running risks….
>
> When the actual bombing starts, or the sound of gunfire is alarmingly near, go into meditation, if possible assuming the meditation posture. Now this may seem impossible of achievement during the din of a raid, and so it would be for the untrained mind; but if preparations have been made in advance, it will prove unexpectedly easy, for the stress of an air raid heightens psychic perception, and many a person will witness the parting of the Veil and see into the Unseen who, under normal conditions, might have to work long before they achieved such an experience.
>
> Each person should compose for themselves a short mantram, or rhythmical sentence of invocation of the Masters to be present and protect, and should repeat it silently like a litany until the mental turmoil ceases and it is possible to perform meditation proper. If the turmoil can be stilled even for a few seconds, it will be possible to pick up the inner contacts with every probability of vision opening and enabling us to see the work going on the Inner Planes, for the Invisible Helpers come very close to earth at these times.
>
> Try and make contact with these, not in order that they may

protect you, but that you may co-operate with them in helping
those around you. You will then find them very ready to avail
themselves of your co-operation, for their problem is to establish
contact with the people they are trying to help, who, not being
psychic, are very difficult for them to influence. It is in such
circumstances as these that the value of steady, regular meditation
shows itself, and if you have learnt to discipline the mind and
enter into the quiet amid the distractions of everyday life, which
so many people allege prevent them from meditation, then you
may have the great experience of seeing the heavens open when
the stress of the moment has given just that extra turn of the
screw that makes consciousness change gear.

During our meditation on Sunday, we were conscious of the
coming of a Messenger, and it is probable that steps are being
taken to establish contact and co-operation with those who work
as Invisible Helpers in close touch with the earth-sphere. It would
therefore be well, when danger threatens, to formulate the Rose
Cross in the same way that you would put up a notice indicating
that there is a stirrup pump in your house, so that any Invisible
Helper who is working in your environment may know where to
look for co-operation, but remember that to do this involves
willingness to sacrifice yourself if necessary.

A stirrup pump was a simple water pump and short hose, operated
by foot and hand, that could be placed in a bucket of water to direct
a jet at a fire or incendiary bomb. They were liberally issued by the
government to the civilian population in towns.

Two weeks later the Queensborough Terrace headquarters was
straddled by a stick of four bombs, but apart from a good shaking,
escaped damage, the second time that this had happened in the near
vicinity. If she felt that this was a result of angelic or other forms of
spiritual protection she was sadly disillusioned the week following
when they were bombed out of the place and the roof fell in. The
house was pronounced unsafe and the residents had to evacuate to
a maisonette further down the road. They drew consolation from
the fact that although everything was thrown off the altar in the
sanctuary, the statue of the Risen Christ remained standing on its
pedestal, though shifted to the very edge. In a situation where, in
this month alone, 6350 civilians died and 8700 were injured as a
result of the bombing, small sparks of comfort like this, whether or
not coincidental, are a considerable comfort. Fortunately they

suffered no casualties in the house on this occasion and the following week were able to move back in, the walls being structurally sound and the roof having been rendered weatherproof.

They retained a sense of humour. As Dion Fortune remarked, she had often been alleged to be a Black Occultist but on this occasion the allegation could not be denied as she and the librarian looked like a couple of sweeps through the difference of opinion with the roof, which fell on them but tactfully refrained from hitting them. Miss Lathbury's abiding memory of the time was having to cope with rescue workers who, somewhat to their amazement, kept pulling voluminous black robes with hoods from the rubble and wondering what they were for.

So, throughout all of this, the weekly letters continued, and the meditations went on, in a kind of permanent extended astral working. The "Inner Light Magazine" had to suspend publication in August 1940 because of paper rationing but fortunately not before Dion Fortune had completed a series of articles entitled "The Circuit of Force", one of the most practical works that she had written to date, and which owed something to the conversations on Tantra that she had enjoyed with Bernard Bromage.

In May 1941 she was able to announce that the Fraternity was resuming its Outer Court teaching activities and that particulars of the study course could once more be obtained from the Secretary. This was the time when those who were to become the post-war leaders of the Fraternity joined.

With the entry of America into the war, the tide of battle turned, and eventual victory seemed in sight. From this time on the tone and content of Dion Fortune's letters turned from immediate exigencies to planning in the post-war era, which was looked forward to as a time of opportunity for building a New Aquarian Age.

Typical meditation subjects were now not so much the symbolic images of the early weeks of war but forward looking aspirations such as "The rising tide of the new life", "Letting bygones be bygones", "A new spirit in human affairs", "The possibility of having to change our way of living for the sake of social justice", "The new man in the New Age", "The coming of the Aquarian Age", "The illumination of the mass mind", "The ideals behind the plan".

In October 1942 the Weekly Letters came to an end, just three years after their commencement. Looking forward to the Fraternity of the future, the final group meditation was "The nucleus of dedicated and initiated."

An attempt was also made to recommence the old Monday evening lectures. Dion Fortune officiated once per month and the other slots being filled by new members of the Fraternity, but the experiment did not last for more than one term.

In the meantime Dion Fortune was extremely active on three different fronts, in concert with her old teacher Maiya Tranchell-Hayes (formerly Curtis-Webb). Of this, more later. It led to an intensive series of trances producing a body of teaching known as the Arthurian Formula. Another initiative was an attempt to form a broad alliance of the occult and spiritualist movements. The third line of activity was to attempt to revitalise the esoteric healing work of the Master of Medicine.

On top of all this she began writing a series of Monthly Letters as a stopgap for the old "Inner Light Magazine". They took up as much precious paper as the former Weekly Letters but gave the opportunity for longer articles. In these, following upon the more practical line she had followed in "The Circuit of Force" in the last issues of the "Inner Light Magazine", she launched upon "Principles of Hermetic Philosophy" and "The Esoteric Philosophy of Astrology" dealing, amongst other things, with the formulation of astrological elements within the astral aura. Whether she realised it or not, for this was before Frances Yates made the roots of the Hermetic tradition more accessible, she was, in this approach, going back to Renaissance roots in the Western Esoteric Tradition, and the type of natural magic advocated by Marsilio Ficino in the Florentine courts of the Medici.

33
THE RETURN OF
MAIYA TRANCHELL-HAYES

A strange series of transcripts survive, commencing August 8th 1940, in which the participants are just two in number, "D.F. & I." The "I" stands for "Ishtar" and turns out to be none other than Maiya Tranchell-Hayes, Dion Fortune's early mentor in the Alpha et Omega Temple of the Golden Dawn tradition. The series of trances that follow, somewhat disjointed and not in the same tone as Dion Fortune's usual contacts, are a strange re-run, on a higher arc, of the very first scripts recorded when the two of them worked together in January to March 1921.

In the intervening period Dion Fortune had gone on to build her own Fraternity on her own contacts, after being expelled from the Alpha et Omega by Moina MacGregor Mathers and then being re-affiliated and subsequently disaffiliated from the Stella Matutina by Hope Hughes after the Israel Regardie debacle. Maiya had apparently remained loyal to her original affiliations through all of this but, along with most of the other dwindling Golden Dawn Temples, had suffered a devastating blow when Israel Regardie began to publish the Order papers in 1937.

In despair she buried all her regalia in her cliff top garden and after the death of her husband assumed she had come to the end of the road as far as that kind of magic was concerned. However, something brought her and Dion Fortune together again in 1940 and we have the strange situation of the two of them working together apparently trying to re-establish her old Golden Dawn inner contacts. Those contacts that Israel Regardie insisted did not and could not exist, but which had been very strongly in the background, not only in respect of MacGregor Mathers "Secret Chiefs" but in the more or less overt claims of Dr. Felkin in the early days of the Stella

Matutina in 1903 with a being called Ara ben Shemesh. Brodie-Innes also, as R.A.Gilbert noted in "The Golden Dawn: Twilight of the Magicians" *"was supposed to have had contacts with the Sun Masters."*

It is just such a "Sun Master" that Dion Fortune and Maiya Tranchell-Hayes were trying to contact in August 1940. The contact came through at first in a somewhat stilted, not to say high handed, fashion, and addressed to Maiya, or Ishtar of the Star, as she was called in this series of scripts. The identity of the "M" referred to is not known.

You must build in existing conditions: use the name. The temple you belonged to has ceased to exist. Much was given there but the teaching was not complete as it was broken by death.

M. is with you in this and wishes you to carry on the work. You are to be head and she is to be your medium; secrecy is to be strictly observed and no teaching given out till she is on your level. At present I am hampered by her lack of knowledge.

I have not spoken before but am one of Them behind the Order. I will accept responsibility with you for the teaching. You do not need a medium to communicate with M.; hold his writings in your hand. Others can communicate with you by letter. Later others may come and speak to you face to face. Work at Q.T. Locality is important for certain work; when a change is needed I will tell you. D.F. made the place not knowing what it was for and you found it ready made. Can you want more proof?

These temples are sections of the Light.

The implications of this are quite staggering. The communicator seems fully to be expecting a complete take over of the Fraternity of the Inner Light, with Dion Fortune regarded as very much a second fiddle, and not a very good one at that, who has fortuitously prepared the place to hand over to the new work.

This series of meetings went on under conditions of intense secrecy, although somewhat infrequently in the beginning. Another meeting was held in December in which general plans were revealed as to what was to be known as "the Nameless Order" – the title chosen for the sake of dignity and because names had been so much abused in the past.

It was to have various grades: of Sun, Moon, Earth and Ether. The Sun grade would be devoted to high abstract mystical knowledge. The Moon level would be concerned with magical knowledge. At the Earth level would be gathered the knowledge of magnetism of the physical plane. The Ether grade signified space, and "non-being", that is to say knowledge of that which is beyond form. It was not be confused with Elemental magic, which was of historic interest only except in matters of pathology and "spirits in prison".

It was necessary to have a Lesser Mystery system in which people were prepared, and in this respect the existing Fraternity of the Inner Light could provide what was needed. The Greater Mysteries would be re-shaped for the coming age and consist of two grades. The first would bring down the Higher Self into union with the Lower Self by means of ritual. The second would concern raising the adept to new life by particular sacred formulae.

A significant point was emphasised regarding Elemental initiations, which were held to have caused problems in the past within the Golden Dawn.

> It is a mistake to work with the Elemental forces till full Adepthood is gained – the Initiation of the Elements which comes after the raising to new life of the Adept. Working with the Elements is not the same as working with Elementals.
>
> The reason for so much trouble in the old Order was that they gave the Elemental Initiations to the unregenerated. But under this [new] dispensation there will be no Elemental Initiation, but Adepthood being gained, the Adept will study the art of the Elements. For till he is full Adept the Elements are his masters and you see the mistake that was made. Forces were called up that were beyond the power of the candidate to control.

At a meeting in February 1941 the Communicator revealed himself not so much by name as by the title of his office, which was "Shemesh" which means the Sun.

> I hold the office of Shemesh but am not the Shemesh you knew. You have no doubt recognised the identity of the Force and the similarity of the influence. At the present we are engaged in remaking the Order for the Aquarian Age. The contacts are not yet established nor the personality, mask or persona fully formulated. I am the Shemesh of the Aquarian Age.
>
> There is always a Shemesh, the Teacher, and Hakim, the Healer – he is still to come. We build the Temple of the New Age.

At this point he was apparently asked if W.K.Creasy, the most senior initiate within the Fraternity, and with whom Dion Fortune was currently working, could be introduced to these meetings. Permission was somewhat grudgingly given, and not without reservations.

The decision is yours and mine. If you take the responsibility you must be prepared to face the consequences of a mistake and so must I. If you do not take a risk you can do nothing. We have therefore to consider the question of necessity. These papers are at your discretion to be given to suitable persons and you must wait until you are satisfied. Remember hearsay is not good enough, so make it your business to find out.

Because your comrade needs his co-operation for her function and because she works with him it does not mean that you need work with him. There is much that you and she can do together and only you two; you must go through the papers to form the foundation for the new era.

The past era was the mastery by man of matter; the coming one the mastery by man of mind. The old teaching was expressed in terms of Physics; the new is to be in terms of Psychology. To this end was your comrade trained.

The reference to physics as a mode of teaching would seem to refer to the alchemical tradition. Anyhow, the Shemesh agreed to allow Creasy into the next meeting.

At this point it may be as well to try to review the other inner work that was currently being undertaken by Dion Fortune at this time and the attitude of other residents of the house, which was still regarded from the inner plane point of view as a Community.

At a meeting called of all residents of the house on December 16th 1940 there were three men and five women, besides Dion Fortune herself.

Of these Miss Lathbury, Miss Brine and Miss Barlow – "Dragon", "Briney" and "Doodah" – had been in the Fraternity since 1929, Hilda Leach since 1932 and Helah Fox, the relatively new girl, since 1935. It is she who was one of those interviewed by Janine Chapman in "The Quest for Dion Fortune". Of the men, J. Buchan Ford is something of a mystery, not appearing on any lodge records, but these exist only until the end of 1936. Loveday had of course been in on things since the very beginnings in 1922, whilst W.K. (Chris) Creasy had entered in 1934. Of about the same age as Dion Fortune he was a bank manager and at this time had risen to be virtually Vice-Warden of the Fraternity. Dion Fortune had apparently chosen him as her latest magical partner following the departure of both Dr. Penry Evans and Colonel Seymour. Loveday, although used in this role in the past, seems now to have been deemed unsuitable. It is possible that the early symptoms of Parkinson's Disease may already have set in. Miss Lathbury was Secretary and Miss Brine the Librarian.

They were called together to have certain things explained to them. One of these was the reason for Dion Fortune making contacts with people outside the Fraternity as compared to her previous more cloistered existence in pre-war days. The other was the nature of her close relationship with Mr. Creasy, who was the only person, apart from the hired cleaner, allowed to enter her room. This had apparently caused some kind of improper speculation, as had dogged Colonel Seymour and Christine Campbell Thomson before.

Erskine, speaking through Dion Fortune, laid down general guidelines as to how they were expected to conduct themselves within the house. They were enjoined to respect each other's freedom and privacy, and to try to look upon their fellows with the eyes of the higher consciousness rather than the personality standards of the outer world. He pointed out that the bond that existed between them was not necessarily one of personal liking but of a common dedication.

Community life within the house was the nucleus of the Fraternity, and whilst personal feelings and convenience should rightly be considered as far as was possible, life there was not organised to provide them with happy homes and congenial companionship. When any question of the good of the work arose such might well be disregarded.

At the present time there might not appear to be very much inner plane work going on but nonetheless they lived in a highly charged and stimulating atmosphere. This in itself gave opportunity for inner growth that was not available elsewhere. They were therefore by no means wasting their time, even if for the present they seemed to be pursuing only fairly menial tasks. Such inner gifts as they possessed would be called for when the time came.

They could still, if they wished, pursue magical work of their own devising, and in pursuit of this he gave them the following practical advice on how they might go about it.

I have told you there must be privacy and freedom in your individual lives, but equally you will find in all magical work that nobody can work alone, and according to the work you want to do you will work in polarity, or triangle or circle.

For the formation of such a group, the first consideration is atmosphere – to be in harmony with the people you work with, for you cannot do practical occult work unless you have happy conditions. You may have to wait a long time; for magical working must be as balanced as a choir.

Form such groups among yourselves, but your leader must require to know what you are doing. She will not interfere unless you do something injudicious, but if you are wise you will consult her before attempting any new departure, because of her experience and knowledge. As your leader she must hold all threads in her hands, driving on a loose rein, but she must hold the reins. Therefore organise nothing without consulting her. If important, she will consult with another or me.

In circle work you will get the best results if you have a balanced proportion of the sexes. Never have a greater proportion than two to one of the negative factor to the positive, otherwise the work becomes unduly negative. Polarity is the key to all magical work. Even in circle working you always get one to sit opposite the leader of the circle, and unless the leader finds a suitable person, the force will not start to flow. He must have capacity and understanding of the matter in hand, and once the flow begins between the leader and one person, it starts the current of force in circuit.

The principle of polarity is of special importance. It is one of the basic principles. Polarity means the function of flow and return of force. It is not fixed. It is an alternating current and therefore constantly changing. Sometimes one or another is negative.

He was at pains to point out that this matter of polarity was universal and concerned all human interchange. In an esoteric context it was particularly relevant to the matter of teaching. Their leader would have to be "negative" to the relatively "positive" teacher on the inner planes, but then became "positive" to her outer group in passing on the teaching received to them. The previously "positive" teacher on the inner planes would meanwhile take on a "negative" role in accumulating more teaching to pass through.

By this same token it was necessary to change polarity periodically, for if it were fixed for too long, the two parties would cease to be magnetic to one another. He illustrated this by example.

You have seen how your leader seeks contact with persons outside your group. It is for the sake of reversal of polarity. And as she finds someone who is equal and to whom she can be negative, so she becomes re-magnetised.

Also, polarity was not a case of "all or nothing". This was an unrealistic situation. In practice it focussed upon specific mutual interests or concerns.

This means that you take a person and pick out one particular quality – one facet in which they are superior, and work on that one aspect only – all other aspects being inhibited. This is an important point in practical work for it enables you to work with a wide range of experience. There are few you can accept unreservedly to polarise with completely; it is asking too much of human nature.

So each one of you will polarise with this or that person – with this or that quality - according to the knowledge they possess.

This effectively ruled out popular ideas of "soul mates" and ecstatic physical liaisons.

The personal union on which the once-born pin their hopes is unworkable in magic, so don't attempt it.

Polarity, moreover, ran through the whole of life and a misunderstanding of it was the cause of difficulties in organisations of all kinds in the world at large. Right handling of it was the secret of all inspired leadership. It was not just a matter concerning persons of opposite sex, although this obviously could be a factor.

In the esoteric field certain magical work might depend on the physical sex of the operators but only because the inner vehicles of a man or a woman are better suited to carry certain voltages. A woman could work with a woman and a man with a man, but it was seldom as satisfactory as a man working with a woman. Nonetheless, a female guru had originally initiated Dion Fortune. (This presumably refers to Maiya Tranchell-Hayes being in the East at her Golden Dawn initiation of 1919. There is reason to believe that she became a Golden Dawn adept in 1917).

Another point he asked them to bear in mind was that every soul is bi-sexual, both aspects being present in the Higher Self. In the developing adept both aspects became functional in consciousness, which is a perfectly natural process, having nothing to do with any psychological or sexual abnormalities.

In the undeveloped person one aspect only is developed. In the anomaly, one is repressed and the other developed at its expense. But in the adept, the second aspect is developed until it matches the primary. You see the difference?

Occasionally you get a type of man, the kind tied to his mother's apron strings, and there the male aspect has been repressed; but frequently you get women in whom the female aspect is repressed and they are masculine in mind and often in body.

A very important part of the knowledge of occult work and human relationships lies in the law of alternating polarity and the re-magnetising of each other.

You can establish relationships with many different types by dissecting out a given quality in a person. These are important clues to practical work. And remember you need to exchange polarity with anyone you are working with regularly in order to get the best results. You also need to have polarity with many different persons for full development of experience and function.

You can get exchange of magnetism between two of the same sex, but the trouble is that the flow thus exchanged cannot flow in circuit.

Let us put it this way. The flow and return in a pipe is like a normal magnetic relationship. With two of the same sex, each one has half the pipe and they are not joined up. It is this leakage of magnetism that is dangerous, for, from the magnetism thus discharged, certain elemental forms are built up.

The same applies to auto-sexuality.

Erskine concluded with some specific comments upon the various men with whom Dion Fortune had worked in the function of polar priesthood and what it had (and had not) entailed.

If you observe the working of all the rites you have seen, you will note how polarity is carried out. The positive and negative maintained – a man and woman opposite each other when possible.

Now when it comes to the practical work, the same principle prevails, and as I told you before, you will all in turn get the opportunity of the experience of all the aspects of the work as they are built up and made available.

Your leader has first to get the archetypal ideas. Then give them form on the physical plane, and when that has been done they are available for everybody. Now when she is doing that she works by the law of polarity. First she will have negative relations with whoever on the Inner Planes is the Master concerned, in which he gives, and she receives.

Then she reverses and works with someone on the physical plane. She gives and he receives, and in order to achieve that reversal, she usually works with a man; and she has worked with various men, some you know, and some you don't, and she will always do so.

In the days when her husband afforded her protection there were no difficulties, but now that protection is withdrawn the group must afford her it. She must be able to work thus without being exposed to scandalous tongues, therefore the wisdom and protection of the group must serve to guard her, just as the bees in a hive guard the queen bee – the layer of eggs – the one creature in the hive that can lay eggs. That is why group formation is essential for the work so as to make conditions and give the necessary protection.

Now, my son, the Priest, you had experience of the work for several years. Did it ever give rise to scandal?

Loveday:　　Never.

Was there ever anything in that relationship that could have justified scandal?

Loveday:　　Nothing.

When that phase of work was finished, were you left uncompensated?

Loveday:　　No, I was fully compensated.

There you have his testimony. Since then your leader worked with another priest, [Seymour]. The relationship served its purpose, fulfilled its end – gave her what was needed and ended, but the priest has not been left uncompensated, nor will be.

Now a third priest works in a third relationship, [Creasy], and I would ask you to assist and protect that work, for it is necessary for bringing through the teaching, and he who receives it passes it on again, not to one, but to all. And in asking you to assist in that work by making a circle of protection around it, I give you my assurance there is nothing in that relationship to cause scandal or bring disgrace upon the work. It is a magical relationship. For this it is necessary that persons should be in sympathy, but as I told you before, the personal factor does not come into it.

I have exemplified three cases of polarity in which your priestess has been used, representing the three Rays of this Fraternity; in each case the work was undertaken as work. Personal relationships had to build up to enable the work to be done, but in each case the relationship was entered upon for the work and not for personal ends.

I may tell you further, there was a delay of several years before the first priest was found, though the priestess was ready. And before the third priest was selected, two others were tried and discarded. These matters are entirely to do with the inner work of the Temple. There is nothing personal in them. It is not easy for people to understand who have not known the impersonality of Temple work.

The man who gave the princess her initiation on the physical plane – her husband – was fully cognisant of the aspects of her work with the Priest of the Graal and the Priest of Isis, and had no fault to find and no complaints to make in the matter.

This, besides settling wagging tongues, which were also adjoined to secrecy about this type of work to those outside, serves as an excellent summary of most of the polarity teaching that Dion Fortune hinted at in her novels and in her later articles such as "The Circuit of Force".

On 1st May 1941 Creasy was duly invited to a meeting with Maiya Tranchell-Hayes and and introduced to the Shemesh. He was given a magical name, Sandalphon of Earth, and future plans were outlined for a three-tier system of Lesser Mysteries, Greater Mysteries and an Inner Order as well as the development of the healing work, which is described below as Esoteric Therapeutics.

There followed a long series of trance communications that eventually came to be known as the Arthurian Formula. It came through in a series of fifteen or so sessions between April 1941 and February 1942 and formed the staple for the Fraternity's Greater Mystery work after the war.

The body of this teaching was pushed through at a great rate, expecting the recipients to fill in gaps with their own reading and study. It was based upon the somewhat startling assumption that the Arthurian Legends were based upon race memories that had their origin in Atlantis. That they had been brought to the western seaboards of Europe by Atlantean settlers after the last great cataclysm of the ancient continent. Upon it therefore, a pure and ancient form of Mystery training could be based.

A system of Mystery training was envisaged with three grades, that of Arthur and the Round Table Fellowship, that of Merlin and the Faery Women, and that of Guenevere and the Forces of Love and beyond that the Mysteries of the Graal. It was in many respects a higher and deeper analogue of the pyramidal symbolism that had recently been developed in the Sunday meditation group based on the Weekly Letters. It was however coming from a profounder level and with considerable implications for the future. It finally saw the light of day in the public domain in 1983, by being incorporated into "The Secret Tradition in Arthurian Legend" by Gareth Knight following some practical work on it conducted at Hawkwood College in 1981.

In the esoteric set up put in place while this new material was being revealed there was a threefold function of the three of them, designated by Star (Maiya Tranchell-Hayes), Moon (Dion Fortune), and Earth (W.K.Creasy) with the Sun represented by the Shemesh upon the inner planes.

The former might also attend other meetings of the group but did so incognito, veiled, arriving before the others entered and staying until after they left, wearing a star headdress – not for the sake of glamour but as a reminder of the presence of the inner planes being behind all the work that was being done.

Upon the inner planes there was said to be a senior office known as the Hilarion, representing a background influence, with an executive triangle below consisting of the Shemesh – as Lord of Wisdom; the Metatron – as Lord of Power, and the Hakim – as Lord of Love and Compassion.

This last office was also concerned with healing, and strenuous efforts were made to reactivate the work that had previously been done with the Master of Medicine and Dr. Penry Evans. This entailed finding a qualified doctor who could be the recipient for this kind of work.

There was no one within the Fraternity adequately qualified, so they sought a medical practitioner from outside who might be sufficiently open minded to take part in this kind of work. A Dr. Vasifder was suggested, a 49 year old Indian practising in this country, and although they might have preferred one of their own kind in terms of nationality, they invited him to attend an experimental séance.

They were listed in the report of the occasion by their mundane names, and besides Dr. Vasifder and Mrs. Evans, those present were recorded as Mrs. Hayes, and W.K.Creasy. Things could hardly have got off to a worse start as the doctor proceeded to ask test questions to ascertain the medical knowledge of the communicator.

His first question was "What is the best way of treating a burn?" to which the reply came that the inner plane communicator was not a doctor and so could not help very much in that matter, but would welcome questions on general principles.

Dr. Vasifder therefore asked what light could be thrown on the causes of cancer.

The communicator was happier to deal with this and put forward a theory that had been favoured by the Master of Medicine in earlier days. This was that there were two kinds, one caused by karmic problems in which there had been great sexual vigour misdirected, often with a streak of cruelty, that led to a frustration and misdirection of the life forces. The other was in the form of a parasitic astral entity that could pass from one victim to another, either in the same family or in the same locality looking for another host.

Dr Vasifder then returned to more specific medical questions, asking to be told the treatment for high blood pressure. Again the reply was that the communicator was not a doctor.

Mrs. Tranchell Hayes then led the questioning and the conversation went off into more speculative areas which eventually became as general as Dr. Vasifder asking for light on the progress of the war and when it would be over, to which he received a rather stonewalling answer, and thenceforth the talk passed to matters of post-war reconstruction with the doctor playing little further part in the conversation.

The inner plane opinion of Dr. Vasifder, after the meeting, was that despite other fine qualities, he was not advanced enough in esoteric tradition. Accordingly he was not asked back. The following month another doctor was found, referred to as "Dr. C", another Indian it would seem, who proved much more sympathetic to work with.

At times the conversation became quite technical and specifically clinical, and it was explained that this was because the communicator could tap into the medical knowledge of the doctor. It seemed also that by the same token the Master of Medicine had come back on stream but there was never quite the same quality of interchange that had been the case with Dr. Penry Evans.

At the same time, as had occurred many years in the past with regard to "The Cosmic Doctrine" other inner contacts might take over unannounced, so there was never any specific identity on the other side. A particular instance of this was called to their attention after one particular meeting, when the communicator said, before leaving:

We have been honoured tonight. We have been fortunate enough to have the presence of one who does not very often communicate. He can give you what I cannot. You no doubt noticed the point at which the change took place. He is not a very ready communicator.

By the end of the year the principal communicator behind these discussions announced that he would prefer to give straight lectures rather than further interrogative work with doctors who were not initiates of any great advancement.

There was sufficient quantity of this material for a series of small booklets to be run off, entitled "Esoteric Therapeutics" during the war. They were apparently circulated only to approved recipients and subtitled "Teaching received from the Inner Planes by the Fraternity of the Inner Light" and marked "Confidential" and to be returned to Dion Fortune at the Queensborough Terrace address. They included some material that had been received in earlier years under the aegis of Dr. Penry Evans.

After the war the whole corpus of material was worked over by those members of the Fraternity who were suitably qualified, medically and esoterically. It proved an extremely demanding task editorially and a matter of fine judgment as to just how much was suitable for open publication. Therefore it never got as far as book publication. Some of the diagnostic techniques, such as reading the Tree of Life within the aura, were used however in a non-medical context by sufficiently able clairvoyants, such as Margaret Lumley Brown.

Subsequently it has been discovered in neglected files and what seems suitable for publication sorted out for publication as "Principles of Esoteric Healing" by Dion Fortune. (Sun Chalice, 2000)

34
SPIRITUALISM REVISITED

Another new initiative that was aided and abetted by Maiya Tranchell-Hayes at this time was the vision of a post war united front between occultists and Spiritualists. The high hopes for the post-war era had all the enthusiasm and idealism that fifty years later greeted the new millennium, or the coming of the Aquarian Age.

The editorship of "Light", a leading Spiritualist journal, published as a weekly newspaper at that time, was held by Charles Richard Cammell, a post which had recently come his way. He happened to be in Maiya Tranchell-Hayes' large circle of esoteric friends and acquaintances and this was no doubt the seed that set the following events in train.

He was invited to attend a series of private séances at which Dion Fortune was the medium, and to meet the Master who was working behind her. Two such meetings with the Magus Innominatus occurred in October 1941 which considerably impressed him, and he decided to run a series of editorials and articles based upon these communications.

Accordingly for the issue of January 15th 1942 he wrote an Editorial under the heading "Unusual Communications", in which he stated:

It has been the present writer's recent privilege to obtain certain communications of an unusual character. The Medium is a person of high literary distinction, whose remarkable psychic gifts have never been employed professionally and are known only to a small and strictly limited number of friends, each of whom is a serious student of the occult and spiritual sciences, and with whom the Medium's secret is in safe keeping. The Communicator from the Other Sphere desires also to remain nameless, as far as the public is concerned. According to his statement, he had attained the grade of Magus in his life upon earth. I need only add that, on the occasion on which I was present, the Medium was in deep trance for a period of three hours.

Under this introduction he gave an edited transcript of the meeting with the sub-headings "The Secret Tradition" and "London as a Spiritual Centre." He concluded that he hoped to publish more extracts from the same source from time to time.

The unusual sense of power that he felt to be behind this material led Mr. Cammell to expand upon the circumstances of his recent appointment to the editorial chair of "Light", which he began to feel had been arranged from a higher source.

That sources beyond and above his control he could not fail to suspect. That this was, in fact, the case, was later confirmed by various psychic communications in no way connected one with another.

Last summer, in the West of England, the writer saw in a dream a personage whose identity he recognised, although neither in life nor in a portrait had he ever seen this person. Some months later, in London, he was invited, in a curious manner, to meet the small and strictly limited circle, students of occult and psychic science, referred to in our former article. Among its members he immediately identified the personage of his dream.

That is to say, Dion Fortune – not that he mentioned her by name at this point, but he gave the gist of the message that had been communicated to him. This was that there had always been a tradition of the Secret Wisdom, which, in the third quarter of the 19th century, had come through a new impulse. These were the first ripples of the Aquarian tide, part of which was the Spiritualist movement. The 1914-18 war marked the end of the Piscean age and we were now entering upon a new phase of enlightenment for which the Spiritualist movement, now past its experimental phase, would be a channel. It would bring through the archetypal plan from God, through the great archons and angelic hierarchies, through the souls of just men made perfect and the adepti, who live in seclusion, and thence to the people.

Britain occupied a position of great importance in the spiritual history of mankind. In the past there had been holy centres where spiritual forces have come through to the world, Rome, Jerusalem,

Thebes and Lhasa. In the new age such a centre would be London.

An organ most suitable for such a revelation was unquestionably "Light" which for more than sixty years had been a pioneer of psychical, occult and mystical research. The war currently being waged was not only a conflict against material forces of prodigious power but also a spiritual war. To wage this effectively an important section of the intelligentsia of the nation must progressively be taught more of occult, mystical and spiritual science.

It was of paramount importance therefore to keep this channel open, through "Light", for this vital teaching. Attempts would be made to close this channel but it was incumbent upon all who believed in its mission to give it their support. Malignant forces on the Other Side were in operation against human progress, interested in closing every channel of occult and mystic power working in the service of humanity. Weak minded persons, serving their own ends of petty ambition, jealousy or simple dissatisfaction were easy prey to such forces; unconsciously the cat's paws of evil intelligences, pawns in a perilous game.

His Editorial of February 26th 1942 was given over to a verbatim record of the trance of October 27th 1941 which gave very precise details on the modus operandi of trance communications. Almost a do-it-yourself guide in fact.

Still no mention was made of Dion Fortune but on April 23rd the first page was dominated by a signed article from her, entitled "The Secret Tradition". It was serialised over three issues and began in forthright fashion:

Let me commence by answering the very reasonable question: what have Spiritualists to do with the Ancient Wisdom? More than most of them realise, for Occultism is traditional Spiritualism. Whether we study the Delphic Oracles or the witch trials of the Middle Ages, we encounter authentic psychic phenomena. Spiritualists would find themselves on familiar ground if they penetrated to the caves of Tibet or the temples of Ancient Egypt, for the Secret Tradition has been built up by generations of psychics and spirit-controlled Mediums.

The antagonism between modern Occultism and Spiritualism arose owing to the tendency of two of a trade to differ somewhat drastically. Followers of the ancient wisdom-religion saw unauthorised trespassers investigating their preserves, and were neither helpful nor polite. Mme. Blavatsky and MacGregor Mathers, the principal exponents of the Eastern and Western Traditions, both decried mediumship; but Mme. Blavatsky was herself a Medium, and a very fine one, as witness "The Mahatma Letters"; and MacGregor Mathers made use of the mediumship of his wife, sister to Henri Bergson, in reconstructing the rituals of his famous "Order of the Golden Dawn." I cannot speak concerning what goes on nowadays in the Esoteric School of the Theosophical Society, but mediumship and clairvoyance were to my knowledge made use of in the higher grades of the "Golden Dawn", the deprecation of these practices by occultists being of the nature of a smoke-screen.

Initiates of the lesser grades may take these denials seriously, but those who are acquainted with the practical work of the higher grades know what value to set on them. While I am entirely in agreement with a policy of caution in developing gifts that are by no means without their attendant risks and drawbacks, I am not prepared to endorse deliberate mis-statements. Spiritualism and Occultism are much closer akin than spiritualists realise and occultists will admit.

She also gave her views on secrecy in no uncertain terms, which must have caused a certain twinge to Maiya Tranchell-Hayes.

The deeper occult teaching circulates in manuscript form among small groups of people pledged to secrecy. It is a great pity that the occult teachers, even if they consider it undesirable to make their teaching available to an unselected public, should not pool it among themselves; but the tradition of secrecy is so ingrained in the movement that it is not easily abrogated.

Moreover, people are generally bound to this secrecy by traditional oaths concerning which nobody seems to have the power to give dispensation, even when such oaths have been made ridiculous by the advance of popular knowledge. When I was initiated I swore to keep secret from all uninitiated persons the methods of the Hebrew Numerical Qabalah, that curious technique for the interchanging of numbers and letters to yield magical formulae, upon which nowadays several scholarly books are available. I also swore to keep secret certain astrological data which modern astrologers would consider a first course for beginners.

The occult dove-cots, however, were badly fluttered a few years ago when the secret papers of one of the most famous of the occult fraternities, the "Golden Dawn," were published in four volumes in America; but any one who reads these books in the hope of learning the occult secrets will be sadly disappointed, for they are quite incomprehensible to the outsider, though an invaluable encyclopaedia of reference for the initiated.

I had all this material in my possession many years ago, laboriously copied by hand. I had to learn it off by heart in order to pass the tests of the grades; no explanation was ever given me concerning its real rationale and use – these are Lost Secrets in the "Golden Dawn" today; but a very old, bed-ridden woman gave the key when she whispered in one of her rare intervals of consciousness – "Study Yoga and the methods of the spiritualist circle."

It was in the light of this hint, and my previous knowledge of psychoanalysis, that I was able to find my way through the Valley of Dead Bones to which I had been admitted by virtue of my initiation. Yoga, spiritualism, and the psychology of the unconscious are the three keys that open the gates of the Ancient Mysteries to modern thought.

One would dearly like to know the identity of this obviously highly respected bed-ridden old woman, whose remarks also inspired much of what she wrote in "The Circuit of Force".

These attempts to bring the spiritualist horses to water did not, however, persuade them to drink. Charles Cammell remained sufficiently interested to include a brief introductory section of the Arthurian Formula into a subsequent editorial, but he began to feel increasingly out of sympathy with the whole project, and in July 1942 wrote to Mr. Creasy to say that he was not interested in participating in any further trances.

Dion Fortune continued gamely with a series of lectures for the Marylebone Spiritualist Association and also publicly admitted her own trance mediumship in the first of the Monthly Letters of October 1942.

The mediumship of Dion Fortune has been a well kept secret within the Inner Group of the Fraternity, but it has recently been decided to make a secret of it no longer in order that certain of the teachings thus received may be made available for all who follow the Path.

There followed an address received through her mediumship and the intention was expressed that similar extracts from a great wealth of unpublished material would be released for publication. In her Monthly Letter of December 1942 she wrote a long article, putting forward her current views on Spiritualism, which modified some of the criticisms she had made about the movement in "Spiritualism in the Light of Occult Science" and "Through the Gates of Death" a decade before.

In this article she stated quite unequivocally that the Masters of the Great White Lodge had given instructions to the brethren charged with the direction of both movements that the time for co-operation had come, and the two movements were to make contact at their periphery, like two circles meeting and slowly blending. More specifically she spoke of the mediumship of various occultists, including Brodie-Innes, the head of the Alpha et Omega Temple of the Golden Dawn tradition, into which she and Maiya Tranchell Hayes had been initiated..

> *That Occultism has owed much to mediumship is witnessed by the tradition of the Oracles and the well-known life story of Madame Blavatsky; after whose death C.W.Leadbeater, her student, continued to keep open the lines of psychic communication. The lesser known history of MacGregor Mathers, the great English occultist, who used his wife as his medium, and of his collaborator, Brodie-Innes, who was himself mediumistic, confirm the tradition.*
>
> *The question is frequently asked as to whether the Fraternity of the Inner Light makes us of mediums and psychics, and whether Dion Fortune, its Warden, is herself a medium. Hitherto information has been refused on this point to all save those in the higher grades of its own organisation. The time has now come, however, to give an answer.*

The gist of this answer was that the Fraternity trained its students, to begin with, in the philosophy of the Esoteric Tradition and in meditation. They then, in the next grade were developed psychically and taught how to enter the inner planes by the traditional methods. Advancing further they studied the art of operating the astral forces, all members taking their part in skrying (or clairvoyance) according to their capacity, but they were not encouraged to act as mediums for one another but to learn to make direct contact with the Masters by means of the meditation methods in which they had been trained.

However, a line of direct communication was always kept open, operated from the inner planes, and Dion Fortune at present held this office, an office which she took over from her predecessor and teacher *[presumably Moriarty]* who likewise received it from his teacher. Members of the Fraternity did not sit for development in mediumship although individual members from time to time, according to capacity, might have experiences that enabled them to test for themselves the inner plane contacts claimed for their Fraternity. These contacts had also been counterchecked recently by mediums belonging to well known Spiritualist organisations.

One of these would have been a well-known medium of the time, Mrs. Methuen, who had a Red Indian guide called "White Wing" and with whom Dion Fortune had had a consultation on the afternoon of August 31st 1942.

Some points in her account of the meeting are of considerable biographical interest and somewhat at variance with the image of supreme self-confidence that had impressed Bernard Bromage.

> *Before going to the sitting I had invoked my own guides, asking that a check-up might be made on my own psychism, for one of my chief troubles has been lack of self confidence, and the fear that I may be deluding myself and others owing to subconscious contents getting mixed with my psychism. The control dealt with this point at considerable length and very explicitly, giving me much valuable advice and reassurance, of which I was much in need.*
>
> *He proceeded point by point to deal with the topics on which I had recently been having counsel and instructions from my own controls, thus counterchecking them in a very interesting and evidential manner.*

"White Wing" confirmed that she had much psychic power and a great mission to perform, with more help available from the inner planes than she realised or of which she was ready to avail herself. Something of her apparent great self confidence remarked upon by Bromage may well have had much to do with this faith in her own destiny and those who ruled it.

*He described accurately the difficulties I had encountered in
life, and should continue to encounter, but said I had ample help
from the inner planes to enable me to drive through them. I have
always been conscious of this, and have often likened myself to a
ship driving through a heavy sea with decks awash, but coming
up after each plunge.*

Some of these difficulties were referred to more specifically later
on:

*White Wing described accurately my relations with my parents,
which have never been very helpful or sympathetic, and my
separation from my husband; saying, in my opinion correctly,
that neither of us desired to re-contact the other, and would never
do so, as our evolutionary paths would not touch again. He said
that I had learnt much and taught much through the marriage
relationship, and that I had done well. I was glad to hear this, as
I had no means of assessing my own conduct objectively.*

Prognostications about the immediate future did not turn out to be
very accurate. White Wing said there was some man working with
her, aged about 65 who would want to marry her, but advised against
marriage as it would hamper her work. However, although there
were several men working with her, Dion Fortune could think of
no-one of this age, nor who was in the least likely to fulfil this
prediction. She evidently gave no thought either to Colonel Seymour
or to Charles Loveday, who were respectively 62 and 67. The first
had in any case recently departed. Creasy, the only other man of
note at the time was about her own age of 51, and C.U.A. Chichester,
with whom she later did some work, had only just arrived on the
scene and was in any case about ten years her junior.

A trip to America after the war was very definitely forecast.
This of course never came to pass because she survived the cessation
of hostilities by only a few months, unless the strong impression of
a far trip is regarded as a euphemism for death.

Another interesting point was White Wings' repetition of a
warning about certain people who would be ready to sap her energy
like a leech. He repeated the expression "like a leech" several times.
Here again, could this have been a foreknowledge of the leukaemia,
the cancer of the white blood corpuscles, that caused her death in
January 1946?

He also encouraged Dion Fortune to take up healing work as she had gifts in this direction, and there were doctors upon the inner planes who wanted to work through her. She was of course already working along these lines with the renewal of the Master of Medicine contact but was not so sure about her own gifts as an alternative healer, although Bromage had also thought about her positively in this respect.

> *The presence of healing power recently I had begun to suspect. My constitutional scepticism however had prevented me from trying to make use of it.*

It is possible to regard this streak of scepticism as one of the saving graces of Dion Fortune's contribution to occultism. She was able to deliver the goods without necessarily falling into the uncritical credulity that mars the work of many other psychics. However, from another point of view, this could be regarded as a lack of faith in her own powers. It would seem that the ideal, as in most things esoteric, is to find the middle way. At times she felt that she could have done better in this respect, but it is no easy assessment to make with regard to the whole woman and the whole work.

> *White Wing had much explicit advice to give me concerning an inferiority complex which he said robbed me of self-confidence and prevented me from doing my best work. Of this I have long been very conscious, and his counsel and confirmation were very helpful to me.*

One fleeting reference is intriguing towards the end of the session when, at the more usual spiritualist type of level she was asked if she recognised a grey haired lady with thin face and blue eyes who had had heart trouble. It was suggested it might be her mother or a grandmother but neither of these fitted the description. She remarked however that one of her "initiators" answered in all particulars – "except that she had massive features." It would be interesting to know whom she had in mind.

In summarising this unusual consultation between a leading spiritualist and a leading occultist, she concluded:

> *I found the interview very helpful; firstly by the stimulus to my own psychism it afforded, which was an extremely valuable*

experience to me; secondly, by the confidence it gave me in finding
so close a check-up on my own communications and methods. It
is clear to me that Mrs. Methuen and myself use exactly the same
methods.

At the end of 1942, in the December Monthly Letter she made a
formal statement about the current attitude of the Fraternity of the
Inner Light to Spiritualism.

To those who have knowledge of both movements it is obvious
that they are the two sides of the same coin. Spiritualism is
empirical Occultism. Occultism is traditional Spiritualism. The
methods and tone of the two movements differ, the one being
propagandist and the other exclusive. In the past both had their
separate tasks to perform, and could only perform them
separately. Occultism had to keep alive and increase our heritage
of psychic knowledge, and Spiritualism had to introduce the same
concepts to the popular mind in a form that could be appreciated
by people whose past incarnations had given them no
subconscious aptitude for understanding the invisible realities
and who were making their first approach to the Path. Both
movements were under the jurisdiction of the Great White Lodge,
but were carried on by different groups of Masters on the Inner
Planes and their servers and pupils on the physical plane.

Independent organisation was necessary, as the one movement
aimed at the widest possible publicity in order to influence
popular opinion, (which it has done successfully), and the other
still needed to remain in seclusion till public opinion had
undergone the preparation that was the work of the Spiritualist
movements. During the last great war Spiritualism came into its
own and accomplished its mission, and its contribution to human
thought is now an accepted part of our culture. In this war
Occultism is coming into its own in turn, consolidating the ground
pioneered by Spiritualism.

The Masters of the Great White Lodge have given instructions
to the Brethren charged with the direction of both movements
that the time for co-operation has come, and the two movements
are to make contact at their periphery, like two circles meeting
and slowly blending.

However, things were never going to be quite so easy. However
noble the aspiration, there remains, half a century further on, little
sign of a grand amalgamation of the two movements. Although it

has to be said, particularly after the remarkable decade of the 1960's, that there has been an increasing public awareness of the inner side of things, and less tendency to compartmentalise categories of belief. A more egalitarian society and increasing ease of travel and communication have been steadily eroding the old divisions.

35
POLICING THE JURISDICTION

The middle of 1942 saw the beginnings of the rebuilding of the Fraternity in preparation for the post-war period.

Bernard Bromage had recently met Dion Fortune once more. She now lived in a basement maisonette just down the road from her headquarters. He felt a certain change had come over her personality and that she had become less of the recluse than in the Belfry years. She was getting out an about and meeting a greater assortment of people. In short, he felt that she was trying to move with the times.

Her previous scarlet gown and wide brimmed hat had given place to a more mundane and highly becoming dress of black satin. Her reception room was however exotic with coloured silks and elaborate hangings.

She had asked him to call because she had in mind a project for a united front of leading occultists in London, and eventually Europe for that matter, whereby they could get together and pool esoteric knowledge and resources to enrich the common stock. From his own knowledge of contemporary occultists Bromage felt such a scheme likely to be somewhat optimistic but she said that she would let him know in due course how she got on with the enterprise.

It may have been partly in this spirit that she went down to Hastings to meet Aleister Crowley. In the Belfry days, when he had turned up to one of her meetings, she had somewhat cold-shouldered him in public. However he lived in Hastings where, coincidentally, her father also lived along with her stepmother, having re-married after Sarah Firth's death in December 1936.

However, Kenneth Grant was present at their meeting and does not think she was visiting her parents, for he recalls waiting for her train, in a thickening mist, and after the meeting seeing her back to the station.

She had ostensibly gone to consult Crowley about a ritual, although as it allegedly involved the sacrifice of a cock it seems highly unlikely to have had anything to do with her own ritual practice, although it makes a good story in Thelemite circles.

They seemed to Grant's eyes to get on very well together, spoke very much as equals, and to have more in common than might have been thought from her books. Indeed when Crowley later heard of her death he wondered seriously about the chances of taking over her Fraternity. However he had obviously read too much into an unexpectedly cordial meeting. The fact that she may have asked his advice over some technicalities of magical practice did not imply that she acknowledged any esoteric authority on his part.

She evidently made a good impression on the young Kenneth Grant who recounted to Alan Richardson some thirty years later that he still remembered the sparkle in her eye when she countered Crowley quip for quip. She accidentally dropped a brooch consisting of two wyvern-like creatures supporting a green stone. Crowley remarked that ten years before he would have consecrated it for her. She replied that ten years before she would have done it herself.

There was also a flurry of correspondence between the two during 1945 but this was eventually strayed, stolen and destroyed. Its contents therefore remain a mystery but as we know from her track record, she would have done nothing without direction from her inner contacts. Why then would they have encouraged her to visit Aleister Crowley?

The answer may lie in another somewhat surprising contact she made with a Mr. Tom Sumpton who, under the more resounding name of Dr. Antony Greville Gascoigne, had begun to develop a sizeable following, and published a "Golden Dawn Magazine" to which Dion Fortune contributed. He had also written a book "The Way of an Initiate" which is strongly reminiscent of her "Training and Work of an Initiate." Referred to in the script as "the man from the North", he was invited, with two of his colleagues, for an interview with the Magus Innominatus at Dion Fortune's headquarters. He left the country soon after, as the result of some problem with the police.

A long trance interview of 5th December 1944 provides an explanation for this particular uncharacteristic contact. The Magus Innominatus, revealed to Creasy and Chichester that as a member of the Great White Lodge he was responsible for the occult jurisdiction of a particular geographical area and it was this responsibility that had caused him to wish to interview "the man from the North". Chichester, who had not been present on that occasion, was provided with a brief account of the circumstances.

Well, now, it concerns the management of a jurisdiction, and I happen to be the person in charge of this jurisdiction, and this group is my "point d'appuie" on the physical plane, which I have through long years been engaged in building and getting ready for certain work, and we have had to use it for various matters before it was fully formed – that could not be helped.

But in this particular instance you had a Teaching School developed, or developing, and the man at the head of it had had a considerable amount of training in the Eastern Tradition which he was applying in the Western jurisdiction. He had no proper Western contacts but he had a good deal of knowledge. His Western teaching he got out of books, and he was using the "Golden Dawn" formulae, though not a "Golden Dawn" initiate, but he had sufficient knowledge to use them with power – so the position was a peculiar one.

Here was a man, Eastern trained, and with power, using Western formulae with power but without contacts, therefore not under control; responsible to no one, unguided, undirected, and unprotected. Had he not had a group of students he could merely have been left to his own devices, but he showed every sign of building up an organisation, growing strong and getting a number of people into difficulties. Now there were two factors, or there were really two aspects of one factor in his work which lifted him out of the realm of ordinary quackery and made it a much more serious matter. He had been taught the Eastern method of sublimation and conservation of kundalini – the sex force.

Now this is a true teaching when it is done by men in the second half of life who have performed their duty to the race in leaving sons to perform the ceremonies which every good Asiatic has performed at his death; older men in whom the full development of the personality and the glandular system has taken place. They can use this method when they are in the second half of life and the tide is falling on the physical plane, but young men cannot – and this man was taught the method as a youth, and when it is taught in such circumstances certain [auto erotic] *practices are also taught which Westerners consider are not of a desirable nature – Asiatics regard them with indifference. The truth is halfway between the two.*

In this particular case the "man from the North" made use of this technique partly as a means of disposing of his unused force, partly as a means of satisfying his emotional needs, partly to gratify his love of power. So there was being developed in this jurisdiction, in a teaching school operating on a fairly large scale, a very undesirable technique.

It was the same thing that had been developed in the Theosophical Society some years previously, and it broke the Society. [The reference is to C.W.Leadbeater and the young Krishnamurti which resulted in a scandal and court case.] *It is a condition that it is not desirable should be developed in this jurisdiction and, as always when such a condition develops, steps are taken to stamp it out – and that you have seen done.*

In order to deal with it we have to make contact with it. Now the contact has to be made through some link formed on the physical plane. In the case of the Theosophical Society it was dealt with twice. On the first occasion it was dealt with through a man who was an initiate of the Western Tradition and a member of the Theosophical Society, but the trouble started again, and on the second occasion it was dealt with by directing your present leader, the Pythoness, into that organisation to make the link, and when the work was done she was drawn out. The history of that transaction you know, the whole condition was cleared up and has given no trouble since.

In this matter of the "man from the North" we were dealing with a very much smaller organisation than the Theosophical Society, and our own organisation was very much more highly developed than it was in those days, so we did not send anybody into their organisation to make the contact, we sent for the leader, and he came.

So that whole story was a matter of the discipline of the jurisdiction, of the nipping in the bud of undesirable factors. Things that it is not expedient should spread through the group mind of the race. Ordinary charlatanry is negligible but now and again there are magical factors which could be really serious and could start a corrupt Tradition, and these we deal with.

Ordinary rascality we don't deal with. The many personal shortcomings of the man known as "the Ace" [Aleister Crowley] *we have left to the law of the land. But now and again spiritual wickedness starts, and that we deal with, as speedily as may be, because it can spread and corrupt.*

He was asked how they first became aware of this spiritual wickedness.

Let me put it this way. Whoever is in charge of a jurisdiction visualises it as spread out like a map below him, and that map is illuminated in places. There are spots of spiritual power which light up – this is all astral imagery – and to the vision of the watcher they light up with different coloured lights; so he becomes aware of what is going on in the mental atmosphere in his jurisdiction because the particular spot will glow, and if you get a particular spot glowing with what I call a smoky light, then you bring it into focus and find out what is happening.

For instance, supposing in a particular instance there is a red light with smoky black streaks in it, one would know here was a magical power factor with something wrong. Or again, one might see the green light of the elemental contacts streaked with various swirls of black smoke. Now that blackness is caused by the disintegration of force which would normally take place in the Qliphothic spheres. So the watchers, when they observe that, check up on that centre, and just as you would focus a pair of opera glasses or a telescope on it, they focus, and get the details and inspect it at close quarters.

Asked if they could pin down the house so that they could observe the human being without any physical human contact intervening, the M.I. replied:

Yes, they get it all right. Once you have established your district you have got it fairly well located. You focus on your district and then you soon get your house – if the house is a place where an atmosphere is built. Having got that it is not difficult to get the persons concerned, but to make a contact itself on the physical plane, physical plane means have to be used.

Now it is always possible to deal with the whole situation from the inner planes and break the whole thing up from that level, but it is always, if possible, desirable to give the person concerned the chance to put things right. And this is especially the case where a person is of mixed, good and evil, character, which most humans are, and so, instead of breaking the whole thing up from the inner planes, it is our practice to send an initiate in to make a contact and see whether the condition can be cleared up; and if possible to help rescue individuals who are being innocently victimised.

Now because you did not get immediate results from that contact, or any similar contact, do not think that nothing has been achieved. The person who has been contacted, although they do nothing about it, may not necessarily have forgotten it, and the leaven may work quietly. But we never turn on the destructive ray until we have given opportunity to even the most unpromising material to reform if they want to – somebody is always sent in to make the contact.

In the light of all this one may well wonder about the real purpose behind the talk of bizarre rituals and the accidental dropping of magical jewellery on a certain day in Hastings.

Another interesting point arose at this particular address from which we have extensively quoted. The Magus Innominatus was asked whether the inner plane communicators behind Dion Fortune had remained pretty well constant over the years.

The reply was that they had – but that they evolved, just as did those upon the physical plane. He went on to say:

My position now is very different from what it was when I served the person who was referred to as the "old Greek".

From thus it would seem that back in 1923 the inner plane Master who really called the shots, despite his humble demeanour, was the one known as Socrates. He was responsible for the team that brought through "The Cosmic Doctrine" between 1923 and 1925, which is a more significant text than many people think, who have only given it a cursory reading.

It also implies that the work of Erskine and Carstairs, particularly in 1922/33 was the subsidiary one of preparing Dion Fortune and C.T.Loveday for that event. However, since then, it was principally Erskine who had gone on to forge the group into a Fraternity.

Above, left: Dion Fortune, from a group photograph in the mid 1930s.

Above, right: Contemporary print of Thomas Erskine as a young lawyer in the late 18th century.

Below: Advertisement for the Christian Mystic Lodge in *The Occult Review* for February 1926. Also an early advertisement for the Community (later Fraternity) of the Inner Light, probably in 1928.

Christian Mystic Lodge
OF THE THEOSOPHICAL SOCIETY.

President : DION FORTUNE (Miss VIOLET M. FIRTH),
3 Queensborough Terrace, Bayswater, W.2.

PUBLIC LECTURES— Mondays at 5.30 and 8.15, the latter being a study group conducted by the President.

Read the Transactions of the Lodge, price **3d.** or 3,- per annum post free, a monthly magazine dealing with ESOTERIC CHRISTIANITY. Editor: DION FORTUNE.

Sane Occultism, Independent Outlook, Active Practical Work. Specimen copy and syllabus of lectures free. Apply—*Secretary.*

COMMUNITY OF THE INNER LIGHT
Warden - - *DION FORTUNE.*

The Community of the Inner Light is a fraternity whose purpose it is to pursue the study of Mysticism and Esoteric Science. Its ideals are Christian and its methods are Western.

It maintains a Lecture Centre and Library in London at 3 Queensborough Terrace, Bayswater. Public lectures are given on Mondays at 8.15 p.m. by Dion Fortune throughout each term. Syllabus on application. Admission to all lectures and study groups is free, all contributions being voluntary.

THE CHALICE ORCHARD CLUB, Glastonbury, Somerset, is maintained as a hostel and pilgrimage centre. It is open from Whitsuntide to Michaelmas. Terms from £2 12s. 6d. a week.

"THE INNER LIGHT." Edited by Dion Fortune. A monthly magazine devoted to Mystical Christianity, Esoteric Science, and the Psychology of Super-consciousness. Price 6d. 6s. 6d. per annum, post free. Specimen copy sent free on request.

BOOKS BY DION FORTUNE.
"Esoteric Philosophy of Love and Marriage." Rider. 3s. 6d.
"Secrets of Dr. Taverner." Fiction. Noel Douglas. A Study in Esoteric Medicine. Cheap edition, 2s. 6d.
"The Demon Lover." Fiction. Noel Douglas. A Study in the abuse of Occult Power. Cheap edition, 2s. 6d.
Syllabus of the lectures, tariff of Chalice Orchard Club, and all information may be obtained from the Secretary, 3 Queensborough Terrace, Bayswater, W.2. Tel. Park 7217.

Dust jacket for *The Demon Lover* (1927) designed by Mary Bligh Bond.

"The Thing came out into the moonlight following the girl across the garden." (See 'BLOOD-LUST' inside)

Above, left: *Royal Magazine* cover of 1922 featuring 'Blood-Lust', the first of the Dr. Taverner stories.

Above, right: Illustration of Dr. Taverner by Leo Bates.

Below: Group photograph at Chalice Orchard in the mid 1930s. W.K. Creasy standing on his own, centre, Miss G.P. Lathbury and C.T. Loveday fourth and fifth from left in front row. Probably Colonel C.R.F. Seymour seated alone at front.

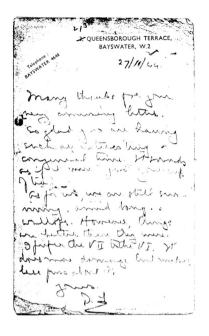

Left: Postcard from Dion
Fortune to Margaret Lumley
Brown (holidaying in Scotland
in November 1944) when
London was still under
bombardment by flying bombs
and rockets.

Text: *Many thanks for your very
amusing letter. So glad you are
having such an interesting and
congenial time. It sounds as if it
were just your cup of tea. As for
us, we are still surviving, amid
bangs and wallops. However,
things are better than they were.
I prefer the V.II to the V.I. It
does more damage but makes
less fuss about it. Yours, D.F.*

Below: Fragment of some
student verses by Violet Firth at
Studley Horticultural College.

V. Firth. Poultry Dept. 19..

I wish my mother could see me now, with a
                    hen-coop under my arm
And very short skirts & very big boots & blisters
                        all over my palm,
Cuddling a broody old hen by the wing, for we're
                    moving the ...... from B.
( ) used to go to receptions once
Dances, theatres & concerts once
Knitting, races & rest cures once
But now I am only P.D.

My nose is all spotty with freckles, my skirt is a
                    waistband & frill.
And the things I've used my penknife for would
                    make my sisters ill.
But I jolly well know how the poultry's run & where
                    things ought to be.
( ) used to be massaged & manicured once
Powders, face creams & lotions once
Puffs & switches & pin-curls once
But now I am just P.D.

That is what we are known as, we are the persons
                    to blame
For begging the loan of a tin-tack & fitting a
                    shed to the same
Can't even look at the dairy — or they grab all
                    the milk-pails & flee
Though they pasture their cows on our hen-food
                    For nobody loves the P.D.

36

ON THE THRESHOLD OF THE FUTURE

The first steps in preparing for the rebuilding of the Fraternity in the post-war era became evident in March 1943 with the announcement of a new Study Course for those who aspired to membership. She explained in a Monthly Letter the kind of members they wished to attract and the type of work they might be expected to do.

The Mystery Tradition has often been likened to an iceberg, of which but a small proportion is above the surface and the great mass out of sight. But a small part of an esoteric Order exists on the physical plane; all the greater and more important aspects are on the inner planes. The mundane aspect of an Order is practically nothing but a training school wherein mind training is done – a mind training designed to serve spiritual ends, for schools of the Right Hand Path are most careful that their training shall never be used for ends of personal power and aggrandisement. Those who are fully trained learn to use the channel of communication with the inner planes for the receiving of teaching and instruction and the bringing through of that concentrated form of spiritual force that enables the service of God and man to be performed with power. It is obvious that such work can only be entrusted to carefully chosen and trained persons, but we found in the days when we threw open our doors during the Siege of London that the tensions of war had brought spiritual growth to the nation en masse, and that a very great many people were ready and able to co-operate in the work of the Mystery Tradition.

She went on to say how getting into touch with the Mystery Tradition depended on two things, knowing where to look, and having the right approach.

The right approach was not only having a selfless desire to serve but also a willingness to observe a discipline.

The right place to look was on the inner planes.

> *Granted the right kind of character, it is only necessary to indicate where to look in order for that the search may be rewarded; for those who approach in the right spirit carry the key in their hands. The place in which to look for the Mystery Tradition is on the inner planes. We turn inward, into the Silence, to make our contacts, not to any spot on the physical earth.*
>
> *The contact with the Masters on the inner planes is made by thinking about them. The pictorial imagination is one of the principle instruments used in esoteric work, and by careful training and constant practice it is brought to a very fine edge. In consequence, it is possible to build up very clear-cut and detailed mental images. These images are, in reality, astral thought forms, and they are the channels through which the invisible forces work. In order to enable the imagination to get to function, it has to be provided with the material, just as a novelist who wanted to write an historical novel would study the period in which he proposed to lay his scene until he could picture it in all its detail of dress, architecture and customs.*

The basis for such an imaginative approach, she suggested, was contained in her two little books "The Esoteric Orders and their Work" and "The Training and Work of an Initiate". Accordingly they formed the basis of the Study Course which they were now providing.

> *These books give a general concept of the Mystery Tradition and its workings and the student who has read them, and thought about them, especially the latter, can, if he has the right kind of character, pick up his contacts with the Mystery Tradition on the Inner Planes. Or to be more precise, the Tradition will pick him up.*
>
> *To discuss the ideas contained in these books under the direction of a teacher or group leader is the best way of getting into contact with the Tradition, but where personal presence is impossible, we are arranging for students to correspond with members of our Fraternity and so make a personal contact, even if an indirect one. We are not asking those who join our Initial Training Course to pass examinations, but only to think about, and either write or talk about, the ideas in these two little books.*

This may seem very simple and unexacting, but it is not quite as haphazard as it looks, for unless there is the "right approach", nothing will happen. But those who bring to the altar of the Mysteries acceptable gifts of character and dedication will, sooner or later, and more often sooner than later, find that in a sudden flash of reality the Masters have made contact.

From the beginning, and right through to the end, in her plans for the Fraternity of the future, contact with the Masters was the fundamental rock upon which Dion Fortune based her occultism, and she expected this contact to be made, in some form or other, by all who rallied to the call.

Such a flash is usually a brief moment of illumination; it is impossible to hold it for longer than that in any intensity; it may, in a less intense form, or as the aftermath of such a moment, continue for some days as a state of spiritual insight and exaltation, but it never by any chance continues long. If it did, it would disorganise the mind by its intensity, for the untrained human mind is not built to carry such voltages, hence the prolonged training that is necessary in order to attain to the higher grades of initiation. But some sudden sense of reality there can and should be as a result of study along the lines indicated. It may be as faint and elusive as the fragrance of flowers in the dark; but it will nevertheless be something outside the ordinary range of experience and it will convey the sense that the Invisible Realities are real – that they have been known at first hand, and that one is no longer dependent upon second hand testimony for knowledge of the Secret Wisdom and all that proceeds from it.

Once this flash of reality has come – and gone – the student is in an entirely different position, for he has been "contacted"...

Those who follow the Mystery Tradition do not need to depend upon second hand evidence. Ours is not a school which teaches a doctrine only. Unless we can give first hand experience we consider we have failed to initiate.

Of those who were already within the Fraternity at this time and had joined during 1941 when Dion Fortune still contrived to give occasional lectures, one was Charles Arthur Chichester, who was later to succeed Dion Fortune as Warden of the Fraternity.

Born in 1904 into a semi-aristocratic Irish family he had been educated at Stonyhurst, the Roman Catholic public school which the men of his family had attended since Elizabethan times. He had, however, broken away from family traditions at an early age and emigrated to Canada, through which he travelled in a succession of jobs, nearly freezing to death on the way, until in 1926 he became an executive of the Asiatic Petroleum Company in Japan. Here he must have begun to take an interest in esoteric subjects for there exists a copy of Dion Fortune's novel "The Demon Lover" with his book plate and signature and the inscription "Tokyo 1927" the date the book was newly published.

He was back in England when the 2nd World War broke out and joined the Royal Air Force. He was made an intelligence officer on account of his Far Eastern experience and posted to the Air Ministry in London. This allowed him to make contact with Dion Fortune, to one of whose lectures he turned up.

He was at first disappointed with what he found and frankly told her so, saying that he had come seeking bread but she had only offered him stones. She was however apparently impressed by his character and demeanour and invited him to investigate a little further. This he did, and soon made his mark, working closely with W.K.Creasy and Dion Fortune. She came indeed to look upon him as her "young Sun priest". Creasy, then and later, was more respected for his "Earth" contacts.

In a letter to me of July 8th 1970 Arthur Chichester recalled the circumstances of those times.

> These were the war years and the absence of many members and restrictions generally made workings rather difficult.
>
> After becoming Magus in 1943 I did special work with Dion Fortune and indeed saw much of her. There was research into Atlantean origins, and much teaching from the Chancellor now available in our papers and reflected in policy. She was also interested in psychology and its application especially on Jungian lines – hence what were once called "Green Ray" workings. As some sound knowledge of Greek, Egyptian and British mythology

was needed and the Group remarkably uneducated in these
matters she and I were the only workers. This, however, did not
touch the Group or its basic policy as she had not completed her
psychological research though she had had some analysis. She
was considering writing a "Psychological Qabalah" but died
before she could start it. The Greater Mysteries then were not in
being save for a few members specially enrolled, but the Grail
contacts had been made, though not used in any depth. There
was also the very Christian "Guild of the Master Jesus" open to
the general public.

The Guild of the Master Jesus had begun its Sunday services again
in the Spring of 1942, and the Monday evening lectures were also
recommenced. Dion Fortune spoke on the first Monday in each
month, the other Mondays being covered by whatever members of
the Fraternity happened to be available. This included members of
the old guard, such as the librarian Miss Brine on "Merlin and
Tintagel" and Katherine Barlow on "Christianity and Magic" and
"Wisdom and Fairy Lore". New members were represented by
Arthur Chichester, who spoke on "Entering upon our Heritage"
and Rosina Mann on "Magic".

Rosina Mann's talk received a rave review from Charles
Cammell, editor of the Spiritualist newspaper "Light", although
from his remarks it was obviously not so much about magic as an
approach to mysticism based upon the innocence of the child.

The theme of Mrs. Mann's lecture was Magic, and she approached
that tenebrous and vexed subject in a manner the most original,
yet on this very account, with a comprehension that was profound.
For it was in childhood that she found the key to the science of
the Mage; it was the Child whom with absolute vision, she
recognised to be the true Seer, the master Magician. In perfect
purity and essential spirituality she discovered the true and
straight path to the kingdom of that higher Imagination which is
the temple of Transcendental Magic, the one and only Magic
worthy that exalted name, all others being deceptions, base
travesties, false coin.

This requires mention in the light of later developments when she
played an influential role in the Fraternity's affairs from 1962 and
became its virtual head in 1979.

She had joined, with her husband, at much the same as Arthur Chichester, and acted as scribe in work with Dion Fortune, Creasy and Chichester, and was appointed Magus in 1944. She ran into some difficulties with Dion Fortune, however, during 1945, who accused her of some misdemeanour, apparently quite unjustly.

Although shortage of paper did not allow republication of "The Inner Light Magazine" Dion Fortune began to use her Monthly Letters as a vehicle for long articles that could be eventually made up into book form. These comprised "The Esoteric Philosophy of Astrology" between November 1942 and February 1943 and "Principles of Hermetic Philosophy" between April 1943 and March 1944, in the latter building on from the practical considerations of "The Circuit of Force" which had dealt with the etheric vehicle, to work upon the astral aura and building elements from the astrological birth chart within it.

In 1944 she also restimulated her interest in Jungian psychology. She had first made acquaintance with Freudian theories as early as 1914 when they were attracting popular attention in this country, and although she had realised them to contain some truth felt that they were essentially incomplete as a statement of the condition of the human soul, as were Adler's rival theories. It was not until she came to the study of Jung's Zurich school that she found a psychology that could be correlated with esoteric psychology.

She had of course been in correspondence with leading Jungian psychologists for some years, but was much encouraged by the publication of an introductory book "The Psychology of C.G.Jung" by Dr. Jolande Jacobi. This was soon added to the essential reading list for Study Course students and so remained for some years.

Nor did Dion Fortune consider psychology a substitute for the occult tradition, as so frequently happens when even quite advanced students abandon occultism for psychology or try to explain occultism in terms of psychology. As Dion Fortune had already remarked in connection with her fiction, she had long gone through the stage of trying to explain occultism in terms of psychology, and had moved on to trying to explain psychology in terms of occultism. In her Monthly Letter for May 1944 she sought a common language and bridge between the two disciplines.

With Jungian psychology the ancient Mystery Tradition can join hands. They may not speak the same language, but they have the same outlook. All that is needed is a Rosetta Stone bearing parallel inscriptions in different languages, the known and the unknown, to enable translation to begin and an immense wealth of data and experience to be made available for both sides of the council table

Psychologists have long been at work trying to penetrate the mystery symbolism from the hither side of the Veil of the Temple. Unfortunately they made use of the Freudian reductive technique of "nothing but", and the Temple of the Mysteries soon lay in a heap of rubble at their feet, its beauty destroyed and its significance lost. They were then able to explore at their leisure the drains and cess-pools under the foundations and discover to their delight that the soul, like the body, has certain needs that require sanitary arrangements; but is such a discovery, absorbing though it may be to those who have a taste for such things, any adequate substitute for the domes and spires of the architect's vision?

Let us, for a change, approach psychology from the yonder side of the Veil of the Mysteries. It will be an exercise not without its practical value, in my humble opinion. I would say to my fellow occultists, who love me not because of the amount of debunking I have done in my time: "Here is something by which you can check up on your findings and learn what is true and what is not, if you have a liking for such a proceeding."

To the psychologists I would say: "Here is no poor relation, no illegitimate child of orthodoxy, but an heir to great estates, born of ancient lineage, coming with both hands full of jewels."

As a beginning to any such approach she suggested the study of Dr. Jacobi's introduction to Jung's psychology in conjunction with "The Mystical Qabalah".

Throughout the time of reconstruction of the Lesser Mysteries Dion Fortune continued to give trance addresses at the Equinox and Solstice lodges. From these it is apparent that this building process started at the Autumnal Equinox of 1941 when the 1st Degree was instituted from scratch once again. In subsequent addresses through to the Autumnal Equinox of 1943 detailed attention is given to ritual technique and performance, sometimes with instruction, occasionally with admonition.

Something of the mode of operation of the inner workings of the
Fraternity was given at the Winter Solstice address of 1943.

*The work of the Mysteries is performed by a group of adepts
and initiates making an organisation, preparing candidates,
instructing students, building a Temple, gathering together
books and manuscripts, making the symbols, arranging all
mundane affairs in connection with the studies and work
undertaken: but all this is as an unlit fire or dead ashes unless
the Masters direct the forces into the form thus built. Equally,
the Masters can only contact rare and highly gifted individuals
unless there is an organisation for training and instructing
neophytes and bringing them to the point where they are ready
to receive initiation.*

*The two aspects must always work together, otherwise forces
cannot manifest and form is inert and lifeless.*

*You have patiently wrought your form, you await the influx of
power to make it functional. We, for our part, await the completion
of the form in order that the power may be poured in.*

At the Vernal Equinox of 1944 they were told that they had come to
an end and a beginning. They had achieved ritual working of great
excellence. They stood in the darkness of a dawn with the rim of the
rising sun just appearing above the eastern horizon. Affairs would
move fast now, as tides of affairs on the inner planes were now
flowing. What was built now would stand.

Those who had remained faithful through the long hours of
darkness and slack water under great difficulties, in many cases in
great danger, were thanked. It was harder to keep the night watch
than to advance with the dawn, and there was a special blessing on
those who had kept the night watch.

They were now advancing to the dawn of a new epoch. Old
things were passing away, all things were becoming new. And as
Our Lord had said "I have yet many things to tell you, but you
cannot bear them now."

Dion Fortune's last trance address was given at the Autumnal
Equinox of 1945, and the first in time of peace after the years of
war in Europe. It was also marked by a number of resignations,
upon which the communicator commented. The late war years were
times of radical change and a number of resignations were only to
be expected. Some who had served long and well now needed a

desired rest, whilst others had not grown with the work, or were not readily able to adapt to the necessary changes that had to be made.

His peroration in this talk were the last recorded words of Dion Fortune in the flesh:

Think of the Elder Brethren as men more evolved than you are and without physical vehicles of manifestation. They are neither angels or gods, but human souls standing higher than you do on that great stairway, that ladder on which the souls of just men made perfect come and go between the planes. For there is a brotherhood in the Mysteries between all servers whether they serve in the body or out of it.

There is a comradeship of the Path between all who have trodden it whether upon the Sacred Mountain of ancient Atlantis, or in the Temple Courts of Egypt, or the crypts and the secret meeting places of the Mysteries that exist even unto this day.

All are brethren. All meet in the brotherhood of the Lodge, each according to his grade in the hierarchy of the Mysteries. Each equally under discipline.

Every brother among us has the right of appeal to the Masters, none is refused access if he claims it. If he claims it worthily he learns that which he wants to know. If he claims it unworthily he will learn that which he needs to know. Thus do the Mysteries live on with the Eternal Life on both planes together.

Dion Fortune felt unwell and was unable to give an address at the Winter Solstice meeting of 1945. Two members present had come up from Chalice Orchard, where they lived and which they maintained for the Fraternity. They were Mary Gilchrist and "Uncle Robbie", a retired dental surgeon.

Just after the meeting, Robbie was asked to go up to Dion Fortune's room to look at an infected tooth that was giving her trouble. He came back down the stairs ashen faced, bursting out to Mary Gilchrist, "She's had it!" Apparently from what he saw he was able to diagnose leukaemia.

Within a fortnight, on January 6th 1946, Dion Fortune was dead. Her remains were taken from the Middlesex Hospital for burial at Glastonbury, where they still lie, with those of Charles Loveday close by, who followed her shortly from the Bethesda Nursing Home at Glastonbury. The burials of both of them were conducted by the vicar of St. John's, Glastonbury, that great champion of Christian Avalon, friend of Bligh Bond and Alice Buckton, the Reverend L.S.Lewis.

Ex Deo nascimur – In Jesu morimur – Per Spiritum Sanctum reviviscimus

Epilogue

THE POST MORTEM HERITAGE
1946 – 1999

37
THE GREATER MYSTERIES

The Fraternity of the Inner Light thus passed into the post-war era under new leadership, and on seeking status as a charitable institution, its name was changed to the Society of the Inner Light, a legal refinement rather than a signal of any change in policy.

Arthur Chichester and W.K.Creasy found themselves to be the principal members, with Mr. Creasy in the senior position, having previously been Deputy Warden and a member since 1934.

An immediate problem was to find a replacement for Dion Fortune to function as a medium, or "pythoness", so that verbal contact could be maintained with the inner plane adepti. One possibility was Margaret Lumley Brown, although this seemed at the time something of a forlorn hope.

She had joined the Fraternity in 1942 and a number of eyebrows had been raised when Dion Fortune gave her accommodation in the house. This was seen largely as an act of charity towards someone who was somewhat disorganised and thought incapable of looking after herself without the support of her sister who had recently died. She had not distinguished herself at all in ritual work, to say the least, and justified her existence in the house as a somewhat inefficient parlour maid and short order cook.

However, it was recognised that she had some natural psychic abilities, and so, banking on this, she was relocated in Dion Fortune's old apartments and told to try to develop her mediumistic abilities as best she could, in preparation for giving a trance address in three months' time at the Summer Solstice meeting of 1946.

In some trepidation, this is what she set out to do, spending at least an hour each morning and afternoon on the task. Fortunately her diaries have survived, giving a detailed account of her experiences. She succeeded in making contact not only with Erskine, who was referred to in those days as the Magus Supremus, but even with the late Dion Fortune herself, who began to coach her in the task that lay ahead.

Thus in her diary for 18th April 1946, we find a record of Dion Fortune, apparently as large as life, giving her detailed instructions:

> We are entering the Solstice in two months. By then I hope you are able to continue my work transmitting in Lodge. It could be, I think, by then. You will have to be a great deal more sure of yourself as a medium. I note that you are still afraid of getting a wrong sentence. You will have to work yourself up to it as I did. You must count yourself a genuine medium of the occult type – that includes bringing through these messages from Masters and Entities as well as inspirational messages from the inner planes. It is entirely different from what is known to Spiritualism.

And again on 6th May:

> Now that we are approaching the Solstice you will be able to see better how we work and not to be so unhappy about it. Your first efforts were "inward" words and that is good but it is wiser to get a message telepathically, as you are now beginning to, sentence by sentence. I want you to feel that you are able to hear far more surely! Don't regret the long time spent in learning a different way! I want you to be strong enough to take responsibility for working in harmony with the higher forces yourself, and not to be always doing it with dread. The Magus Supremus is doing all he can to condition you. I want you to get the work into good shape and not balk at it.
>
> ...Are you able to understand that though I am not seen, I am fully able to see you and all done here? Try to realise better all you have found in this work and do not treat it as a side issue, and the material things first. I should like you also to realise that now you are a medium as I – a cosmic one – not merely a psychic transmitter, and that is what we are doing to you to make you receive these matters day by day.

It would thus appear, that whatever rumours may have been circulated about Dion Fortune being something of a spent force in her latter days, she was certainly showing little signs of it after her death!

Margaret Lumley Brown was not her only contact however. She had apparently been training another, younger medium, before her physical demise. This was Anne Fox, whose future role and status was outlined to Margaret Lumley Brown in a contact with the Magus Supremus on May 4th:

As to your actual work, I am about to define that. You are waiting still a little for the worker in touch with you to come forth too – I speak of the young priestess. She will make a new grade soon, as she will be in the High Priestess's [i.e. Dion Fortune's] *place – incognito, as it were! – and you must be her follower along the path itself, towards Eternity. You will find her actual knowledge far deeper than your own and her actual development a good deal better; but you have got higher up the scale lately as a result of entering the Greater Mysteries. She will also be a medium of help for you too by means of her actual connection with the High Priestess. I would like to say we who are here do not care about the physical age or the distinctions of the mundane plane. We refer solely to the inner life and the experience of it. In that she is your senior. Nevertheless you have, as well, a great deal of the physical seniority as regards your knowledge and experience of the world and also your intellectual realisation and attainment. That is why I can use you more completely before I have trained you as, in her case, the High Priestess had already trained her fairly well before beginning. We who are here realise the discrepancy of this and you have a good deal more to learn before being proficient in the actual working of the trance.*

Do not let this worry you because all of us have to wait and learn before we are able to contend with greater work.

In the event, Margaret Lumley Brown successfully delivered the Summer Solstice address and went on from strength to strength over the years. As Charles Fielding and Carr Collins remark in "The Story of Dion Fortune" she was *"probably the finest medium and psychic of this century, although the public never knew her. She raised the arts of psychism and mediumship to an entirely new level and the high quality of communication that came through her has not been equalled."* Examples of her work have now been prepared for publication, together with something of her life story, in "Pythoness" (edited by Gareth Knight, Sun Chalice Books).

The role of Anne Fox was rather different from that of Margaret Lumley Brown. She undertook a very close inner relationship with the late Warden, in the interests of trying to finish off certain work that Dion Fortune had left undone. There was, however a certain risk in such close involvement, which became, in effect, almost a complete overshadowing of her personality. This could only be a relatively temporary arrangement and it came to an end in 1950.

For her part, Margaret Lumley Brown became the principal amanuensis for Erskine, the Magus Supremus, and was given the major project of developing the Arthurian Formula that had been instigated by Dion Fortune and Maiya Tranchell Hayes.

By 1947, aided and abetted by promptings from Dion Fortune, mainly through Anne Fox, it was strongly suggested that Arthur Chichester should take over as Warden of the Fraternity. After the initial shock W.K.Creasy stood aside with good grace and remained a stalwart member of the group until his death some twenty-five years later, acting during this time as its Honorary Treasurer.

Chichester set to work to impose a discipline of smooth working within the domestic and office functions of the Fraternity. Such indeed had been the first requirement in the very early days when Erskine had impressed upon Penry Evans the need for smooth running of the mundane organisation for there to be any chance of higher spiritual work.

Gradually they built up a full system of three Lesser Mystery Degrees, as had been in place before the war, although now they were probably worked at greater depth. It took at least a year to work through the curriculum of any grade, and for some members far longer than that - a far cry from the three months that was possible in earlier days.

Something of a crisis occurred in 1950 in the breaking of the close inner contact with Dion Fortune. It is not clear whether it all became too much for Anne Fox or too much for Arthur Chichester, or possibly a combination of both. By this time Anne Fox was no doubt feeling the strain of being a substitute Dion Fortune, and Arthur Chichester was apparently also beginning to feel that he was now capable of acting as Warden without need for detailed oversight from the previous one.

This cutting of the contact, apparently in a somewhat peremptory manner, came as something of a shock to all immediately concerned, not least to the discarnate Dion Fortune, and caused a certain amount of what was later called astro/etheric congestion. A concern that others might try to renew the contact in a like manner, with no very good results to themselves or anyone else, brought about an edict to destroy existing photographs of Dion Fortune. This was generally perceived by those outside the group as a somewhat draconian attempt to prevent the development of a personality cult, but had its reasons somewhat beyond the apparently obvious.

The general direction of the group now became the development of a Greater Mysteries system as a communal effort, which was something of an innovation within the Fraternity. Certainly work at Greater Mystery level had always been performed by Dion Fortune herself and her immediate colleagues, but now the aim was to achieve this through the function of an organised group of trained initiates rather than to rely on the gifts of talented individuals.

By the mid 1950's the Greater Mysteries was working in two grades, an Outer and an Inner. In the Outer the Adeptus Minor was encouraged to write his or her own workings for performance by the group, and there were also one or two set pieces based upon the Holy Grail traditions and some of the early Glastonbury scripts. Initiates in this Degree no longer had an aspirational motto for a Mystery Name but were known as Son or Daughter of a particular deity or archetype. This name was conferred upon them at their Greater Mystery initiation when offering their unreserved dedication to the work, and represented the evolutionary type of their Essential Self.

In the Inner Greater Mysteries a new Mystery Name was conferred that at this time was based upon some particular aspect of a character from the Arthurian Legends. This line of work had its origins in the Arthurian Formula and the idea behind it was known as "the redemption of the archetypes". This had to be achieved by the initiate's realisations and life in the world, and was not quite such an invitation to quasi-romantic posing as might be supposed.

With the intense pressures that can come upon the initiate in advanced esoteric work it was felt advisable to continue to seek some kind of psychotherapeutic support. Unfortunately traditional Jungian analysis had proved impracticable, on grounds of time and expense, although Dion Fortune had taken a great deal of trouble to try to find ways of adapting this form of psychology to esoteric ends.

This was the motive behind an interest in dianetics and scientology that appeared on the scene in the early 1950's. This interest began and continued cautiously in the course of the subsequent years, coming to a climax in 1962, although tapering off after that, and several members of the Society became trained in its techniques. There was also interest in other therapeutic systems such as the Alexander Technique of muscular re-education that has etheric extensions that are by no means always recognised. Another activity upon the alternative scene that was also investigated at that time was a movement known as Subud.

Thus the Society was by no means unaware of or unconcerned with other movements upon the esoteric scene but on the other hand it no longer continued its previous mission of actively taking its message to the public; it published no magazine and laid on no lectures.

However, as to its inner organisation, despite the higher power levels of the work, it was less enclosed than it had been in earlier days. In the earliest days the Society had started out with the name and ideals of being a Community and although the name was soon changed to Fraternity this conception was ever in the background. In Dion Fortune's day, and also for some years after, those at the hub of the work virtually lived the lives of a contemplative religious order, with ceremonial robes being worn within the house for most of the time and members' rooms being virtually esoteric chapels as well.

Arthur Chichester gradually encouraged a more open and relaxed mode of work, in the belief that initiates should not be cut off from the general concerns of the world at large and group mind of society through living a separate kind of life from the vast majority of their fellows. Adepts and initiates should take their place in the world, not be hived off from it.

Continued publication of Dion Fortune's works was encouraged.

Frank Clive-Ross, a former assistant editor on "The Occult Review" had started up his own publishing company, "The Aquarian Press", and under his aegis the novels and some of the old pre-war titles were reissued. In 1949 "The Cosmic Doctrine" finally saw the light of day as a published book.

At Wednesday evening discussion groups, "The Cosmic Doctrine" and "The Mystical Qabalah" were studied. For those who lived near the headquarters there was a plethora of activities in which to join, with five degrees being actively worked apart from approved individual initiatives and the general chores of keeping a house, study course, and library running, together with the constant typing up, duplication and circulation of papers that were the inevitable result of the mediumistic work of Margaret Lumley Brown and others.

In 1956 a completely new work by Dion Fortune was published, her novel "Moon Magic". She had probably started to write this before the war, but had some difficulty in making it gel. She made no less than six unsuccessful starts before, on starting to write it in the first person, she found it began to flow remarkably well.

The new work attracted much attention and restimulated interest not only in Dion Fortune herself but also in her powerful heroine Vivien or Lilith Le Fay Morgan, and raised a certain amount of speculation as to how closely Dion Fortune might have become identified with this character. She herself had made some quite provocative remarks in this respect in her Introduction to the book.

Who and what is Lilith, and why did she live on after the book about her was finished, and insist on appearing again? Have I furnished myself with a dark familiar?

and:

I can only know that Lilith lives after a curious manner of her own; she lives for others as well as for me; and it may well be that to some of those who read these pages she will come as a shadowy figure half-seen in the twilight of the mind.

This is great publicity material, and also has more than a grain of truth within it, although the only readers at the time this was written would have been her immediate friends and associates.

However, the ability of certain fictional characters to come alive in the imagination, not only of the author, but of readers as well, is not uncommon. Some authors are better providers of such characters than others. Charles Dickens or Shakespeare are supreme examples, but there are many fictional characters produced by lesser writers that are capable of seeming vividly objective, such as Sherlock Holmes, James Bond, even Superman or Tarzan. Such characters often answer, in the function of modern myths and legends, to certain unfulfilled needs of the soul in a greater or lesser number of people.

It seems that Vivien or Lilith Le Fay Morgan fulfilled these characteristics for some people on the esoteric scene. Indeed, this had been Dion Fortune's intention in writing her occult fiction, even if after "The Winged Bull" she thought she might have failed. It would seem, however, that in the protagonist of her last two novels she at last succeeded.

Some thought that the character might represent certain parts of the author's personality or even inner self, either cut off or repressed and seeking expression or compensation – perhaps fulfilling a function imposed by personal karma or destiny. Either way, it could have a powerful effect upon others who were sufficiently attuned to it.

It caused a fair amount of speculation. Arthur Chichester, for instance wondered, only half in jest, if in her last days he had not hastened her death by encouraging her to identify with the character she had created. There is a certain amount of conflicting evidence with regard to this. Bernard Bromage reckons that on the last occasion he met her she was no longer power dressing in the old "Sea Priestess" way of long cloaks and floppy hats as in the pre-war years.

At any event an attempt was made to clarify the minds of members as to which was the real Dion Fortune and which the fictional projection, by performing the old Rite of Isis. This was a moving experience for some people, including myself. Unfortunately, for those who had not known her in the flesh, the lack of a photograph of the physical Dion Fortune now proved something of a handicap in sorting fact from fiction, for the fictional character tended to make the more vivid impression upon the imagination. The few photographs that have gradually come to light over the years did not do so until some time later.

However, if one had read a great deal of Dion Fortune's other writings, one was more likely to be able to home in on to her essential self. This, if one were seeking for an image, might be better represented by the famous statue of the Demeter of Knidos. Bernard Bromage's assessment of her character on the lecture platform confirms this, as did Arthur Chichester in conversation with me. Or, if one were to think in terms of Tarot Trump images, she contained more of the Empress than the High Priestess.

I had a particularly strong experience, and a salutary realisation of just how powerful magical images could be, when on the way home from the first of these Rite of Isis evocations when I had to undertake a bicycle ride at night westward along a long country road when the horned moon was setting. To my stimulated imagination a great figure of Isis kept building up underneath the crescent, rather like Apuleius' vision of the goddess in "The Golden Ass". This was all very well and reasonably under control until I noticed a red jewel upon her horned moon crown, which was so vivid as to seem physically real, and I thus began to fear I might be hallucinating. However, as Mr. Creasy reassured me with a newspaper cutting in response to my subsequent report, what I had seen was in fact physically there, it was a lunation of Mars, visible in the late evening of 6th February 1957. I do not regard astrology as a very exact science but it is synchronicities such as this which cause me to retain a certain respect for its possibilities.

From here on Margaret Lumley Brown was deputed to make a series of regular contacts with Dion Fortune, in a series that extended from February through to August of 1957. These were not at the intense personal level as had been the case with Anne Fox several years before. There was still, however, a strong personal element in the communications. One of the first recalled an unfortunate incident with regard to Rosina Mann. The diary entry reads:

I was profoundly aware of a mirror with a chain on it building up and realised the appearance of one I had forgotten which figured in an unfortunate episode about twelve years ago – owing to the late Warden's taking a prejudiced action in the matter thereby causing a grave wrong to be done to another. She said that she wished it known that she was most ashamed and sorry about the matter.

She not only specifically asked that this message be passed on but referred to it again the following week to ask if this had been done. Oddly enough it was this same year that Rosina Mann departed for the United States, not to return until the end of 1961. The late Warden also remarked that she felt troubled about some of her actions during physical life and felt she had been unfair and "over-powerful" to some within the group. She also regretted that she might not have aligned herself sufficiently with the Christ-force but had followed an inclination to concentrate more upon the Green Ray.

She repeated what she had once written before about her novels, that properly understood they were esoteric formulae that could be used as meditation subjects or directed visualisations if the reader identified with a character in the book or an associated god-form or ritual figure. The male god-forms were positive in "The Goat-foot God" and "The Winged Bull". The female god-forms were positive in "The Sea Priestess" and in "Moon Magic". In the two last books the heroine was a High Priestess; in the first two books a priestess. Much teaching about Isis came through in "Moon Magic" and "The Sea Priestess", their theme being the archetypal reappearance of an ancient high priestess of the goddess ensouling a modern figure.

She also resumed a subject that concerned her when she wrote "The Circuit of Force", describing how the Positive and Negative Forces interact all the time upon all the planes. The two forces could represent Higher Self and Lower Self in the same person; or alternatively the Lower Self and a god-form of opposite force.

Two personalities of opposite sex could also adopt appropriate god forms, and although this was perhaps the easiest form to be understood by average people it was also the most likely to be misunderstood, for the earthing of the force in the familiar ways of physical sexual intercourse was not essential to magic, except perhaps in the ancient fertility cults. Auric work of this kind required, however, very great development of character and profound esoteric knowledge. (This is not too far distant from what Moina MacGregor Mathers had written to Paul Foster Case many years before!)

She was glad that "The Mystical Qabalah" was being studied in the Wednesday discussion meetings but wished that she could write it again.

Referring to "The Cosmic Doctrine", she said that the Master behind it had *"much to do with the scheme of things to come,"* and had put the teaching into the symbolism of space rather than into the symbolism of mysticism as this method brought home the truth more easily to some people. (In this respect it was no coincidence that the Society's library in those days had a large section devoted to science fiction.)

She also said that within her deepest self she represented the great Feminine Power of ancient times and there was still much to bring through about this. Indeed, in the light of more recent realisations about these matters, particularly with regard to the work of R.J.Stewart and others, it would appear that what she was saying implied that she came from one of the very ancient and remote Sisterhoods that are concerned with the Feminine Principle.

In this respect lies the implication that Sarah Jane Firth's odd belief about the strange events surrounding her daughter's birth may not have been far from the truth. That is to say, that the Higher Self that inspired the work of Dion Fortune was not of the usual type, but of considerable spiritual remoteness and antiquity that could not easily project its own personality into the modern world. The personality projected into the embryo had therefore come from another, less remote, Higher Self, that after birth had withdrawn for the other to take over and perform its mission in the world. This somewhat unusual process would also have had its disadvantages, which need not detain us in a general book of this nature. Part of all this, however, lay behind the ease of confusion between Dion Fortune and Lilith le Fay.

It was felt that more teaching along the lines of the old novels might perhaps be brought through via the mediumship of Margaret Lumley Brown, who, however, felt somewhat dubious about the likely success of such a scheme through lack of her own fictional abilities. Nonetheless an attempt was made at the end of July 1957 and the resultant story was "The Death of Lilith Le Fay Morgan". This, it was felt, might also help sort out some of the aforementioned problems of identity, and it duly appeared in the public domain as "an epilogue to Moon Magic" in a collection of old Dion Fortune articles called "Aspects of Occultism" (Aquarian Press 1962; Samuel Weiser, 2000).

It is tempting to regard this fragment as something of a *roman á clef* and try to identify characters within it, in which case, to my mind Anita Warburn represents Anne Fox, Lena Rees represents Maiya Tranchell Hayes, and George Brendan, who *"had shown a curious independent enlightenment which did not come from my own sources"* is likely to be Arthur Chichester. He is mentioned in connection with an alleged account of Sun magic among her secret papers, which successions of enquirers still ask about. I had always assumed this to refer to "The Cosmic Doctrine" but on later close reading of Margaret Lumley Brown's diaries I incline to the thought that it was something yet to be written, for if this post-mortem literary experiment had been a success, other projects in mind, included *"something about the Sun and the Stars"*.

The results so far were apparently not thought sufficiently promising for the experiment to be continued with, although this was not the end of contacts from Dion Fortune. A paper issued in April 1959 contained various notes:

> *The late Warden had the following to say recently: She is aware that quite a new epoch is beginning for the group; though we are getting rid of Chalice Orchard there may well be more rather than less responsibility for us in the future. She thinks we shall eventually have some new premises.*
>
> *Since her death she says she has been in a position to see the inner plane position of other brethren who have died. She herself, Art O'Murnaghan (the "Hibernian Adept" whom we invited in his lifetime to some meetings here), Lt. Colonel Seymour, Mr. Loveday and Miss Brine, though by no means always together seemed to be much more quickly in touch with higher conditions even if they could not remain in these for long periods at a time. The usual periods of meditation and realisation were "sharper" but also shorter and more fruitful than for those who had not been initiated in life and there were remarkably few periods of the "lethargy" through which the average dead man passes in long intermittent periods.*
>
> *Miss Brine was much more advanced than might be thought by people who knew her personality only. It was expected that she would help Dion Fortune and Art O'Murnaghan with certain work on the Irish contacts for she had always had a strong contact with the Celtic forces.*

Dion Fortune thought that Western initiates could find more help by visualising the after-death conditions in the manner of the Ancient Egyptians rather than those of orthodox Christianity. The "Judgement Hall of Osiris", though full of personalised forces, did provide some explanation which could be of use to the dead man himself and could help him to accept help when offered and to help himself far more deliberately than the Church taught.

She went on to say: "I see the rising and expansion of this Fraternity as a teaching body especially belonging to these Islands of Britain – expressing the Western Mysteries and their links with the people of these Islands. When I see how much has been achieved since I left you, under the present Warden, I am grateful and bewildered for I had not expected the work to grow quite as it has done."

Dion Fortune turned up again a couple of months later on the occasion of my initiation into the Greater Mysteries, appearing in a blaze of moonlight to the clairvoyant sight of Margaret Lumley Brown, in what was described as "the Eleusis of Britain", to announce that the young man who had just been admitted was "her pupil", although she declined to give a reason.

That must form part of another story, at the hands of another biographer, but one unexpected eventuality very soon after was my being commissioned, completely out of the blue, to write "A Practical Guide to Qabalistic Symbolism". This gave an opportunity, as she had wished, to update "The Mystical Qabalah" to a certain extent, although not with any pretension to replace it. This marked the birth of "Gareth Knight", so called because this particular archetype had also begun to make its presence felt in vision and in my affairs.

The disposal of Chalice Orchard has been mentioned above. Whatever its glories in the past it had become something of a neglected outpost by this time. It was sold to the two Society members who still occupied it, F.G. Roberts, ("Uncle Robbie") and Mary Gilchrist, and eventually passed in ownership to another dedicated Avalonian, the historian Geoffrey Ashe.

Another property disposed of was situated at St. Albans, at Brickett's Wood, that had been part of a naturist colony and which was now used only as an occasional country retreat for residents of the London headquarters. This had been acquired in 1948, probably in connection with the renewal of work with the Master of Medicine by Dr Edward Gellately, who had joined the Society while still a medical student, and for some time worked closely with Margaret Lumley Brown. As well as his formal medical qualifications he had made himself extremely knowledgeable in many areas of alternative medicine, and was considered for some time to be a future Warden of the Society – although in the light of events this never came to pass.

The change in premises predicted by Dion Fortune came about at the end of 1959 when the Society moved its headquarters from the west to the north of London. This was the culmination of a gradual process of social and economic change in the Bayswater locality. The big terraced houses that well-off gentlefolk used to occupy in 1924 began to be split up into rented flats which brought about a general decline of tone in the neighbourhood including the occasional minor vandalisation of visiting members' cars.

Just as in 1924, when the acquisition of a house was said to have been assisted by inner plane influence, so the move of 1959 was blessed with happy synchronicities. An advertisement in "The Times" led Mr. Creasy to inspect a property which he went to view only because it seemed very reasonably priced for its locality. When he arrived, he was amazed to find it had two large studios attached that were ideal for the group's work. Furthermore, the owner, recently bereaved, was anxious only for a quick sale and so was asking a sum far below the market value. Creasy, being a man of scrupulous conscience, drew his attention to this fact, but although thanking him for his honesty, the vendor stuck to his original price.

The change in venue was also the forerunner of a fundamental change in the Society's esoteric work. In certain respects the general atmosphere within the group had begun to become somewhat abrasive in a way that had all the elements of power levels getting too high for the comfort and ability of those who were called upon to carry them. Much the same situation had occurred before in the problems that beset the Golden Dawn at the beginning of the century and no doubt in many other less well-documented and more ephemeral groups.

Things did not get so bad as open schism but there was a general tendency to lack of trust and mutual respect between members. One senior member was peremptorily expelled from house and group for reasons that never became clear. Others appeared to be failing to maintain a sufficient level of impersonality in polarity work.

One element in all of this may have been the expansion of a new type of work that had commenced at the core of the group a little earlier but started to come on stream in the Inner Greater Mystery degree in 1959. It was called the Lemurian Formula and aimed at identifying and rectifying very ancient causes of sin and unbalance, some from remote stellar sources, and this may well have helped to upset the apple cart. Soon after, whether as part of the dynamics of causation from the remote past or as a deliberately induced remedial effect, a very powerful Christian influence started to pour into the group, although even this had its unbalanced elements.

In the face of this complex situation by the end of 1961 Arthur Chichester concluded that emergency action had to be taken. The whole edifice of Mystery grades, Greater and Lesser, was reduced to one single mode of working, the 1st Degree.

This is standard esoteric practice that applies to individuals and to groups. If things go wrong the remedy is to stop all active operations and let things lie fallow for a space – in severe cases for as long as seven years. In dire cases, even longer.

38

THE INITIATION OF THE NADIR

Esoteric work did not in fact completely cease, it was simply pegged back to a level of safety. In other words, the pressure of steam was lowered in the boiler.

Practical work continued in the 1ˢᵗ Degree, thus indicating the reliability of a long practised ritual pattern. The basic pattern and practice of the Lesser Mysteries is like a flywheel that gives at the same time momentum and stability, and much the same might be said of the liturgical traditions of the established churches, which put much faith upon their ceremonial. It was in the advanced and experimental work within the Greater Mysteries that, although breaking new ground for the future, at the same time had a greater degree of potential instability and risk.

A three-year plan was announced for group and individual reassessment, along with a few organisational changes. The Warden, who had been somewhat beleaguered with a plethora of duties, esoteric and mundane, now became called the Director. This was largely in the sense of being a Spiritual Director, a function borrowed from the practice of enclosed religious communities, where the spiritual welfare of the members is under the supervision of a religious superior.

The post of Warden became entirely an administrative function and was filled by Richard Mallock, a long serving member who had first joined in 1938 and studied under Colonel Seymour on the Study Course. He had served in India during the war, and on demobilisation from the services, being of independent means, was able to serve as Honorary Secretary, Director of Studies and general factotum for the Society through the subsequent years.

Anne Fox remarried, and departed to spend the rest of her life in psychotherapeutic practice. Margaret Lumley Brown was relieved of her function as Pythoness, partly on account of her age, as she was now well into her seventies. She had continued to provide sterling work right up to the end but under the new dispensation came the assumption that the type of mediumship she represented should now be a thing of the past.

Rosina Mann, who had been resident in the United States since 1957 studying scientology, was asked by Arthur Chichester to return to active service within the group. She virtually took over from the previous mediums, using a technique of conscious "mediation".

This was the logical outcome of a trend that had been going on for some years. In the days of Dion Fortune and for some time after that, the medium lay prone upon a pastos to receive communications. In the course of time this gave way to a spinally upright sitting position, and in the case of the latter day mediumship of Margaret Lumley Brown, the type of trance seemed very light, and a condition that was entered and left with considerable facility.

The group as a whole began a period of intensive self-examination, and for a time the old discussion meetings gave place to psychotherapeutic exercises.

The work of the group began to change in a radical fashion from its earlier days, and apart from "The Cosmic Doctrine" and "The Mystical Qabalah" there began a certain distancing from the former works of Dion Fortune.

One or two publishing projects already in hand, collections of articles from the old "Inner Light" magazine, were allowed to proceed and appeared in 1962, and other old works of hers continued to be reprinted by interested publishers. Now however they contained a printed announcement that their contents might not reflect the Society's current aims and views.

The works of the late Dion Fortune were written a long time ago and since then a great deal more has been understood and realised so that many of the ideas then expressed are not now necessarily acceptable. Also, much of what she wrote was written from the viewpoint of the psychic. Psychism is simply one type of inner awareness and there are other types at least as valid and as common. Non-psychic readers, therefore, can translate experience in terms of psychic imagery into terms of their own inner awareness.

The publication of these books continues because there is still much of value in them and because they can act as valuable pointers to seekers.

The principle behind this notice was to emphasise that inner contacts need not be the exclusive prerogative of rare individuals with mediumistic gifts or the "second sight" as was popularly supposed. Such contacts and personal spiritual realisations could come to anyone through the processes of intuition via meditation and contemplation. Indeed, far from being a mark of spiritual advancement, natural psychism, particularly if uncontrolled, could be the symptom of an atavistic throwback.

The keyword for the new work of the group was Regeneration – or more specifically - the Path of Redemption in Earth. In metaphysical terms this was closely connected with what might be called the Initiation of the Nadir.

That is to say, one of the problems that afflicted esoteric groups and individuals in the past had been a tendency to try to turn to psychic, astral or quasi-spiritual regions as a flight from the problems of daily life in the world.

In traditional esoteric terms, the life-wave that comprises all humanity is seen as coming down the planes to the physical from the plane of spirit. This is the process of *Involution*. After due creative expression of spiritual principles in Earth it then returns up the planes in the process of spiritual *Evolution*.

From this, it follows that a successful turning of the corner, the bottom-dead-centre of the involutionary/evolutionary process, is absolutely crucial. So much so that as well as being termed the Initiation of the Nadir, it was also, in terms derived from "The Cosmic Doctrine", seen to be the divine Logoidal Impress upon the individual human spirit, from the very heights, as it turns the dangerous corner.

In practical terms this means that to pursue an interest in the higher worlds before the Nadir has been successfully reached and passed will be a retrogression and degradation of the soul rather than an evolutionary way forward. One look at the occult lunatic fringe may be sufficient to see the effects of this starkly demonstrated. However, the occult world does not hold a monopoly in exemplary failures in this respect, which can be found in any amount of distortions and abuses, particularly within the religious field.

The larger picture also concerned the stewardship of the human race towards the other forms of life which share the planet. This is a metaphysical underpinning for all concerns with the environment. It obviously embraces all forms of human, children and animal welfare, but with the extended awareness of occult philosophy, includes concern for the elementary units of consciousness that go to make up the inner side of nature. That is to say, from traditional local Elemental beings to the great Generating Elemental and provider of forms of the Earth itself. In the terminology of the Society this was called the Planetary Being, (or in certain other schools, and in the original "Cosmic Doctrine" script, the Planetary Spirit). Others have come close to the concept in the figure of Gaea.

Upon the personal level this meant that until and unless one were capable of a spiritually mature approach to daily life in the world, one had not passed the crucial point, the Initiation of the Nadir. No manner of grand esoteric titles or high-sounding initiations is any substitute for this. What is more, for various metaphysical and cosmic reasons, there is a considerable number of ways and means by which reluctant souls try to avoid these essential rites of passage.

Rosina Mann produced a searching analysis of some of the symptoms that might be found, particularly in esoteric circles, of what might be called these "spiritual pathologies".

Typical symptoms would include:

1. *difficulty in finishing a job or a cycle of activity completely; giving an impression of other-worldliness, or spiritual "top heaviness";*

2. *a reincarnationary record demonstrating sequences of lives spent withdrawn in religious or occult orders occasionally interspersed with a life of extreme violence – in short, lack of balance in life expression;*

3. *a mind dominating the feelings, thus having no real warmth of "heart", even when outwardly apparently kind and considerate;*

4. *difficulties in relating to the opposite sex because of a compulsion to be independent, aloof, self-sufficient;*

5. *a tendency to be unmarried, or else married to a similar type with little interest in children or domestic and family life;*

6. *very often in the right, but intolerant of imperfections in others*

or themselves;

7. *at heart lonely and unfulfilled, seeking "higher" consciousness to
    compensate for the hollowness of expression and experience at the
    lower levels.*

The work of members in the Society now became very much a
matter of self-examination and working upon themselves to achieve
right living in the world, rather than the traditional graded structure
for developing magical techniques or modes of inner consciousness.

With this new emphasis the Society seemed to be well on the
way to becoming a religious sect rather than an occult fraternity in
the traditional sense. Arthur Chichester maintained however, that
whatever the appearances, the work of the Society was still upon
the lines laid down in Dion Fortune's day, and what is more,
considerably further advanced along them. He did not much care
for any continued association with the Golden Dawn tradition, nor
did he like being regarded as an occultist. If label were required, he
preferred to think of the Society as an association of Christian
Qabalists.

Traditionally minded respondents might be somewhat
surprised at his assertion but if the principle behind the work of
Dion Fortune be regarded as the observance of three strands of
tradition, then that principle could still be observed at work. In the
terminology of the earlier days these three strands of tradition used
to be called the Blue, the Green and the Purple Rays. That is to say:

1. Hermetic philosophy and ceremony,
2. the Elemental contacts,
3. the line of Christian mysticism.

In the earlier history of the Society the *Hermetic Ray* was expressed
in ritual work on co-Masonic lines and study of the Qabalah.

The *Green Ray* was celebrated in the association with
Glastonbury Tor, the Chant of the Elements and the content of the
novels, particularly the "The Winged Bull" and "The Goat-foot God".

Devotional Mysticism was the motivation for "Mystical
Meditations on the Collects", the Guild of the Master Jesus and
later Church of the Graal, to say nothing of the concerns of the
Christian Mystic Lodge and early contacts with the Company of
Avalon.

Within the new parameters, the Society's practice still embraced all three.

The *Hermetic* side was represented by the continued use of the 1st Degree ritual with its basic Masonic structure and the background of Qabalistic symbolism. It is true that only one Degree was now being worked, but this placed necessary emphasis upon Malkuth, the Earth Sephirah, and its immediately related Paths. Whatever the apparent limitations in terms of higher consciousness, this discipline served to concentrate the sacramental and talismanic ceremonial work of the group upon the immediate concern in hand: the regenerated expression of human life in Earth.

The *Green Ray* had its place in the particular concern for the Planetary Being. This was a term coined in the days of the discussion groups upon "The Cosmic Doctrine" when it was agreed that the term "planetary spirit" within that work, would be better changed to "planetary being", for it was more of an etheric entity than a 7th plane spirit. Arthur Chichester liked to describe it as a "generating Elemental".

Just as it had always been an occult tradition that it was the duty of the adept to train and spiritually educate Elemental beings, so, to the new way of thinking, this was a duty of all humanity, whose failure in spiritual stewardship in this respect did countless harm to these less evolved beings.

The general idea has since been taken up in the many public concerns for the environment. The special place reserved for the welfare of the Planetary Being in all practical workings of the Society deserves a special mention in that it may well have had the magical effect of permeating these concerns through the group mind by psychic osmosis.

The *Purple Ray* was expressed in the new mode of the Society by the insistence that Jesus the Christ was the Master of all the occult Masters. In a sense this is but a restatement of Dion Fortune's concerns when in the Christian Mystic Lodge.

However, there was now also a recognition of the feminine side of divinity, expressed in a particular devotion to the Virgin Mary, in all her aspects, not simply as listed in the famous Litany of Lareto, but in many other manifestations of the divine feminine principle. St. Joseph as head of the holy family also received special formal recognition in terms of concern for the welfare of children.

After Arthur Chichester's death in 1979 Rosina Mann remained consistent to her views on magic expressed in her celebrated lecture of 1942. She resisted all attempts to open up the higher grades and the type of Greater Mystery work of former days, even though one or two senior members who remembered those times felt that much had been lost by the abandonment of such work over so long a period. Her view was that it contained elements of glamour that could lead to very subtle temptation and abuse. Not least that it could provide a distraction from the fundamental purpose of the Mysteries, which was Regeneration.

39

THE FLIGHT OF THE PHOENIX

In metaphysical terms the dilemma that faced the Society was a matter of force and form. Or what Dion Fortune might have described in homely terms as the danger of throwing out the baby with the bathwater. However, within the genuinely contacted Mysteries there is an automatic balancing action, that tends to preserve equilibrium. As the Society had turned away from the form side of magical techniques within, so teaching and knowledge about such techniques increased and expanded without, and very largely through members who left, to teach what they had learned within the Society in the first place.

This pattern of action and reaction is succinctly described within "The Cosmic Doctrine". If the work of the Mysteries is symbolised by a circle, it contains within it a dynamic polarity between the central point and the circumference. The one is under the Law of the Attraction of the Centre (deriving from the Ring Cosmos) and the other the Attraction of the Circumference or Outer Space (deriving from the Ring Chaos). The centre pertains to a "pattern of perfection", that may be likened to a Central Stillness. The circumference pertains to an urge for new experience and growth.

Were one to put this into the terms of the legendary primeval traditions favoured by Dion Fortune's mentors in the early days, the first is akin to the Sun Temple of Atlantis, the latter to the Withdrawn Temple of the Sea and the Stars.

Thus is was that at the time of the new dispensation, or fairly soon after it, whilst a number of members felt happy to continue in their allegiance to the centre, and so remained for many years, there were others who had the call to leave and go forth to take what they had learned out into the world. This was, after all, the decade of the

1960's, with its huge efflorescence of awareness of the presence and validity of the inner side of things.

If the enclosed part of the Society of the Inner Light retrenched to preserve the spiritual principles of Dion Fortune in a condition of pristine purity, so, after another manner, did the spirit of Dion Fortune or rays from the Inner Light move out into the world.

Despite the apparent diametrically opposed directions of endeavour, there was also a common element in them both. For just as the centre returned to working just the 1st Degree, so too did those who moved out into the world of necessity have to start back at the beginning, dealing for the most part with untrained people barely capable of working even at the level of the 1st Degree.

The full story of this movement needs a broader history than can here be told. For just as the work of Dion Fortune had developed out of the pioneering work of others – Barrett, Lytton, Kingsford, Mathers, Moriarty, Brodie-Innes and the like – so did the pioneering work of Dion Fortune and the Fraternity of the Inner Light spawn forth other groups and movements. This is the way that the Wisdom Tradition works, it will never be a great coherent institutional monolith, and it spreads like the seeds from dandelion clocks.

Thus in the space of thirty years from the inception of outgoing seeds from the Inner Light, one could compose a list of derivative groups or individuals: Helios Course on the Practical Qabalah (Butler and Knight), Servants of the Light (Butler and Ashcroft-Nowicki), the London Group (Adams), the Star and Cross (Adams and Collins), the Ibis Fraternity (Butler and Geiki), the Order of the Lamp (Rice), Sangreal Foundation (Gray and Collins), Gareth Knight Group (Knight), Avalon Group (Harris and Berg), Companions of the Inner Abbey (Mazonowicz), Broken Arrow (Carpenter), Magical Christianity (Whitehead), Sacred Science (Brennan), Company of Hawkwood (Matthews), Invisible College (Green), Pharos (Goddard), and one could go on. Not all of course following a line that the original Society of the Inner Light might wish to subscribe to, or even to be associated with, but nonetheless a generation of teeming offspring owing its existence, at least in part, to the coming together of Dion Fortune and Charles Loveday in a union of esoteric parenthood in 1922.

Speaking for myself I retained the ambition to build an active group that would replicate the Greater Mysteries worked by the Society of the Inner Light that I knew in my salad days. My old friend and colleague Alan Adams, or "Charles Fielding" did the much the same. When invited to lecture in public I tried to introduce techniques I had learned within the Grades of the Society to a wider audience. This was, to my way of thinking, another aspect of what the Tibetan Master called the "externalisation of the Hierarchy".

In 1979, in a weekend devoted to "The Tree of Life" I conducted a multiple "path working" a "rising on the planes". It was the first time ever, so far as I know, that such a technique was tried in public. In subsequent years it has become almost commonplace, in workshops around the world, and is also widely used as a psychotherapeutic technique. I make no claims to originality, I was merely one of the first of a large wave, that also had its exponents in Dr. Roberto Assegioli and his "Psychosynthesis".

In 1980 my subject was "The Works of Dion Fortune" with a particular emphasis upon the novels, not least the figure of the Sea Priestess, and here I introduced some public ritual work also, although somewhat in disguise, in plain clothes and more in the outer form of a play reading, but with hidden dynamics.

In 1981 it was the turn of "The Arthurian Tradition" and this was largely based upon the Arthurian Formula of Dion Fortune's provenance, along with Maiya Tranchell-Hayes. This turned out to be an extremely powerful weekend, and set a great number of dynamics going, leading to the publication of "The Secret Tradition in Arthurian Legend" in 1983, so at last getting much of the original material out into print after a lapse of some forty years.

From 1982 we continued the Dion Fortune tradition with "The Chymical Marriage of Christian Rosencreutz", "The Mysteries of Isis", "The Celtic Mysteries" and things escalated from there, leading to two major meetings per year, attended by leading occultists of a new generation, and going on to cover new ground such as the works of C.S.Lewis, Tolkien, Charles Williams, and also the Tarot, supported by published books "The Rose Cross and the Goddess", "The Magical World of the Inklings", "The Treasure House of Images", etc. There followed commitments to overseas workings, in Paris, Auxerre, Dijon, Athens, New York and the books on

Qabalah, the Arthurian Legend, the Rose Cross and the Goddess were translated into major European languages spreading the Dion Fortune influence wider.

The culmination of this outward flow probably came in the Centenary celebrations of the birth of Dion Fortune, on 6th December 1990, wherein all who had participated in these works of the previous decade were invited to acknowledge her influence behind it all in a concerted meditation rather after the fashion of her old Wartime Letters imagery. That is to say, of the Cavern under Glastonbury Tor with its blazing Rose Cross and Seven Lords of the Rays.

Proceeding up a spiral pathway to the top of the Tor one looked out over Glastonbury, aware of the two thorn trees, one on Wearyall Hill where Joseph of Arimathea traditionally first struck his staff, and the other by the chapel wall in the precincts of the Abbey. One visualised Dion Fortune, with Joseph of Arimathea, striking a third thorn staff into the top of the Tor, which grew immediately into a miraculous tree. A triangle of white light ran between the three trees which then formed the base of a pyramid the point of which was a blazing star high above, among seven other coloured lights, the colour of the robes of the Seven Lords seen below in the Cavern. Many people took part in this, as individuals or in groups, in England, Wales, Scotland and the United States. Typical of the visions experienced were the following:

> Circle dancing on the top of the Tor, rhythmic and very physical, barefooted in mud wet and warm, aware of the earth beneath us and the spiritual energy coming down through us. The roots of the tree throwing out energy in the underworld. Most important was the connection between the earth and the stars. Aware of the different constellations, especially the Plough and Great Bear. As on an axle, spinning with my feet fixed in the earth and feeling the energy beneath me and of the spiritual energy above me. A mirror image on the land of all the twinkling coloured star constellations above, energy pouring up and down.

> Energy built as we climbed the Tor, swirling and more concentrated as we reached the top. The planting of the staff produced a great tree, its roots deep in the earth, its branches stretching skywards. The dance which followed took the form of a May dance – the tree decked with ribbons, each person spiralling inwards, weaving in and out. I felt a rush of energy

upwards through my body, and the whole scene turned on the
axle of the tree. The whole meditation had an elemental feel.

These experiences had a certain resonance with the Chant of the
Elements experienced by Dion Fortune and her friends on the Tor
in 1926. There was also a more serious note, reminiscent of the
time of the War Letters, in a fragment of communication.

"All individuals must act responsibly as a nexus of great events
is occurring or about to occur. Resonances were set up half a
century ago (7 x 7 years) to save these shores and the wider
kingdom. The work should be carried out again. Do you not realise
that energy is not, within the greater sphere of the earth, created
or destroyed? That as the power mass shifts, new stresses arise."
Following this came the image of the islands of Britain, green in
a blue sea, outlined in light, a silver line around the edge of the
land. Four winged figures hovering in the four directions – the
lion, the eagle, the bull, and the man. The feathers on their wings
eyed, and yet unlike peacocks, and the feathers so beautiful as to
cause the observer to lose oneself in looking at them.
"Be awake, be aware" came the watchword from the
communicator.

Another angle upon all of this came from a colleague who, on the
6th, happened to be in the vicinity of Llandudno, visiting the places
of her childhood. He wrote:

The upshot of this was that leading up to and especially during
Christmas I became aware of "little Violet" in our home being
very much a normal child among our kids, cats and dogs. This
may be seen as part and parcel of an "initiation/rebirth" for her,
a going back to roots in a sense, both to a stage where all those
adult compromises with original innocence have yet to be made
and love, warmth and laughter are as natural as breathing. It is
of course this sort of thing which exorcises the ghost of the
supposed "mighty priestess" more effectively then anything.
Violet was just another child who joined in the rough and tumble
of our own family Christmas. Having said this, it is difficult to
see where D.F.'s individual "initiation" ends and another step in
our national or even cosmic initiation begins, but "childhood"
is obviously the link. The fact that D.F. and Joseph were jointly
planting the staff certainly points to the considerable status of
D.F. as a "racial adept" at a vital time.

To another, another aspect of her post mortem condition became apparent,

> She had not fully entered the Second Death because she had been called back and back, not by her direct magical heirs so much as by her magical grandchildren born after her death, with whom she had a very close bond. These were the many "children" who were awakened often by first reading her novels or the Mystical Qabalah and she could no more abandon them than a lioness abandon her cubs until they were able to stand on their own feet, and that there was a process which she was overseeing that needed to continue until such time as she could "give up the ghost".

However, the feeling of her moving on from a past level to a new one was referred to in a number of reports.

> She seemed to say that she has now been able to complete her own work and can pass on to the inner levels. I felt that we all now had to take on what she has given us. I think we have all been given something.

> Another felt that she had moved away and the spiral had once more turned. Certainly a sense of departure was indicated.

> The meeting on the Tor felt like a real reunion, there were so many people there who I have come to know over the past years. The unexpected bit was that the Priest of the Moon came down from the Star direction between the coloured spheres and taking D.F. by the hand in a formal ritualistic way, took her back with him to the upper regions.

> It started rather solemn, then it became light hearted, very much like a happy reunion of friends. I had a feeling that the celebrations would go on until the late hours, but my own conclusion was that D.F. is now very much of the past.

> From chatting to various peers since the event it does seem that with this passing that there was over the time of the centenary, a degree of gifting by D.F. – whether that be in the form of giving specific tasks or jobs to get on with, or in the form of some symbolic token in recognition of the work that had been undertaken.

Whether or not one wishes to take all these statements at the foot of the letter, all, together with those that have not been quoted, bear witness to the fact that Dion Fortune retained a respect and affection from a large number of people that stretched over all the intervening years. Certainly amongst people beyond the originating centre of the Society of the Inner Light. But it would appear that her influence was now on the point of flowing back inward. The ripples that had started moving outward from the centre in 1960 had struck the periphery of the pond in 1990 and were starting on their way back.

The central point now began to pulsate and expand. A new Wardenship and a new team came about. The foundations of the former magical edifice had now been thoroughly cleansed and grounded in Earth. That is to say, the Initiation of the Nadir had been talismanically passed upon a group level of the Mysteries. The time had come for rebuilding a new structure upon the foundations that had been maintained.

Rome was not built in a day and nor can a graded Mystery be set up instantaneously, but over the ensuing decade steady progress in the rebuilding was steadily made.

The physical headquarters were completely refurbished. Plans were laid for new publishing. This included a new edition of "The Cosmic Doctrine", going back to the original text and incorporating the diagrams that had been prepared by C.T. Loveday. Selections from the War Letters of Dion Fortune were commissioned for publication under the title of "The Magical Battle of Britain". A trading arm of the Society was set up to maintain old Dion Fortune titles in print, including the novels and also a revised edition of "The Mystical Qabalah". The old "Inner Light Magazine" was relaunched, in bright coloured covers, as a quarterly, some of its articles latterly displayed upon the internet.

A formal rededication of the work and of its resurgence was performed at Glastonbury and some of the old ceremonies were dusted off, refurbished and reworked. Step by step the 2nd and 3rd Degrees were opened up again and eventually the Greater Mysteries.

During this time I gradually became aware of this intensive work, at first upon the outer levels and then upon the inner. When approached to edit the War Letters of Dion Fortune I regarded it as a compliment and a privilege but saw it simply as a straightforward editorial job. As I got to work on the text however, it started to open up inner contacts tapping into the former ones of Dion Fortune, together with an increased facility to channel them. I began to receive a great raft of dictated material that enabled me to form an inner structure of advanced work for the Gareth Knight Group, a group that I had been developing for twenty years past as a means to re-establish the kind of Greater Mystery group that I had known in the Society of the Inner Light.

At the same time the magnetic pull of the Society began to increase as I was invited to contribute articles to the "Inner Light Magazine". This gradually became a regular feature and indeed, it seemed, an inwardly driven duty. Then one or two others in my group began to pick up on inner contacts that had worked with Dion Fortune in the early days, in particular David Carstairs, who went so far as to virtually dictate a play about life in the trenches in the 1ˢᵗ World War, "This Wretched Splendour", which against all the odds received immediate amateur and professional productions.

When I was invited to visit the old Society headquarters, it was the first time I had crossed the threshold for thirty-four years and it felt just like going home. I also now began to realise the purpose behind this long circular journey over all these years of questing in the outlands. It had been to learn many magical techniques and contacts that were new, or old and had been forgotten, and which could be brought to fruition to be poured like wine into the waiting cup that had been prepared for it.

My long held ambition to build a Greater Mystery lodge like the one in which I had first learned my trade came to paradoxical fulfilment in returning to help to restore one within the original source. I at any rate had come full circle, or perhaps more accurately arrived at a higher point upon the spiral. For I also left behind me a Greater Mystery lodge that had taken me twenty-five years to build, re-named the Avalon Group, in token of the earliest contacts made by Dion Fortune and their inner and outer location.

After nearly forty years, it seemed to me that the reasons were now disclosed behind the cryptic suggestion perceived to be said by Dion Fortune at my own initiation. It also seemed that a phrase that had been uttered by the Priest of the Moon in "The Death of Vivien Le Fay Morgan", was also about to come to pass:

"... as the work has been good in standard, it will not die, but following seeming defeat will rise again in another manner... "

— APPENDIX —

RECTIFIED ASTROLOGICAL BIRTH CHART
FOR DION FORTUNE

Born 00.55 G.M.T. 6th December 1890 at Llandudno
Drawn up and interpreted by Sander Littel

The only birth chart for Dion Fortune so far published seems to be the one in Fielding and Collins *"The Story of Dion Fortune"*. In the absence of a time for actual birth the house and planetary positions for Noon on 6th December have been used, as is generally common practice in such cases. However, as we have the testimony of Sarah Firth that she sat with her new born child in her arms during the dark hours before dawn, it would seem that a more appropriate time would have been some time after midnight, almost twelve hours before.

A more precise time has been taken based upon certain key dates in Dion Fortune's life, the technical details for which I provided at the end of Sander Littel's interpretation.

Gareth Knight

It is always a little tricky to delineate the birth chart of somebody whose birth time is unknown. Yet in Dion Fortune's case, of whom it is known that she was born in the early hours of the night of the 6th of December 1890 in Llandudno, we have a few valuable dates from her life history to enable a so-called rectification, (or preferably, an "educated guess"), at her horoscope.

Based on these dates a seemingly appropriate birth time for her is 00:55 GMT which shows the 27th degree of Virgo Rising. I often use the Sabian degrees, as described by Marc Edmund Jones and Dane Rhudyar, to see whether they contain some valuable information that I would otherwise miss and I believe the degree is worth while mentioning in this case:

"A group of noblewomen, who are in function at the court, come together during ceremony."

Dane Rhudyar says about this degree: *"The capacity to accomplish an honoured tradition, in order to maintain the standards of what is considered sublime in a culture."*

This strikes me as a very apt description of her activities and thus seems to confirm the calculated birth time to some extent.

One of the first conspicuous things in Dion Fortune's chart is the fact that there is no occupation of the so-called Water Signs. This implies that a lot of her life energy will have been aimed almost obsessively at trying to connect herself with the deepest and most hidden aspects of her own emotional nature, and consequently with the emotional level in general. Most probably this will have had its roots and reflections in her upbringing and early childhood.

A lack of Water often reflects in youth as a conscious negation on the parents' part to accept the feeling nature of the child. In such instances the education and the cultivation of the mind have been designed to make the child a master of its own fate, often by stimulating the denial of the chaotic or the seemingly threatening impact of emotion and feeling.

The imprint of this on the child's character can have many different effects. For instance there can be a tendency to compensate for this in adult life and to become wrapped up in all-pervading emotions and sentiments, without finding a satisfactory connection with the inner self. However, there is also possible a different and much more constructive response to this compulsive urge: one is compelled to investigate consciously one's own emotional nature, or, eventually, emotional nature in general, and try to find ways to merge these findings into the overall outlook that was taught and experienced in youth, thus bringing order into chaos and a more balanced attitude.

As Dion Fortune's Ruler, the critical and curious Mercury can be found at the deepest point of her chart. It looks as if all of her energy was aimed at finding her "real" roots by ordering the past in a primarily intellectual and analytic way. This primal energy is principally of a fiery nature: Mercury, Sun and Venus all have a Sagittarian colour: wide perspectives and always new horizons were necessary to develop her inner being, her mind and her affections, and this is combined with a central Mars in Aquarius which wants to strip the forthcoming energy of the all-too-personal elements and bestow it with universal, more "humane", qualities.

Her feeling nature itself, her receptivity, was always present and alert, as the Moon is to be found in her first House, which pictures her appearance and way of behaviour; and because the Moon represents the element water in a very active way, this counts as a firm counterweight to the above mentioned lack of Water.

The Moon is just entering the sign of Libra and stays close to the Ascendant. The aloofness and critical outlook of Virgo rising became softened and redirected by a strong need to feel emotionally secure and thus the Moon here made her rather sensitive to appreciation by others in the environment. She wanted to feel that others needed her and therefore she would sometimes comply temporarily to others, particularly to people that she considered authorities, while at the same time she could be somewhat changeable and moody, though always within rational bounds and essentially craving for ultimate harmony, order and justice.

The most interesting feature of the chart is perhaps this Moon entertaining a smooth aspect in her chart with the outstanding planetary conjunction of Neptune and Pluto, the other two so-called "Water" planets, placed in the 9th house of expanding consciousness, indicating her obvious receptivity (Moon) to "higher" otherworldly knowledge and her capacity to bring that down into reality in an orderly way (Virgo).

Neptune and Pluto belong to the superhuman or supernatural realm, and are forces that can not normally be handled consciously by most mortals. As Dion Fortune was gifted with the trine of the Moon and of Jupiter to this 9th house configuration, she was able

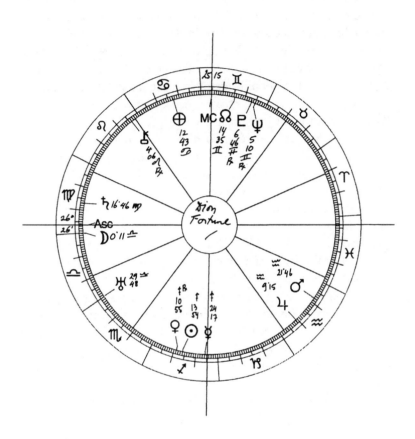

Rectified birth chart for Dion Fortune

to tap information from these higher levels and to translate it into very clear and concise language.

Communication of her ideas has not always been without problems, as Mercury (of words) is conflicting the Ascendant, and she might sometimes have overstrained herself, or have had a wrong understanding of the mental receptivity of her audiences. This could at times also have had an adverse effect on her own mental balance and nervous constitution. Nevertheless she managed in a cautious way and in a clear style to create a new order which was based on the most essential of traditional knowledge.

Most of her planets are in positive, male signs, indicating that she experienced a strong urge to project herself out into the world. With jovial Jupiter and wilful Mars in the fifth house (of centre stage), she was keen to play a central and leading role if necessary. To become a spiritual leader in a forceful and enthusiastic manner did fulfil this need to a great extent, although, as Saturn (of outer authority) in the 12th house (of hidden causes) squares the Sun (of inner authority), she must always have felt a certain basic insecurity when forced to exert (or suffer) authority.

Generally speaking, this whole chart breathes a strong uplifting and visionary enthusiasm. It is burning with zeal and aiming at the highest possible spiritual goal, at the same time picturing a more struggling and practical attitude in order to ground the complex message and to put what has been grasped mentally into words.

The Part of Fortune in the 10th house (of responsibility taken) is in the feeling sign of Cancer, the sign of "the first cause", and it is right on the mighty star Sirius, brightest star of all, which essentially accentuates the ultimate value and meaning of what she has brought to the world.

Sander Littel Oudelande, 21 February 2000.

CHART DETAILS

Birth place and time: Llandudno 53N19 3W49 00.55.30 GMT
                          06.12.1890 Startime 05.39.19

Placidean House system: 11th 2LEO08 12th 2VIR32 2nd 19LIB26
                          3rd 18SCO58

Asc:	26VIR26	1st House conj Moon sq Mercury
Sun:	13SAG54	3rd House [Dec –22.28]
Moon:	0LIB11	1st House [Dec 4.36]
Mercury:	24SAG17	3rd House sq Moon [Dec –25.18]
Venus:	10SAG41 R	3rd House conj Sun [Dec –22.12]
Mars:	21AQ47	5th House sext Mercury [Dec –15.29]
Jupiter:	9AQ15	5th House sext Sun semisq Mercury sext
Venus	[Dec –18.40]	
Saturn:	16VIR46	12th House sq Sun sq Venus [Dec 6.56]
Uranus:	29LIB48	2nd House semisq Sun sext Mercury [Dec –10.54]
Neptune:	5GEM10 R	9th House opp Sun tr Moon opp Venus tr
Jupiter	[Dec 19.31]	
Pluto:	6GEM46 R	9th House opp Sun tr Moon opp Venus tr
Jupiter	[Dec 9.43]	
N.Node:	14GEM35	9th House R opp Sun opp Venus tr Jupiter sq Saturn sesq Uranus [Dec 22.33]
Cheiron:	4LEO06	11th House sext Moon opp Jupiter sext
Neptune sext Pluto [Dec 11.57]		
Pars Fortuna:	12CAN44	10th House
Midheaven:	25GEM20	10th House sq Moon opp Mercury tr Mars sesq Jupiter tr Uranus sq Ascendant

Fire:	Sun Mercury Venus Cheiron [36%]
Earth:	Jupiter Ascendant [24%]
Air:	Moon Mars Jupiter Uranus Neptune Pluto N.Node Midheaven [40%]
Water:	Pars Fortuna [0%]

Cardinal:	Moon Uranus Pars Fortuna [18%]
Fixed:	Mars Jupiter Cheiron [14%]
Mutable:	Sun Mercury Venus Saturn Neptune Pluto N.Node Ascendant Midheaven [68%]

Positive: Sun Moon Mercury Venus Mars Jupiter Uranus
              Neptune Pluto N.Node Cheiron Midheaven [76%]
Negative: Saturn Pars Fortuna Ascendant [24%]

*Life events and progressions taken into account in rectification of
chart birth time:*

1. nervous breakdown March 1913:
   pr ASC 13LIB22 sq Part of Fortune 12CAN43, opp Mars/Neptune
   13AR28.

2. starts occult work with C.T.Loveday, Aug 5th, 1922:
   pr ASC 20LIB20 conj cusp II, sesq ruler 7th Neptune 20LIB10; pr
   MC 27CAN30 semsq pr NorthNode 27CAN55.

3. starts Cosmic Doctrine, July 30th 1923:
   pr ASC 21LIB03, sesq pr Pluto 21CAN13, opp tr Cheiron 21AR03;
   pr MC 28CAN30, sesq Sun 28CAN54.

4. marriage, Apr 17th 1927:
   pr ASC 23LIB44 sext Mercury 24SAG17, pr MC 2LEO17 opp pr
   Moon 1AQ44, conj cusp XI.

5. starts Ritual System, Dec 21st 1928:
   pr MC 4LEO00 conj Cheiron 4LEO07, sext pr Neptune 4GEM16.

6. death of mother, Dec 22nd 1936:
   pr ASC 0SCO36 conj rad/prog Uranus 0SCO34; pr MC 12LEO09
   sext pr NorthNode 12GEM09, opp tr Venus. pr Mars 26PIS10 opp
   ASC 26VIR26.

7. maritally separated 1938:
   pr ASC conj pr Uranus at 1SCO19.

8. work recommenced with Maiya Tranchell Hayes, Aug 8th
   1940:
   pr ASC 3SCO07=Venus/MC, sq tr Pluto 2LEO51. pr MC 15LEO50
   conj tr Sun.

9. death Jan 6th 1946:
   pr ASC 6SCO48 inconj Pluto 6GEM46. pr MC 21LEO20 opp pr
   Jupiter 21AQ11 and opp rad Mars 21AQ47. Tr PL 11LEO12 semisq
   ASC 26VIR26.

INDEX

Other titles from Thoth Publications

AN INTRODUCTION TO RITUAL MAGIC
By Dion Fortune & Gareth Knight

At the time this was something of a unique event in esoteric publishing - a new book by the legendary Dion Fortune. Especially with its teachings on the theory and practice of ritual or ceremonial magic, by one who, like the heroine of two of her other novels, was undoubtedly "a mistress of that art".

In this work Dion Fortune deals in successive chapters with Types of Mind Working; Mind Training; The Use of Ritual; Psychic Perception; Ritual Initiation; The Reality of the Subtle Planes; Focusing the Magic Mirror; Channelling the Forces; The Form of the Ceremony; and The Purpose of Magic - with appendices on Talisman Magic and Astral Forms.

Each chapter is supplemented and expanded by a companion chapter on the same subject by Gareth Knight. In Dion Fortune's day the conventions of occult secrecy prevented her from being too explicit on the practical details of magic, except in works of fiction. These veils of secrecy having now been drawn back, Gareth Knight has taken the opportunity to fill in much practical information that Dion Fortune might well have included had she been writing today.

In short, in this unique collaboration of two magical practitioners and teachers, we are presented with a valuable and up-to-date text on the practice of ritual or ceremonial magic "as it is". 'That is to say, as a practical, spiritual, and psychic discipline, far removed from the lurid superstition and speculation that are the hall mark of its treatment in sensational journalism and channels of popular entertainment.

ISBN 1-870450 31 0 Deluxe Hardback Limited edition
ISBN 1-870450 26 4 Soft cover edition

THE CIRCUIT OF FORCE
by Dion Fortune.
With commentaries by Gareth Knight.

In "The Circuit of Force", Dion Fortune describes techniques for raising the personal magnetic forces within the human aura and their control and direction in magic and in life, which she regards as 'the Lost Secrets of the Western Esoteric Tradition'.

To recover these secrets she turns to three sources.

a) the Eastern Tradition of Hatha Yoga and Tantra and their teaching on raising the "sleeping serpent power" or kundalini;

b) the circle working by means of which spiritualist seances concentrate power for the manifestation of some of their results;

c) the linking up of cosmic and earth energies by means of the structured symbol patterns of the Qabalistic Tree of Life.

Originally produced for the instruction of members of her group, this is the first time that this material has been published for the general public in volume form.

Gareth Knight provides subject commentaries on various aspects of the etheric vehicle, filling in some of the practical details and implications that she left unsaid in the more secretive esoteric climate of the times in which she wrote.

Some quotes from Dion Fortune's text:

"When, in order to concentrate exclusively on God, we cut ourselves off from nature, we destroy our own roots. There must be in us a circuit between heaven and earth, not a one-way flow, draining us of all vitality. It is not enough that we draw up the Kundalini from the base of the spine; we must also draw down the divine light through the Thousand-Petalled Lotus. Equally, it is not enough for out mental health and spiritual development that we draw down the Divine Light, we must also draw up the earth forces. Only too often mental health is sacrificed to spiritual development through ignorance of, or denial of, this fact."

"....the clue to all these Mysteries is to be sought in the Tree of Life. Understand the significance of the Tree; arrange the symbols you are working with in the correct manner upon it, and all is clear and you can work out your sum. Equate the Danda with the Central Pillar, and the Lotuses with the Sephiroth and the bi-sections of the Paths thereon, and you have the necessary bilingual dictionary at your disposal - if you known how to use it."

ISBN 1-870450 28 0

PRINCIPLES OF HERMETIC PHILOSOPHY
& The Esoteric Philosophy of Astrology

Principles of Hermetic Philosophy together with *The Esoteric Philosophy of Astrology* are the last known works written by Dion Fortune. They appeared in her Monthly letters to members and associates of the Society of the Inner Light between November 1942 and March 1944.

Her intention in these works is summed up in her own words: "The observation in these pages are an attempt to gather together the fragments of a forgotten wisdom and explain and expand them in the light of personal observation."

She was uniquely equipped to make highly significant personal observations in these matters as one of the leading practical occultists of her time. What is more, in these later works she feels less constrained by traditions of occult secrecy and takes an altogether more practical approach than in her earlier, well known textbooks.

Gareth knight takes the opportunity to amplify her explanations and practical exercises with a series of full page illustrations, and provides a commentary on her work

ISBN 1-870450-34-5

*   *   *   *   *

THE STORY OF DION FORTUNE
As told to Charles Fielding and Carr Collins.

Dion Fortune and Aleister Crowley stand as the twentieth century's most influential leaders of the Western Esoteric Tradition. They were very different in their backgrounds, scholarship and style.

But, for many, Dion Fortune is the chosen exemplar of the Tradition - with no drugs, no homosexuality and no kinks. This book tells of her formative years and of her development.

At the end, she remains a complex and enigmatic figure, who can only be understood in the light of the system she evolved and worked to great effect.

There can be no definitive "Story of Dion Fortune". This book must remain incompete and full of errors. However, readers may find themselves led into an experience of initiation as envisaged by this fearless and dedicated woman.

ISBN 1-870450-33-7

SPIRITUALISM AND OCCULTISM

By Dion Fortune
with Commentary edited by Gareth Knight

As well as being an occultist of the first rank, Dion Fortune was an accomplished medium. Thus she is able to explain the methods, technicalities and practical problems of trance mediumship from first hand experience. She describes exactly what it feels like to go into trance and the different types of being one may meet with beyond the usual spirit guides.

For most of her life her mediumistic abilities were known only to her immediate circle until, in the war years, she responded to the call to try to make a united front of occultists and spiritualists against the forces of materialism in the post-war world. At this point she wrote various articles for the spiritualist press and appeared as a speaker on several spiritualist platforms.

This book contains her original work *Spiritualism in the Light* of Occult Science with commentaries by Gareth Knight that quote extensively from now largely unobtainable material that she wrote on the subject during her life, including transcripts from her own trance work and rare articles from old magazines and journals.

ISBN 1-870450-38-8

ENTRANCE TO THE MAGICAL QABALAH
By Melita Denning & Osborne Phillips.

In this significant new work, Denning and Phillips set forth the essential traditions and teachings of the treasury of mystical and arcane learning which is known as the Qabalah.

Everything that is, ourselves included, is seen by the Qabalah as existing in some or all of four "Worlds" or levels of being.

These Worlds supply the whole fabric of our existence, and we in turn are integral parts of them. It is from this primal unity of person and kosmos that our great aspirations spring: our longing to know and to experience the reality, not only of that mystery which encompasses us, but also of that mystery of selfhood which is within us. For each of these mysteries reflects the other.

This very fact of the reflected likeness gives us a key to both mysteries, a key to mystical and to psychological understanding, It is this fact which makes magic possible. It is this same fact which makes the Qabalah a coherent system in which the aspirant does not follow blindly but with a comprehension ever increasing, and without ever losing that uplifting sense of wonder and of adventure which are rightfully a part of life itself.

With clarity and insight, the authors explore the origins and spirit of this system, its relationship to the Hermetic writings and the Zohar, its great patterns of thought and method, its spiritual sources of power and its tremendous creative potential. The question of evil is addressed in a study of the Qlipphoth and unbalanced force. Here also, among many other vital topics, are considered the role of the Supernal Mother in the cosmic scheme, the structure and functions of the psyche, spiritual realms, the destiny of the soul after death, the nature of the Gods, the way of magical attainment and the crossing of the Abyss.

ISBN1-870450-35-3

THE FORGOTTEN MAGE

The Magical Lectures of Colonel C.R.F.Seymour.
Edited by Dolores Ashcroft-Nowicki

Charles Seymour was a man of many talents and considerable occult skills. The friend and confident of Dion Fortune, he worked with her and his magical partner, Christine Hartley, for many productive years.

As one of the Inner Circle of Dion Fortune's Society of the Inner Light, Seymour was a High Priest in every sense of the word, but he was also one of the finest teachers of the occult art to emerge this century.

In the past, little of Seymour's work has been widely available, but in this volume Doloras Ashcroft-Nowicki, Director of Studies of the Servants of the Light School of Occult Science, has gathered together a selection of the best of Seymour's work. His complex scholarship and broad background knowledge of the Pagan traditions shine through in articles which include: The Meaning of Initiation; Magic in the Ancient Mystery Religions; The Esoteric Aspect of Religion; Meditations for Temple Novices; The Old Gods; The Ancient Nature Worship and The Children of the Great Mother.

ISBN 1-870450-29-9

THE PATH THROUGH THE LABYRINTYH
by Marian Green

The Quest for Initiation into the Western Mystery Tradition.

Underlying the evolving culture of the West there hides a complete strata of folk-lore, of traditional skills and wisdom, of ancient arts and festivals.

These are still emerging in myth and legend, in song and celebrations, each retaining aspects of a very great initiatory system rooted in the land and its magic.

Most available sources tell the reader about the how to of magic, but for the first time this book explores the way of magic, and the what happens when... of modern magical techniques.

In The Path Through the Labyrinth, Marian Green, a highly respected practitioner and teacher of the Western Tradition, examines these questions and guides the reader safely to the heart of the magical maze, and then out again.

ISBN 1-870450-15-9

*   *   *   *   *

PRACTICAL TECHNIQUES OF MODERN MAGIC
by Marian Green

What is the essence of ritual magic?
How are the symbols used to create change?
Can I safely take steps in ritual on my own?
How does magic fit into the pattern of life in the modern world?
Will I be able to master the basic arts?

All these questions and many more are answered within the pages of this book.

ISBN 1-870450-14-0

PRACTICAL MAGIC
IN THE NORTHERN TRADITION

by Nigel Pennick

The Northern Tradition is the indigenous spiritual and magical system of European peoples north of the Alps. With its origin in archaic shamanic nature-veneration, it embodies the observances, practices and tradition of the people of the Celtic, Germanic, Scandinavian and Baltic realms. Practical Magic in the Northern Tradition cuts through the meaningless barriers between people, for these traditions and practices are linked with one another at the deepest level through common themes. The underlying magical principles are identical, being relevant to the same set of environmental conditions.

Many Northern Tradition observances have continued unbroken to the present day as folk customs, rural practices, household magic and the veneration of saints. Now, the Northern Tradition has emerged again in its own right, in a form appropriate for these times. This book is the definitive work of the tradition.

When we view the world in this way, Nature, personified as goddesses, gods and spirits, becomes approachable. It is all too apparent that the materialist ways of modernity can lead only to the destruction of Nature. The Northern Tradition provides another way, one of harmony with the natural world. Northern Tradition magic gives us the tools to bring ourselves into a dynamic interaction with the cyclic workings of Nature. By following the age-old festival customs described in this book, we can become attuned to the natural cycle of the seasons and harmonise ourselves with Nature and our fellow human beings.

ISBN 1-870450-16-7